About the Authors

JOEL MARTIN has worked in radio and television since childhood and is an ACE Award–winning cable talk-show host, producer, writer, and newscaster. He cohosted the top-rated *Psychic Channels* on Long Island's Cablevision network and hosted his own highly rated radio talk show, *The Joel Martin Show,* for twenty years on WBAB-FM. He is a network TV consultant and makes frequent TV appearances concerning the paranormal.

PATRICIA ROMANOWSKI is an award-winning editor and cowriter of more than twenty-three books, including four national bestsellers, *The Rolling Stone Encyclopedia of Rock and Roll, Helping Your Kids Cope with Divorce the Sandcastles Way,* and, most recent, *The OASIS Guide to Asperger Syndrome.* Her work has also appeared in the *New York Times Book Review* and *Rolling Stone.* She lives on Long Island with her husband, the author Philip Bashe, and their son, Justin.

Martin and Romanowski are the authors of *We Don't Die, We Are Not Forgotten,* and *Our Children Forever.*

LOVE BEYOND LIFE

ALSO BY JOEL MARTIN AND PATRICIA ROMANOWSKI

LOVE

BEYOND

LIFE

The Healing Power of
After-Death Communications

||||||||||||||||||||||||||||||||||||||||||||||||||||||||||||||||||||||||||||||

Joel Martin and Patricia Romanowski

HARPER

NEW YORK · LONDON · TORONTO · SYDNEY

HARPER

A hardcover edition of this book was published in 1997 by HarperCollins Publishers.

HarperCollins books may be purchased for educational, business, or sales promotional use. For information please write: Special Markets Department, HarperCollins Publishers, 10 East 53rd Street, New York, NY 10022.

FIRST HARPER PAPERBACK PUBLISHED 2009.

Designed by Elina D. Nudelman

The Library of Congress has catalogued the hardcover edition as follows:

Martin, Joel.
    Love beyond life : the healing power of after-death communications / Joel Martin and Patricia Romanowski. — 1st ed.
    Includes bibliographical references.
    ISBN 978-0-06-017498-9
    I. Spiritualism. 1. Romanowski, Patricia. II. Title.
    BF1261.2.M36   1997
    133.9—dc21   96-46587

ISBN 978-0-06-149187-0 (pbk.)

12 13 ID/RRD 10 9 8 7 6 5 4 3

To Stephen Kaplan, friend, parapsychology researcher, and seeker of the truth, whose work continues in the next stage of life.

—J. M.

In loving memory of Steven Freeman and Michael Dinhofer—beloved fathers, husbands, sons, and brothers. Neither sorrow, nor death, nor time will ever eclipse their light.

—P. R.

CONTENTS

CONTENTS

Authors' Note

These are the true stories of real people. In addition to being extensively interviewed about their experiences, where possible, each subject reviewed our account of his or her story, and each living subject has signed a legal release. Except where considerations of privacy precluded it, we have used subjects' real names. Where we have honored requests for anonymity, pseudonyms appear in quotation marks in the first instance in which they are used. In some cases, we have honored subjects' requests to change certain factual details, such as geographical location, names of friends and family, and other facts, none of them crucial to the core experience recounted here. In addition, we changed a few first names to avoid confusion (for example, there are six subjects named Mary). A handful of cases involve subjects who themselves passed away before we completed this book.

Acknowledgments

Our first thanks go to the hundreds of thousands of readers around the world who make this work so fulfilling and worthwhile. Thank you for your support, your comments, and your willingness to share with us.

In addition to the individuals who generously shared their stories with us over the years, we would like to thank the following for their help in making this book possible: the spirit of Father John Papallo, John and Allison Coughlin, Donna DiBiase, Dottie DiVito and the entire DiVito family, Roxanne Salch Kaplan, John and Barbara Licata and the spirit of David Licata, Joseph Matyas, Rodger McFarlane, Gerrie Menasce, Karen Olivo, Anna Preston and the spirit of Jesse, Marion Rao, Arlene and Michael Rosich, Ashley Scharge, John Smith, Al Vertucci, Neil Vineberg, Rhea White. And Saint Jude, for answered prayers.

I would also like to thank Kristina Rus, whose amazing research skills and constant support proved invaluable; and Patricia Ippolito, whose long support and valued suggestions are greatly appreciated.

Our special thanks to our agent, Sarah Lazin, and her assistant, Marianne Burke. And at HarperCollins, our original editor, Suzanne Oaks, our current editor, Megan Newman, and Diane Reverand, for their unstinting support and encouragement. They welcomed us to our new "home," and we appreciate their kindness and belief in our work.

Closer to home, I would like to thank Sadie Cohen, the late Charles Cohen, and Evelyn Moleta. Mary Moleta's many experiences provided much inspiration for the book, and Linda Le Vaillant transcribed hours of tape, raised many thought-provoking questions, and offered her special friendship.

Finally, my thanks eternally to Elise Le Vaillant, for her continuing support of my work. Her knowledge, strength, and love are my guide and inspiration.

And, of course, Christina Martin, without whom a myriad of tasks could not have been completed for this book. Thank you for your loyalty, patience, and belief in me.

And a special thank-you to my coauthor, Patricia Romanowski, without whom this book would not have been possible and whose partnership I value beyond words.

—JOEL MARTIN

My first thanks, as always, go to Joel, for thinking of me nearly ten years ago and inviting me on board for what's proved to be an exhilarating, inspiring, and always stimulating collaborative relationship. While we spent hours playing devil's advocate, Christina and Elise proved great friends to me as well. They hovered over this book, two unflappable angels bearing advice, commiseration, floppy disks, drafts—and cookies, for my most junior staff member. A million thanks could not be enough.

On a personal note, I wish to thank Ariana Stritzl, Lynda Chieffo, and Meredith Telzer, for giving me the gift of time and unbroken concentration. Carl Aldridge shared his memories generously and helped improve a story with special meaning to me. Mary Johnson, Susan DeMasi, Peggy Dunne, Nancy Inglis, and dozens of other friends and past collaborators: Thank you for sharing your stories. Know that your experiences helped us better understand others'. Our previous editor, the late George Coleman, reminded me many times of how his direct after-death communications experiences changed his life. George, let us know what you think.

I believe I speak for Joel as well in thanking the following people: Elizabeth McNamara, Cathy Sleckman, and Richard Warren. Without realizing it perhaps, they illuminated our path to a higher road.

Closer to the heart, I wish to thank especially, eternally, my sisters Mary Kay and Johnetta and my half-siblings Lynne and Rick, for reminding me daily how beside-normal we are; my nephew Douglas (Student of the Year) Vitro, of whom his mother and father are so proud; and my mother-in-law and father-in-law, Rochelle and Robert

Bashe, for love and support. My husband, Philip Bashe, makes all things possible, and our son, Justin, makes every moment new. I couldn't do it without them, and I would never want to. I love you guys.

—PATRICIA ROMANOWSKI

||||||||||||||||||||||||||||||||||||||||||||||||||||||

Introduction

What happens to us when we die? Do we survive and transcend this physical, earthly existence? If so, in what form? Where do we go? To an after-life, a heaven, an "other side," or simply oblivion? Once there, do we continue our relationships with those left behind? Can we care for them? Help them? Tell them we still love them?

Before 1970, I could have answered any of those questions in ten words or less: When you die, you die. The end. It was not until 1970, when I began hosting a late-night talk show on a Long Island, New York, radio station, that I first paid serious attention to unexplained phenomena. Though our shows covered everything from local and national politics to rock and roll, the programs featuring unexplained phenomena drew the highest ratings. Like it or not, I was spending hours every week traipsing through the unseen world.

As the show's popularity grew, my staff and I received hundreds of letters and calls from people eager to share with us their personal psychic experiences, including premonitions, sightings of deceased loved ones, and haunted houses (of which Long Island seemed to have more than its fair share). Privately, I concluded that people sincerely believed they had been party to something miraculous or mysterious. They genuinely—but mistakenly, I assumed—believed what they were saying. Yet why? Perhaps these "confessions" reflected wishful thinking. Maybe these modern-day ghost stories livened up small talk around the office water cooler.

What my little thesis failed to take into account was that people usually did *not* discuss these experiences with their closest loved ones, much less coworkers, acquaintances, and strangers. Looking back, these people were clearly not seeking attention but validation, some response or feedback that would assure them that they were not alone or crazy. Then, I had no explanation, no words of comfort or confirmation. Today, nearly three decades later, I believe that I do.

PSYCHIC MEDIUMSHIP: A GATEWAY TO THE OTHER SIDE

At that time I remained openly skeptical and worked very hard to find "logical explanations." Even when faced with indisputable, objective if inexplicable evidence—whether it was related to some hauntings, UFO sightings, psychokinesis, spiritual or psychic healing, or ESP—I remained adamantly unconvinced. Psychic mediums, however, presented a special challenge. Some we tested both on and off the air were remarkably accurate when they took phone calls from anonymous listeners, relaying to them information presumably gathered psychically about events, people, and places in the past, the present, and the future. How did they *really* do it? I did not know. However, just because I was unable to identify their psychic sleights of mind did not mean there were none at work. They simply could not be real.

That all changed in 1980, when I met a young man who claimed he could receive messages from the deceased. That young man, George Anderson, is today recognized as one of the greatest psychic mediums of our time, if not the century. He displayed amazing accuracy in messages he brought forth from several of my late relatives. He also revealed many personal details about me he could not have discovered by any other means.

Unlike some other psychic readings I had experienced or witnessed, this one was strikingly free of vague generalities or "fishing" questions. After a decade of interviewing both psychics and debunkers, I knew the tricks of the trade and was careful not to reveal anything to Anderson through my tone of voice, expression, or body language. He relayed information that I personally did not know and was able to confirm only after the reading, so mental telepathy, or mind reading, was also ruled out. In addition, several messages about the future proved true.

Over the next dozen or so years, I witnessed thousands of his readings and studied and interviewed at length hundreds of people who had readings with him and other psychics. In 1988, based on our research, Patricia Romanowski and I cowrote our first study of Anderson and psychic mediumship, *We Don't Die*, which was followed by *We Are Not Forgotten* in 1991 and *Our Children Forever* in 1994.

Since then, we have met other genuine mediums, psychics, and channelers. Although our first three books focused on the work of a specific psychic medium, the thrust of our research and our message transcends the work of any single person, belief, or philosophy. The work of individuals is, we believe, of interest for what it reveals about the broader realm of paranormal experience. In our view, what makes any highly accurate psychic, mediumistic reading significant is not what Uncle Joe, Mom, and Grandma Delores say about themselves or us from the other side. What really matters is what the mediumistic experience—or, for that matter, any form of after-death communication—can tell us about life after death.

GATEWAYS TO THE HEART

Because spirits can communicate to us through someone who has a special talent for receiving those messages, we know that the machinery, the wiring, if you will, is in place. The question, then, is how each of us individually might make that connection. Why some of us appear to be psychically gifted and exactly what that giftedness entails are questions science has thus far failed to answer. That, however, does not change the reality of after-death communications. If the dead communicate through psychic mediums and psychic mediums are human, then it follows that all of us should, at least theoretically, be able to communicate with loved ones beyond.

We are driven to connect, to create a bridge from our consciousness to others, through expression. This may explain why the personal computer–driven "information age" so quickly gave way to the communication age. It is no coincidence that technology is fostering a new sense of global consciousness while interest in the spiritual and the paranormal continues growing. Perhaps we are finally recognizing and acknowledging the spiritual bonds we all share, both here and beyond.

HOW OUR STUDY WAS DONE

The research for *Love Beyond Life* began more than twenty years ago, as listeners, friends, acquaintances, and strangers began greeting me with, "You're going to think I've lost my mind, but . . ."

I began collecting stories informally in the 1970s, as I witnessed and took notes on psychic readings done by guests on my radio program. Between my radio and television programs and group and private psychic readings I have attended, I have personally witnessed more than 11,000 psychic readings. As a broadcast journalist, I have met and interviewed many experts and authors in the field, including John G. Fuller, Melvin Morse, Betty Eadie, Ruth Montgomery, and John White.

By the 1980s my research methods had become more refined. The live audience for my television show, guests on both my radio and television programs, friends, acquaintances, and interested strangers were invited to answer a questionnaire about their paranormal experiences. Over the years, I collected more than a thousand of these. About 80 percent of those who completed the questionnaire claimed to have experienced at least one form of after-death communication.

Through covering the subject for more than twenty-five years in various media and, with Patricia, writing the first three books, the collection of accounts that we deemed reliable grew to more than 3,000. These were narrowed down to 1,500 and then edited again to 500 to eliminate those that were repetitious, mundane, questionable, or ambiguous. In this book we discuss in varying degrees of detail approximately 90 of these cases.

In writing this book, we conducted more than 500 personal interviews with people from across the United States and Canada and from several foreign nations. We reviewed the questionnaires and notes from previous informal surveys and thousands of psychic readings. Since the publication of our first book, we have been deluged with phone calls and letters from people anxious to tell us their stories. In several instances, we followed up and conducted formal interviews; about two dozen of these appear in this book. While some people requested that we identify them with pseudonyms, over half our subjects graciously permitted us to identify them by their real names.

Because we have maintained ongoing, long-term relationships with many people profiled here and in our previous books, we have followed many cases spanning several years that include several different forms of communication and may even involve other living persons who can corroborate aspects of the communication. This massive collection of cassette tapes, transcriptions, notes, and letters has evolved into a large, representative sampling of people's after-death communication experiences. In that sampling we have discovered not only the range and the nature of direct communications, but perhaps its purpose as well.*

This book reflects the enthusiasm and openness of the thousands of people who took part in our research, whether they answered a written survey a decade ago or sat for hours of interviews. As for age, education, economic, social, religious, and ethnic background, the people on whose experiences this book is based are representative of the general population.

OUR PURPOSE

Love Beyond Life is based on true direct-communication experiences but written also for those who have never had such an experience. Dr. Raymond Moody, whose pioneering work defined the near-death experience, has said that "contacting departed loved ones is not only a deep-seated human desire, but . . . also a fundamental part of the grieving process." We agree, and so in these pages we seek to provide

---

*We invite you to share your after-death communication experience with us for possible inclusion in a future book. Please see our questionnaire and our addresses in Appendix II, page 235.

answers to those who ask, "Why haven't I had such an experience?" We believe, and the research suggests, that it is very likely people have many more direct-communication experiences than they realize.

While the vast majority view their after-death communication experience as positive, only a few were totally comfortable with it in its immediate aftermath. For most, it was a puzzling, disorienting, confusing, even frightening time. We write this book in the hope that our readers will learn to regard their direct-communication experiences, both past and future, without fear and confusion and be better able to embrace these precious, golden moments, these bridges of light, with ease and peace of mind.

Because direct communications often come to us when we are alone, people are understandably concerned that their contact was not genuine but instead the result of wishful thinking—a hallucination, a vivid daydream, or a figment of their imagination. These are all plausible explanations, and sometimes they may be correct. Still, the preponderance of evidence from many different types of direct communications in a wide array of circumstances forms a persuasive argument for the reality of communication between the living and the dead. Whether the subjects were self-described religious conservatives or New Age followers, they found their direct after-death communications to be profoundly rich and life afffirming. The evidence is both historical and contemporary, scientific and anecdotal. To those who still question these beliefs, consider this: Of the millions of after-death communications reported, if just one was true, then the survival of human consciousness would be indisputable.

We will examine after-death communications in their most common forms: dreams, apparitions, deathbed visions, near-death experiences, synchronistic occurrences, and such paranormal phenomena as clairvoyance, clairaudience, clairsentience, and psychokinesis. We will also discuss the long, rich, often misunderstood history of direct after-death communications (see Appendix I) and what current research into related phenomena (such as the near-death experience) adds to our understanding. Most important, however, we will introduce you to people just like yourself. As we did in previous books on psychic mediumship, we hope to bring this transcendent human experience out of the shadows and back into the light, where it belongs.

For us as researchers and authors, and for the countless, largely silent millions who have communicated with a deceased loved one, this intertwining of two of life's greatest mysteries offers an unprecedented opportunity to explore direct communications, the true nature of death, and the way love endures. *Love Beyond Life* brings forth a new view of a timeless, universal experience.

JOEL MARTIN

I

BRIDGES OF LOVE FROM THE OTHER SIDE

After-Death Communications

And we have no evidence whatsoever that the soul perishes with the body.

—MAHATMA GANDHI

"I saw my late son standing at the foot of my bed. Maybe I was dreaming, but it seemed so real. I know it was him. I wouldn't tell anyone about it, though. They'd think I was crazy."

"My five-year-old boy insists that his father called him—on his toy telephone. Some things my son says that his father told him he could not possibly have known otherwise. Now I wonder, Was it really his daddy? What should I say to him when he brings this up? If I treat this as 'real,' will my son be helped or hurt?"

"My late daughter came to me in a very vivid dream. I could actually feel her holding me close to her. She was in good health, unlike when she was on earth. She told me some things that had not yet happened. They all came true."

"I was driving when I heard my late father's voice clearly telling me, 'Slow up! Slow up!' I did. Just in time, as it turned out. A moment later, the car ahead of me spun out of control. If I hadn't slowed the car, I would have been in a terrible accident. What if I hadn't listened to my father's voice?"

WHAT ARE AFTER-DEATH COMMUNICATIONS?

We define direct after-death communication as any contact between a living person and the consciousness, spirit, or soul of the so-called dead. The fancy word for contact with the dead is idionecrophany. After-death communications take many forms and can involve any number of paranormal, or psi, phenomena: clairvoyance, clairaudience, psychokinetic activity, and a series of events linked together by synchronicity. The deceased may appear to us in dreams or manifest as apparitions (or ghosts). We may hear their voice, feel their touch, suddenly detect a scent they wore in life, or simply feel their presence. The loved one may announce her visit through psychokinesis (moving objects) or any number of different phenomena that carry a specific meaning. The contact may be fleeting or prolonged; it may happen only once, or several times, or never. Most contacts occur spontaneously, but we do know that through prayer, meditation, and simply refusing to disbelieve, we the living can facilitate if not initiate them.

The purpose and meaning of each direct communication are as unique as the relationship between those involved. Some serve a very definite, often immediate purpose, as in the case of a five-year-old boy who one day announced, "Grandpa says, 'Daddy, drive careful. Don't make the car go fast.'" The boy's mother dismissed the warning as the product of his overactive imagination. After all, both grandfathers had predeceased her son; he had never known them. She reconsidered her reaction later that day, when she learned that her husband had been involved in a car accident.

From beyond the veil of life, our deceased loved ones may assume many different roles: messengers, guardians, protectors, comforters. They may pass on vague, general warnings and advice, or they may actually appear to us and intervene to avert tragedy. They may predict the future accurately or reveal to us elements of our past or their own that we could not have known any other way. Whatever happens, they offer us a chance to heal—from grief, from pain, from loss.

Contrary to a popular misconception, after-death communications are rarely evil, random, or initiated by someone we did not know or were not related to in this life. Judging from the content of the communications and the feelings our respondents reported during and after the experience, the spirits' intention or purpose is often comfort and reassurance, a continuation of the relationship begun before physical death. There are several means of communicating with the deceased, including psychic mediumship, but direct after-death communication offers the subject a different kind of comfort. Because direct after-death communications are private, their subject matter can be more intimate, more personal. Because they can be enhanced, even initiated by us on this physical plane, they are the only form of discarnate communications over which we can exert some control. Because they are so personal, these experiences, though less "corroborable" than psychic readings, are often ultimately more satisfying.

You will notice that we include a large, certainly disproportionate number of direct-communication cases involving precognition. Direct-communication experiences that we can verify are more interesting, if only because they are corroborated by proving true. This does not mean that direct communications that cannot be "backed up" by other events are any less genuine or meaningful. If anything, the true value of provable incidents is that they help us understand that other direct communications with other factors in common are also genuine.

HOW PEOPLE DESCRIBE AFTER-DEATH COMMUNICATIONS

Based on our research, which is supported by other studies of various aspects of the phenomenon, and public opinion polls, we have developed a profile of the factors most common to these experiences:

1. Most people believed they were the only ones in the world to have ever had such an experience.

2. Most people admitted to not believing very strongly in the paranormal, psychic phenomena, or the supernatural. In fact, the vast majority described themselves as initially skeptical or neutral in their opinions of such subjects. Relatively few had expected to have such an experience. Nearly all were surprised when it occurred.

3. Most were reluctant to discuss their direct-communication encounters with others, largely due to fear of being misunderstood or ridiculed. Often, one of us was the first—and sometimes the only—person in whom the subjects confided.

4. Virtually everyone was able immediately to recognize or identify the deceased loved one coming to them. Some actually saw the deceased, as in an apparition; others smelled a scent or heard a song or sound closely associated with that person. Sometimes the subject actually heard the spirit speak audibly or telepathically. Messages from the dead may also come to us as thought forms, or impressions, that seem to have originated somewhere outside ourselves. Typically, someone will suddenly "just know" or sense that the thought or message came through, but not from, themselves. Often, a physical sensation accompanies these thought-form communications, like a sudden rush of warmth, the chills, or a surge of energy.

5. Most communications and visits were from close family members or friends who had died relatively recently, less than two to five years ago. Usually the after-death communications occurred within a year of physical death. However, there are exceptions, as in cases where a grandparent appears to a grandchild who may not have been born in the grandparent's lifetime. There are also many cases in which a spirit makes repeated contacts over many years. We examine several of these highly unusual and remarkable cases here.

6. Most often, the contact lasted between several seconds and several minutes, although those that occur in dreams may seem to go on much longer. While many contacts occurred during dreams, the vast majority occurred while the subject was wide awake and fully aware of his or her surroundings.

7. When direct-communication contacts occurred during sleep, they came as a dream that the subject described as unusually vivid, lifelike, or hyper-real. Dream contacts often contain

important messages or bring the subject a sense of peace or comfort. Given the content of many of these dream contacts, it seems reasonable to conclude that the spirits choose to communicate at a time when our conscious "guard" is down. History is filled with accounts of such contacts, including several experienced by psychologist Carl Jung, who never doubted that they were real.

8. In nearly all cases, the deceased loved ones appeared to be in good health, no matter what their physical state at the moment of death.

9. In many cases, the subjects reported their deceased loved ones predicting future events accurately. Sometimes, these predictions came as warnings and advice. There is also evidence that those still living but near death can communicate psychically through the same channels as the dead, so that, for example, near the moment of her distant father's death, a woman might feel an otherwise inexplicable sense of panic, loss, or comfort (crisis alert), actually see her father appear before her (crisis apparition), or hear his voice or telepathically receive a message from him (crisis communication).

10. Religious or spiritual background, or lack of it, seemed to have almost no bearing on predicting who would receive direct after-death messages. Prayer and meditation, however, seemed to facilitate communications, particularly in the first two years after death. Interestingly, such beliefs often colored the communications' symbolism and language, but not always.

11. Overwhelmingly, those who reported direct after-death communications were grateful for the experience. Nearly all said they were comforted or otherwise helped by it and described it as a positive event. Only a few were frightened or said that they regretted having had the experience. Nearly all said that their direct contact left them feeling "less alone" and that the departed one was "with" them.

CONTACT WITH THE DEAD: THE MOST COMMON
PARANORMAL EXPERIENCE

Although after-death communication, in its various forms, is the most common psychic, or paranormal, experience, it is one of the least understood and most deeply hidden. This is very interesting, since many studies and polls reveal that Americans believe in life after death. For example, a 1991 survey conducted by the International Social Survey Program revealed that 55 percent of Americans believed in an afterlife, while another 23 percent thought it was probable. A 1993 survey from the National Opinion Research Center at the University of Chicago found that "Four of ten [polled] report contact with the dead." Lest anyone assume that these were chance findings, a 1994 Gallup poll reported that 49 percent—nearly half those questioned—"either believe or are open to the possibility that people can communicate mentally with the dead." In a survey released in 1987, Roman Catholic priest, author, and sociologist Father Andrew Greeley discovered that 42 percent of Americans reported visits from the deceased. This correlates exactly with findings from the International Social Survey Program of 1991. A 1994 poll conducted by *USA Today*, CNN, and the Gallup organization found that 90 percent of Americans believe in heaven.

WHO EXPERIENCES AFTER-DEATH COMMUNICATIONS?

Theoretically, anyone can communicate with the dead, but the experience is more common among certain groups. For example, the percentage of widows and widowers claiming to have contact with their deceased spouses is 60 percent, well above the average. In his 1976 book *Death and Beyond*,[1] Greeley published the results of previous studies from around the world. He found, for example, that in 1973 only about a quarter of men and a third of women surveyed claimed to have had contact with the dead. Interestingly, while the percentage of persons claiming to have had "frequent" contact remained a consistent 3 to 5 percent despite sex or race, African-American respondents were nearly twice as likely to have had such contact: 46 percent compared with 24 percent for whites. In addition, the widowed were four times more likely to say they had experienced such contact "often" as opposed to "once or twice" or "several times."

Overall, reports of such incidents have risen. In an early 1970s survey Greeley cites, only 49 percent of widows and widowers reported contact with their deceased spouses; by the 1990s, that figure was 60 percent, more than a 20 percent increase. What does this mean? Have such experiences become more common over the past quarter century, or are people simply more comfortable recognizing and talking about them?

The differences in numbers between African Americans and whites suggests that cultural and religious beliefs may facilitate or hinder after-death communications. Other statistical variations seem to support this idea, for there were significant differences among different nationalities, age groups, religious affiliations, and nationalities. In 1968, 73 percent of Americans said they had had contact with the dead, compared to 38 percent of Swedes. As for age, Greeley found that such contacts were reported by nearly a third of teens surveyed but by only about a fifth of people in their twenties and thirties, rising again through the later years and peaking at 40 percent for those over sixty.

Even among Christians, whom one might presume would accept the concept of life after death, there were marked variations among those who had experienced contact with the dead: 40 percent of Episcopalians surveyed as opposed to 28 percent of Baptists; 26 percent of Catholics as opposed to 40 percent of those who identified themselves as "other" than Protestant, Catholic, or Jewish. Within the same religion, figures varied according to nationality: Italian Catholics were twice as likely to have had contact as German Catholics; contacts were most common among Spanish-speaking and Polish Catholics. Jews, whose religious teachings place far less emphasis on the fate of man after death than does Christianity, reported the same rate of contact as these latter two groups.

One interesting trend, which we address more fully in chapter 7, is the cluster of after-death communications we found among families.

We also discovered that psychic ability or sensitivity may run in families. It is impossible to determine whether this is due to genetic heritage or simply because these children grew up in families comfortable with psychic experience. In several cases, simply having had and recognized a psychic experience, such as an after-death communication, seemed to increase the chances that additional contacts would follow.

While our sample was widely representative in most aspects, we did find that more women than men reported after-death communications. At this point, we are interpreting this to mean not that these experiences are more common among women, but that due to cultural conditioning, men may be less likely to view their experiences as genuine or less willing to share them with strangers. We did observe, however, that neither men nor women had difficulty recalling their experiences in great detail. In fact, if there was anything that people found troubling or wanting about these experiences, it was that they did not last long enough or did not recur often enough.

TOUCHING HEARTS, CHANGING MINDS

Generally speaking, a direct after-death communication experience will influence a subject's opinion about life and death. While, according to people who have had them, most of these experiences are extremely comforting and very positive, we cannot overlook the fact that any belief in an event that we cannot explain or that does not seem to fit our conception of how the known universe operates can be unsettling. We have found that people will reject compelling paranormal experiences out of a need to protect a certain conception of themselves or their world. For example, someone who felt dominated by a father and was somewhat relieved when he died is apt to bend over backward looking for alternate, nonparanormal explanations of an after-death communication. For those who find some sense of comfort or relief in believing their unloved one is "dead and gone," any suggestion that things might be otherwise can be threatening.

One thing we can say with certainty is that virtually no one brings to their first paranormal experience a neutral opinion. Either people believe in life after death, or they do not; either they believe that communication between the deceased and their living loved ones is possible, or they do not; either they believe they may have had such an experience, or they do not. While people may express wide variations in the degree to which they believe or disbelieve, in the end it is often a very clear-cut, black-or-white question.

How they feel about the possibility of transdimensional communication after having what they believe may have been such an experience is another matter. Among the hundreds of people we spoke with, approximately 50 percent claimed that before their experience they did not believe such a thing was possible under any circumstances. Another 32 percent said that they believed it was possible but never expected it would happen to them.

THE "UNPROVABLE" TRUTH

Belief in life after death is a cornerstone of Christianity, and the promise of continued existence is so common throughout major world religions as to be nearly universal. But continued contact between the living and the dead is not an idea encouraged by most mainstream religions. If anything, we find a long history of prohibitions against any form of contact with the deceased, which is often considered evil or the work of the devil (see Appendix I).

Despite cultural bias, religious admonitions, and scientific denial of the possibility or morality of communication with the dead, people persist in claiming they have had such experiences. Why? As hundreds have told us, their personal after-death contacts were of a character and intensity that made the reality simply undeniable. The incredulous reactions of friends and families, old cultural and religious taboos, and even doubts about their own sanity were simply no match for having been in the presence of a deceased loved one, even if for just seconds.

These people knew in their hearts that what they had felt and witnessed was real. Yet when they sought some form of reassurance or corroboration, they found very little. Despite the trendiness of all things New Age, most of our respondents sensed that others would not respect or support their experiences. We also believe that many are influenced by what we term a cultural "suspension of belief," a socially reinforced, almost reflexive denial of anything outside what we consider "normal" experience.

THE NEW MOON

As you contemplate your own after-death communication experience or consider the cases we present here, keep in mind that little in life is absolutely knowable. With the passage of time and increased knowledge, we do not, as some believe, redefine the universe, we only refine our conception of it. What we know is often later revealed to be only a portion—and a small one—of what is.

Take, for instance, humankind's ideas about the moon. For the last 4.6 billion years the moon has been our rough-surfaced elliptically orbiting satellite, glowing in the sun's reflected light, rotating on its own axis, and moving tides. We understand the mechanics behind its phases, the illusion of a lunar eclipse, how to land on its surface. We know that its glow is a reflection, its smoothness an illusion.

Now, imagine sitting down with a group of our ancestors who lived anytime between the dawn of man and yesterday and asking each to describe the moon. Not only would we all seem to be talking about several different entities, but they would dismiss virtually everything you or I might say as impossible, ridiculous fantasy. Still, we would share some thoughts in common, knowledge gained through simple observation. After all, even the earliest civilizations clearly noted a relationship between the moon and the oceans' tides. Could they explain it? Yes, but only in a manner consistent with their conception of the universe *in their time*. The notion of gravity would be meaningless to anyone who lived before Sir Isaac Newton advanced it in 1666, just as the idea of a man walking on the moon would be incredible to anyone who died before July 20, 1969.

In many ways, the mystery of psychic phenomena is our moon.

Looking back through history, we see much about human psychic experience that is incredibly consistent. Of course, the terminology sometimes changes—ghosts become apparitions, witches or necromancers are now psychics and mediums, prophecies are premonitions, some forms of mind reading are now known as ESP—and the acceptance of certain facets, especially mediumship and direct contact, waxes and wanes. Yet we are talking about the same kinds of occurrences. What we don't know—probably cannot know—is where we are in our understanding of them. Is the paranormal universe of after-death communication really like an ancient moon, a smooth gem shining just beyond reach? Or is it in fact a gray, dry, crusty globe few of us will ever touch? Are we scratching arches of crescents and orbs on cave walls or suiting up to plant another flag on its surface?

Scientifically speaking, there is no proof of life after death. However, scientifically speaking again, there is not a shred of evidence that it does not or cannot exist. "Ashes to ashes, dust to dust," cynics will say. But if one believes, as most of us do, that the human body comprises only part of what we consider our human being, the fact that the body ceases to function after death is irrelevant. More important, it proves absolutely nothing about the possible survival of other elements of our being—consciousness, spirit, soul. Since we really do not know what these consist of—energy? information? something we cannot even conceive?—we cannot possibly determine what they can or cannot do. What we can do, however, is what people throughout time have always done, essentially keep charting the moons and marking the tides. And wait for the next theory of gravity. Or relativity.

WHAT DO THESE ACCOUNTS TELL US ABOUT THE WORLD BEYOND?

If a dimension exists that transcends the limits of the human body, then we in the physical world can take comfort in the knowledge that life is eternal and therefore our departed loved ones are still alive. As you will read, a range of related developments in psychology, para-psychology, medicine, and physics have generated new pieces for the age-old puzzle, one we should all very humbly admit we may never see completed.

No living person can fully corroborate the reality of life after death. Despite all that those who have glimpsed the afterlife can tell us, their experiences have limitations. Those who have returned from near-death experiences, for example, stepped across the threshold for a brief moment. Psychic mediums, channelers, and others who receive discarnate communications, while certainly "in touch," are witnesses once removed. You would not expect someone to know the contents of a house by peeking into just one window. You would not believe you had experienced living in Paris just because you phoned your friends there every day. Only those who have crossed into the afterlife truly know.

Still, simply because we cannot claim to know the full answer does not invalidate what we do know. As we said in our first book, we don't die. The evidence gathered in *Love Beyond Life* leaves no room for ambiguity or doubt. Yes, our departed loved ones can and do communicate messages of love to us on earth. They also receive our messages of love to them, our prayers and our thoughts. After-death visits can heal, both in this world and the next. Love between two people does not automatically die with the passing of one.

Why shouldn't a deceased husband return to his wife in a vivid dream to say that his love for her is unchanged? Why wouldn't a departed child come back as a vision, voice, dream, or through another means to comfort a grieving parent? Or a deceased parent return to reassure and help a grieving child?

Rather than turn away from these experiences in fear, doubt, or disbelief, we should learn to embrace and treasure them. While we do not always know the exact purpose of these transdimensional contacts, those who have experienced them gladly attest to the results. Even the most beautifully crafted words barely capture the joy, the comfort, the peace of mind one derives just from knowing that there is something beyond, that life does go on, that no one you love will ever die.

||||||||||||||||||||||||||||||||||||||||||||||||||||||||||||

2

THE CHANGING FACE OF DEATH

To fear death, my friends, is only to think ourselves wise, without being wise: for it is to think that we know what we do not know. For anything that men can tell, death may be the greatest good that can happen to them; but they fear it as if they knew quite well that it was the greatest of evils. And what is this but that shameful ignorance of thinking that we know what we do not know?

—SOCRATES (469–399 B.C.)

Wherever we find life, we find death, a fact that even our earliest prehistoric ancestors observed. We generally believe that among the thousands of species sharing earth, only we Homo sapiens can understand death and realize that we will one day die. Given recent revelations about other species' communication abilities (e.g., dolphins, great apes) and grieving behavior (e.g., elephants, great apes, and some domesticated animals), one has to wonder whether we might one day discover that humankind is not alone in consciously conceiving its future demise. What ultimately may distinguish humankind, then, may be our power to imagine a unique personal existence after and beyond life as we know it. The belief in life after death pervades written history and the archeological evidence that speaks for prehistoric generations. Perhaps no intellectual or religious concept has so dramatically shaped the world and our idea of what it means to be human.

Why do we believe in life after death? One possibility is that such a belief, or hope, is simply part of our neuropsychological makeup, like the sex drive, or instinct. Another possibility is that the notion is so pervasive, we find it impossible to think of death in any other terms.

Or we can look at it another way: Is it not possible that the knowledge of life after death is part of us because it is a reality? In other words, just as we experience a biological response to hunger because we must eat to survive, is it not possible that we are born preconditioned to believe in life after death because it is our destiny?

Nothing brings these questions into focus as sharply as a loved one's death. Before we ourselves experience death, we will mourn many times. How we grieve for our loved ones influences and reflects how we approach death and life. Experts in bereavement, thanatology, and psychology concur that those of us living on the brink of the third millennium are woefully unprepared to deal with death and dying. After years of researching death-related paranormal phenomena and talking to hundreds of people about their experiences with death and bereavement, we believe that contemporary society's denial of death causes tremendous, incalculable pain and suffering. Everywhere grieving people turn, they are admonished for remembering the dead, exhorted to get on with their lives and to avoid anything even remotely associated with death. We are so intent on hiding, disguising, and avoiding death that in the process we turn our backs on those who mourn and those who have died. It is difficult to fathom the logic behind the pervasive belief that the bereaved should hide or give away all their loved one's clothing, preferably as soon as possible. Why? Because it will remind them of their loss? It's as if we believe that our power to ignore death renders it less painful. This is the well-intentioned but misguided thinking that considers regularly visiting a grave "morbid," appropriately alluding to the deceased in casual conversation "obsessive," and preserving a deceased child's room "sick." We avoid the dying, the dead, and the bereaved at every opportunity, and then wonder why we feel so alone when death touches our lives.

All human societies recognize important personal transitions through public ritual and protocol. In contemporary American society, however, we have witnessed a progressively declining participation in and appreciation for funerary and mourning traditions. This has paralleled our declining death rate. For example, if you lived in the mid-1800s, when childhood mortality ran between 30 and 50 percent, you could expect one out of every three of your children to die before reaching adulthood. As a child, you would probably have witnessed the death of at least one sibling and perhaps several. During common epidemics of measles, diphtheria, influenza, and chickenpox, families could lose several or all of their children in a matter of days. As a woman, you faced a one-in-thirty chance of dying every time you gave birth. Faced with such realities, no one could escape, deny, or choose not to deal with death.

Compared with today, death then was not only prevalent, it was pervasive. Until the 1920s, almost everyone died at home, and most funeral services were held in the parlor, or front room, of the house. In fact, the term *living room* originated and was promoted in the early 1900s specifically to dispel the parlor's association with death, dying, and funerals.

Established and accepted mourning customs outlined almost every aspect of the survivor's life, from stationery and attire to the length of the mourning period. Many of these traditions were eventually abandoned as being impractical and old-fashioned, which they sometimes were. Nonetheless, they helped the bereaved come to terms with their loss and establish a new sense of themselves and their lives without their loved one. They also gave everyone around them a clear idea of how to behave toward them and how to provide emotional support. It's interesting to note that when we abandon old traditions, we often replace them with new but equally meaningful ones, and this seems to have occurred with almost every major life passage except mourning.

Therapists who specialize in grief agree that the death of a child is the most difficult loss one can experience. A century ago, custom dictated and the community respected a bereaved parent's mourning for at least two years. Today, someone who loses a child is lucky to get two weeks off from work and can look forward to being told to "get on" with life, dismantle the child's bedroom, and talk about the child as little as possible. Fortunately, the bereaved can turn to peer support groups. The phenomenal growth of such groups is indicative of society's failure to support mourners in their grief, to acknowledge their loss, and to view mourning as a necessary and healthy emotional adjustment, rather than a morbid, aberrant behavior.

One reason much of what we consider New Age seems so new to us is that in closing our eyes to death, we have also failed to see and/or believe our paranormal experiences related to dying, death, and bereavement. Yet for our predecessors, these experiences brought confirmation of religious faith, emotional comfort, and a means of adjusting psychologically to loss. Like many of their contemporaries, President Abraham Lincoln and his wife, Mary Todd Lincoln, knew death all too well. They lost their eleven-year-old son Willie to typhoid fever in 1862. Willie was their second son to die; his older brother Eddie died at three of pulmonary tuberculosis in 1850. In 1863 Mrs. Lincoln shared with her half-sister an incident that we would consider an after-death communication. Such events are particularly common among bereaved parents of every generation, so few would have questioned what Mrs. Lincoln said: "He comes to me every night and stands at the foot of my bed, with the same sweet, adorable smile he has always had; he does not always come alone; Little Eddie is sometimes with him." She went on to assure her half-sister that seeing Willie's spirit comforted her greatly. To a friend, she expressed a view most of her contemporaries shared: "A very slight veil separates us from the 'loved and lost'. . . [assuring us] that though unseen by us, they are very near." Mrs. Lincoln was not alone in believing that her personal experience revealed and confirmed an otherwise invisible reality, and neither are we.

Contemporary psychology's attitude toward paranormal experience continues to evolve in a positive direction of acceptance. In recent years we have interviewed mental health and bereavement experts who support the position that we should accept and use after-death contacts and communications as a means to work through grief.

In 1994 the third edition of the American Psychiatric Association's *Diagnostic and Statistical Manual of Mental Disorders* finally urged mental health professionals to consider more seriously a patient's religious experience. It was a long overdue recognition of the positive role and importance of spirituality in mental health. Psychiatrists Shaun Josh and Colin Ross, writing in *The Journal of Nervous and Mental Diseases*, state, "Paranormal experiences are so common in the general population that no theory of normal psychology or psychopathology which does not take them into account can be comprehensive." This is a welcome change from the not-too-distant past, when anyone admitting to such experiences was declared hysterical, prone to hallucinations, or worse.

WHERE DO YOU WANT TO GO?

In chapter 10, we discuss specific means of facilitating and enhancing direct after-death communications. Here, we offer some general advice for those who have had or believe they would welcome a direct communication. If you decide to become more active in this process, spend some time thinking about what you are trying to accomplish and why. Honestly assess where you are in your grief work and other major areas of your life. Remember, the pain, the loss, and the loneliness of grief are normal. There is no "detour," no shortcut through bereavement. As joyous as any reunion or communication may be, once it is over, you will still miss your deceased loved one. In some cases, you may find the period following a direct communication even more difficult because it so vividly reminds you of what you've lost.

On a very basic emotional level, you may find yourself wishing the death had never occurred and replaying other issues, such as why that person had to die. Mary Vitro, whose son Doug was two when his father died, told us, "All these communications are great, but in the end Doug's dad still isn't here to hug him after a softball game or go with us to walk on the beach. Even though we've learned to accept it, six years later, I still find myself asking why it had to happen, why Rick couldn't still be here with us to be part of our lives here, not over there. To grow up with a mother and a father both alive doesn't seem too much to ask, does it?"

Next determine how you really feel about being more active in the process. For some people, the answer is clear: they are very uncomfortable doing anything to goad the process. For others, praying is fine, but meditating strikes them as a form of channeling. For yet others, anything they can do to increase their chances of hearing from a deceased loved one is fine. Be honest with yourself. This is not a contest.

As you read, you will see that while many people we interviewed wished they could have more direct-communication experiences, an equal number were satisfied with the one or the few they had. We also noticed that people who had a series of contacts also sensed or were told by their loved one that the communications would cease at some point in the future. Time and again, deceased loved ones alluded to a time when their "work" would be done, their "mission" completed. We do not think it is a coincidence that those who had the most realistic attitudes about what their communications could and could not help them achieve here also had a greater number of intense experiences.

Is it possible that our loved ones may sense when we would misuse or depend too heavily on their communications, and so judiciously stay away? Reputable psychics do not encourage people to sit for many readings. They see firsthand the dangers of "psychoholism"—an unhealthy obsession with death and misguided faith in those on the other side to solve our problems. As we have said before, the dead have a place in our lives, but it is their place, and we must respect that. Life here is for the living.

Create Your Own Mourning Rituals

Often, when someone dies, we spend months or years so fixated on their deaths—how they died, when they died, their last months or moments, how the event changed our lives forever—that we lose sight of what they were like when we knew them only as living people.

If you're fortunate, your friends and family members will welcome chances to talk about the deceased, will preserve and cherish their personal belongings, will still exhibit their photograph, and will feel comfortable recalling things they loved to do or often said. If, however, your situation is different—for example, if you or people around you feel that the less said about the dead, the better—then you have some work to do. Remember that there is no one "correct" way to mourn. The bereavement process is a highly individual response. In the same family you may find that some people take great comfort from visiting cemeteries, while others find the experience unpleasant. Neither is right or wrong as long as they are not avoiding the issue and are dealing with their loss appropriately.

Each death raises its own unique issues. Two people mourning the same deceased loved one may have drastically different reactions that are perfectly normal and healthy for them. If your loss was untimely (a child, for example) or involved an accident, suicide, or murder, your grieving may be complicated. It is beyond our scope to address all facets of bereavement, and we recommend that you read up on the subject and consider seeking professional counseling.

Try to integrate the death into your life. Resist the temptation to "black out" significant dates or events. Don't try to pretend that the anniversary of a loved one's death or their birthday is "just another day." Do not follow well-meaning advice to forgo holidays, remove photographs and other mementos, and avoid places, people, objects, or events because they might remind you of your loss. In fact, remembering is exactly what you want to do. We long to remember; we need to remember. And when we grieve in a healthy manner, over time the focus of our memories will naturally shift from what death stole away to what life bestowed upon us. Cherished objects—jewelry, clothing, books—and other precious things, like favorite songs or special holidays, need to be recalled and revisited.

Share Your After-Death Communication Experiences with Others

Many people we have interviewed mention feeling that they can't talk about their after-death communications. Mostly, they fear they will be ridiculed or disbelieved. We urge people to overcome their inhibitions. Sharing direct communications can be cathartic, like sharing any other good news. That does not mean there will not be some who misunderstand or raise a skeptical brow. In fact, we can practically guarantee that someone will give you a hard time. However, you can also count on the support of people who either have had the experience or believe it is possible. Find people you can trust to share with, For some, that will be a good friend, relative, therapist, clergyman, or grief counselor. If your experience is important to you but your therapist dismisses it, consider working with someone else.

If you are attending a bereavement support group, do not hesitate to raise the topic, even if your group is nonsectarian or the group leader seems to have avoided the issue. You will probably find, as dozens of our respondents did, that simply mentioning the subject opened a virtual floodgate. In several instances, people told us that *every single person* in their support group then talked about their own experiences.

Wherever you are, try to keep in mind that people are not keeping quiet about this because they have nothing to say. Most often, they are simply as concerned about being misunderstood as you are. If you feel especially shy, consider going on-line and joining a live chat group, where your anonymity will be protected.

Brace Yourself for Criticism and View It for What It Really Is

One man, a prominent local politician, debated with me endlessly about after-death communications. He did not believe they were possible, and whenever I saw him—whether he was on my show to discuss a new public works project or we were out socially—"it" came up. I was convinced that nothing would change his mind. Then he had an intense after-death communication experience in which his father appeared to him. All that my friend claimed to have believed—or disbelieved—fell away. My friend found the truth in his own time, in his own way.

Begin by accepting that people who do not believe in after-death communications often have compelling reasons for thinking as they do. Their beliefs are as deserving of respect as your own. Their reasons may include anything from strong religious convictions to plain stubbornness. Try not to take skeptics' arguments too personally; they are not directed to you but to the uncertainty and fear your experience may inspire.

Why we believe what we do is a fascinating question. Time and again we have observed a pattern of obdurate disbelief among people who had troubled relationships. For example, children of neglectful or abusive parents are often, even if only subconsciously, relieved that their parents are dead and unable to hurt them anymore. While some such adult children may find hearing from these parents profoundly healing, others do not. We know of one instance where a troubled parental relationship drove someone to pick apart his paranormal experiences until he began questioning his own sanity for ever believing he had them at all. If you enjoyed a tender, loving marriage, you will welcome knowing that your husband still exists, still participates in your life, is still there for you in some way. Yet imagine if your spouse were sadistically violent. You can appreciate why his widow would be less than thrilled about, perhaps even terrified by, the prospect of such a spirit still being part of her life. To press the point with people like these, whose denial serves a psychologically healthy purpose, is presumptuous and cruel. Even people you believe you know well may have issues they've kept secret. When someone resists, back off.

Take it from us, few people switch sides in this debate because of what someone tells them. After all these years, even we have accepted the fact that more often than not we are preaching to the choir. At the same time, we try to help people see that there is nothing new, wrong, or unusual about believing as they do. If it is appropriate, you might want to point out that the New Testament, for example, contains many references to communicating with spirits. Or that such communications have a long, documented though overlooked history. Much of what we include here by way of background and in Appendix I addresses those points.

Sometimes a simple question or analogy will end the discussion on an agreeable note. When people question how reliable psychics might be, we always like to point out the dismal track record of the National Weather Service. Sometimes you may have to call it a draw. Patricia's loving, intelligent in-laws simply do not believe in life after death or the possibility of after-death communication. After years of pursuing a fruitless debate, she finally hit on the right answer. After inquiring about how her work was going with this book, her mother-in-law said, "There's no proof that there's life after death."

"Well, there's no proof that there isn't," Patricia replied. End of discussion. If only out of respect, courtesy, or love, sometimes you must agree to disagree.

Consider Joining a Community of People Whose Experiences Are Like Yours

Sometimes you want to surround yourself with people who do agree. Consciousness about unexplained phenomena has evolved so rapidly that today there are support groups for the subjects of virtually every parapsychological experience you can imagine.

You may learn of these through word of mouth. You might also try exploring what is out there on the Internet. Bear in mind that the Internet's free-market, free-speech ethos virtually ensures that some information you find will be incorrect, misleading, even dangerous. Our advice is to start browsing the websites of established organizations (bereavement groups such as The Compassionate Friends) and educational and research institutions. The Institute for Parapsychology and the University of Edinburgh, two centers of parapsychological research, have websites that are easily found by searching with the word *parapsychology*. In addition, websites usually list related websites and home pages.

Consider Visiting a Reputable Psychic Medium

One of the great beauties and joys of direct after-death communication is that it cuts out the middleman, so to speak. Yet mediumship and direct after-death communications are not mutually exclusive. One experience does not replace or negate the other. In fact, psychic readings often confirm prior direct communications, providing reassuring proof. We recommend psychic mediumistic readings in principle. Unfortunately, it is beyond our scope to address or comment on the thousands of psychics offering their services over the Internet, through 800 or 900 numbers, or in home-hosted psychic get-togethers. If you are curious and willing to part with your money "for entertainment purposes only," as the ads say, fine. However, if you are seeking something more profound and meaningful, we would advise looking for someone you can work with in person, preferably in private.

Years of research in mediumship have taught us that there is much more to being a good psychic than just giving an impressive reading. When seeking a psychic medium, you should consider the same factors you would when considering any other professional: reputation, attitude, and professionalism. Truly great psychic mediums are rare, and good word of mouth travels quickly. Most psychic mediums get nearly all of their clients through the personal referrals of others who have seen them. Psychotherapists, grief counselors, sometimes even clergy and police, can probably recommend a good psychic near you.

Reputable psychic mediums, such as George Anderson, have demonstrated the tremendous value of psychic readings to the bereaved. When comparing a psychic reading with a direct after-death communication, it's impossible to say which is "better." They're very different, and each offers its own benefits and shortcomings. One of the great surprises many subjects get at a psychic reading is their loved one coming through and referring to past direct contacts. Sometimes the subject will recall having had a strange feeling that it was a communication or sensing a spirit's presence but not being certain what it was. Other times, a psychic reading can definitely confirm that an experience that seemed like a direct communication indeed did occur.

Many people have found that having a psychic reading before their direct communication helped them to "go with" the experience immediately without stopping to think, "Is this real?" In that sense, you might regard a good psychic medium as a tour guide, someone who can take you through a psychic experience and help you to feel more comfortable with the whole idea. Dedicated psychics can also offer insight and advice.

These are powerful, potentially life-changing experiences. They can comfort you, teach you, even save your life. Attempts at making direct contact are most likely to succeed if we bring to them the right attitude. First, we need patience. Although we miss them, our departed loved ones live on in a new existence. We must accept that their lives continue there as ours do here. As several of our cases make clear, the departed cannot be at our disposal, ready to answer us in an instant. What we may consider a long time—even a year or more by our reckoning—may be a blink of an eye on the other side. It also appears that the spirits consider carefully when to communicate to us, how, and for what purposes. When we do not hear from them, does it mean they do not hear us or have ceased loving us? No, not at all. As we have seen, we tend to miss many communications. We also know that within the first two years after death, communications are much more common. After that, their frequency and intensity seem to diminish except for emergency warnings.

Most important, we must always remember that we here have lessons to learn and goals to achieve. It's called life. If not for the time, patience, energy, and love we devoted to our relationships on this side, there would be no tie to bind us after death. While there is a great deal to be gained from acknowledging and learning about our destiny after physical death, it cannot become an obsession. The greatest tribute we can pay to those who have moved beyond this life is to be here now—in heart, in mind, in soul—for our loved ones on this plane. Life on this earth is always too brief and precious, something we too easily forget. As one psychical researcher put it once, "We're only on loan to each other in this world. We're a gift to each other."

REMEMBER THAT OUR LOVED ONES ARE ALL AROUND

One of the greatest pleasures of writing our books has been getting to know the people whose stories we have told. The Elliot family—John, Nancy, and their six surviving children—kindly shared the story of their son David with us for our second book, *We Are Not Forgotten*. David died in February 1988 at the age of seventeen after he crashed into a tree while skiing and fatally ruptured his aorta. Interestingly, David's father, John, had read our first book and felt a particular affinity for the story of another teenage boy who died, David Licata. In one of the Elliot family's astounding psychic readings, the two Davids came through together. What made their appearance particularly compelling was that John had dreamed of the two boys together, though all he knew of the Licata boy was what we had written in the book. In the reading, David Elliot spoke of his father's dream in such accurate detail that there is no question but that John's dream was a visitation.

At the time of his son's death, John Elliot was as committed a skeptic as we have found. An engineer and physicist by training, he approached his psychic experiences carefully. Unlike some who doubt the paranormal, John did not feel compelled to discount the unexplained because it challenged his view of the world. Rather, he wanted to be sure that what he sensed was real actually was. Today, he, his wife, and their children believe that David is alive and that he remains a part of their family life. Back in 1990, John told me that he believed David was watching over his family and acting as something of a guardian angel to his siblings. The following experience is but one of several that have convinced the Elliot family of their son's eternal life—and love. It also shows how reacting intuitively to what may be after-death communications can pay off, sometimes when we least expect it.

David Elliot had loved to play soccer, a game two of his brothers, Mark and Jack, also excelled at. Two years after David's death, on the day that would have been his birthday, Mark and Jack were in a soccer game. Both boys played well that day and scored goals. As John Elliot looked on, he could not help but think how promising David's soccer career had been and how proud he would have been of his brothers today. On the car ride home, John sent David the following thought: *You know, it would be really neat, David, if somehow you would share with us that you were here tonight on your birthday.*

Nancy was playing a game of Twenty Questions with two of their younger children, Katie and Michael. The object of the game is for one person to think of an object, person, or place, which the other players try to deduce by asking up to twenty questions. "I've got one!" Nancy exclaimed as the family rode home. John was only half-listening; he was preoccupied with thoughts of David. Suddenly he heard David's voice saying clearly, "It's the dog."

It was David! John was so excited that he immediately turned to Nancy and announced, "The word you want us to guess—it's the dog!"

"How the heck did you know that?" Nancy asked. After all, no one had asked even one question. John explained happily that it was David.

Sometimes we receive communications without consciously realizing it. Patricia recently had such an experience with her late father. "My father had a million card tricks. Because he gambled, I just hated cards—hated to play them, hated seeing them. It goes without saying that I never let him teach me any of his tricks," she recalls. "Recently we were visiting friends, and their teenage son was demonstrating a bunch of card tricks he had just learned. Everyone seemed impressed and at a total loss to understand how he did them. I have no idea how or why I did this, but during one trick I felt like I realized or somehow knew he was palming a card before I actually saw him do it. It was like I said, 'Hey, why's that card face up in your hand' before it registered visually in my brain. But I was right; he was palming a card.

"A few minutes later, after he showed us an elaborate trick involving about a dozen piles of different quantities of cards, it suddenly struck me how he did it. Describing it is hard, but I did not really know it myself. It was like the information just arrived telepathically in my head. At one point I said, 'You're counting cards, right?' Dumbfounded, he replied, 'Yeah.' Then I told him how I thought he did it and I was basically right. If you asked me to explain what counting cards involves or how that trick works now, I couldn't. That night, I felt like I was twelve again and my father, in one of many unorthodox attempts at bonding—which included teaching me to read a racing form——was standing behind me, whispering which cards to throw down from my poker hand. Another reason I feel that my father had a hand, so to speak, in it all was that I'd done something he would have respected and gotten a big kick out of. And I'm pretty sure he did."

WHEN MOONBEAMS WON'T GROW IN PETRI DISHES

For some people, the biggest block to recognizing direct after-death communications is the idea that paranormal phenomena are "impossible," "not scientifically proven," or "wishful thinking." Some feel almost foolish for believing their experience. (See Appendix I, where we closely examine the history of science and the paranormal.)

To the skeptical, after-death communications either do not exist or are unexplained——and unexplainable——anomalies. Some people think that in matters of the spirit, science as we know it is simply irrelevant, that the answers to spiritual questions can never be found in the laboratory. We may one day discover that seeking the proof of spiritual reality through scientific investigation is as pointless as trying to watch your favorite television program on your microwave oven.

Sri Chinmoy is a fully realized spiritual master. Born in India, he entered an ashram at age twelve and in his teens experienced what Hindus consider the highest state of consciousness, *nirvikalpa samadhi*. He came to the United States in 1964 and has distinguished himself as a poet, author, composer, musician, painter, and athlete. He has conducted meditations for United Nations ambassadors and staff, as well as for members of the U.S. Congress. Sri Chinmoy has himself experienced communications from departed souls, as he believes we all can. We asked him how he regarded those who dismiss what they cannot prove.

"There are many things on earth that outwardly we cannot prove. But just because we do not have the means to know something, we cannot say that this thing does not exist," Sri Chinmoy explains. "Let us say that I have eaten a most delicious mango. If you say, 'Prove it!' how will I do so? My joy is in eating, not in proving. If a scientist wants to prove something, he takes us into his laboratory. If we want to prove something on the spiritual plane, we have to take the scientist into the inner world. To enter the inner world, we need a ticket. It's like flying from New York to India; without a ticket, we cannot go. Similarly, without prayer and meditation—which is our inner ticket—we cannot go into the inner world. Is there any scientist ready to pray and meditate like a true seeker and God lover? If so, he will see that communication with beings of other worlds is unmistakably real."

A WORLD—OR TWO—OF WITNESSES

Most of what we know about life after death and after-death communication comes to us from everyday people who never set out to prove or disprove anything. They simply listened and observed.

One of the most publicized and studied after-death communications involved James A. Pike, then bishop of the Episcopal Church. Pike's story is relevant for his faith in his personal experience and his tireless attempts to put aside what he thought he believed in pursuit of the truth. In February 1966, in a New York hotel room, Pike's son, Jim, committed suicide by shooting himself. He was just twenty years old. As his father took great pains to explain in his 1968 best-seller, *The Other Side: An Account of My Experiences with Psychic Phenomena*, Jim was a loving but troubled young man whose difficulties were exacerbated by drug use. In the months before his suicide, Jim had spent much time with his father, who supported him through numerous crises.

Pike was devastated by his son's death, and as he prepared for the funeral services, he writes, "I could not say to myself or to anyone else that I believed that Jim lived on—nor, of course, did I have a basis for believing that he didn't; so I didn't say that either." Clearly, Pike was not expecting to receive after-death communications. Yet shortly after, he began noticing poltergeist-type incidents in the Cambridge, England, apartment he and his son had shared. For example, the bishop and two associates witnessed a mirror that Jim had used move by itself. A broken clock was discovered, its hands stopped at 8:19, the time Jim is presumed to have died.

Jim was apparently trying to get through to his father. Bishop Pike set out to learn all he could from leading parapsychologists and mediums, including Arthur Ford, Ena Twigg, and George Daisley. Considering his position, Bishop Pike had little to gain by publicizing his quest. When he announced that he had received messages from his son through psychics, peers in his church accused him of heresy and the media taunted him mercilessly (one reason he gives for writing his book). Though Pike's search put him in contact with what we would consider the "experts," he repeatedly makes the case for the after-death communication experiences of individuals:

> There are many who would think that an amateur would be imagining things if he reported he was receiving radio signals from outer space on his homemade ham radio set. They would dismiss him as "obviously" engaging in wishful thinking or exaggeration, or assume that he was probably a little "off." Meanwhile, very few in this scientific era will call into question the data gathered by the highly specialized astrophysicists and astronomers, who—with powerful antennas and sensitive recording instruments—make the same report. On the other hand, if in the light of what is now the public knowledge of such scientific data, a ham radio operator today should say he has intercepted pulsations from outer space, the fair-minded person would probably say, "Well, maybe he has. . . ."[1]

A REVOLUTION IN DEATH

Discussing life after death without mentioning the two books that changed the face of death in America is impossible. The first was Dr. Elisabeth Kübler-Ross's *On Death and Dying: What the Dying Have to Teach Doctors, Nurses, Clergy and Their Own Families*. Published in 1969, this seminal work addressed our culture's denial of death and revolution-

---

Throughout the twentieth century, religious teachings and personal opinions about life after death have been diverging in virtually every Western nation except the United States. Moral pundits' assertions to the contrary, statistically speaking, we Americans are the most religious people in the Western world and more apt to accept the premise of life after death than our British, European, and South American contemporaries.

ized our thinking about death and dying. Although most people associate Kübler-Ross with her now-familiar five psychological stages of death, her equally important legacies are the growth of the American hospice movement and a respiritualization of death. Surely, she was not the first doctor to whom dying patients had confided their unusual experiences, such as near-death or out-of-body experiences and deathbed visions. However, she was among the first to take them seriously, though she did not include such accounts in her first book because, as she told *The New York Times Magazine* in 1995, "they would have thrown the whole book out."[2]

In her many workshops and lectures, Kübler-Ross openly discussed the spiritual aspects of what she had observed, but years passed before she wrote about them. Meanwhile, a young physician named Raymond Moody, Jr. became fascinated by the claims of patients and acquaintances who insisted that in a moment of physical death they had died and traveled toward a light. Based on his study of approximately 150 anecdotal cases, Moody wrote *Life After Life*, the first comprehensive overview of what we today commonly know as the near-death experience, or NDE. Moody is careful throughout to state that the phenomenon he describes does not necessarily prove that there is life after death. Yet, understandably, many people—particularly those who have survived such an experience—interpret the NDE as a brief glimpse across to the other side. Many NDE survivors emerge from the experience to report heightened psychic abilities, including those that facilitate after-death communications, such as precognition.

What is most remarkable about these two books is that they touched off revolutions in thinking, not with the discovery of something brand-new but the illumination of age-old phenomena. That they brought taboo subjects to light cannot be overstated. Only seven years after Moody's first book was published, the Gallup organization estimated that approximately eight million Americans had undergone an NDE; today there are hundreds of NDE support groups around the country. Skeptics often ask why there "suddenly" seem to be so many more NDEs than there were twenty, thirty, a hundred, or a thousand years before. Ironically, the advanced medical technology

Kübler-Ross blamed for degrading and compromising the spiritual experience of natural death has created an ever-expanding population of people who have achieved a spiritual renaissance through physically dying and returning to life.

Although near-death experiences have no "witnesses," in a great many cases patients have accurately recalled conversations and events that occurred while they were "dead" and presumably unconscious. Most remarkable and indisputable are those instances in which patients recalled events that occurred in other locations, often at a considerable distance from where they lay "dead." These instances cannot be accounted for by anything *but* a separation of body and consciousness at the instant of physical death.

Over the years experts of many stripes have tried to discredit the NDE, calling it the result of medication, hallucination, or a natural diminution of brain function. Subsequent studies have convincingly ruled out these explanations, perhaps none as effectively as Dr. Melvin Morse's long-term study and resulting book on children's near-death experiences, *Closer to the Light*. Morse's interest in the area began, ironically, in an attempt to discredit Kübler-Ross. This book, based on his study of children's NDEs and those of many other patients, offers what we believe is the definitive argument against the NDE being anything but an NDE.

TOO MANY GHOSTS TO FIT IN THE MACHINE

These pioneering studies virtually revised our society's view of death and the possibility of life after death. Yet they were not scientific studies in the sense that their authors devised experiments that could be reported on and then recreated by others. For all their supporting arguments, these works are based on anecdotal evidence, *what people say happened to them.*

It is simply inconceivable that millions of people have suffered mass delusion or some imaginative, wish-fulfilling grief response. Perhaps there is no explanation as we would understand it. Or perhaps there is an explanation, but one we cannot even conceive. As

Bishop Pike so brilliantly observed in the last chapter of *The Other Side*:

> Suppose Rip Van Winkle had awakened in the electronic age. Suppose he had been instructed to ask a computer a question, had fed in the question, received the answer, and then been asked, "How do you think you got that information?" Surely his answer would have been something like, "A man in there must have looked it up quickly." Nothing in his previous experience would have enabled him to conceive of what are actually the inner workings of such an electronic device.[3]

Pike wrote those words in the late 1960s, when a computer equal in power to an average laptop occupied an entire room. But let's nudge Rip awake in 1997. How will he explain the source of the wisdom lurking inside a Powerbook? Genius insects? Magic dust? Faced with the same phenomenon under different circumstances, he might find some explanation, but it is a good bet we would never convince him it was all zeros and ones dancing around silicon chips. Chances are, Pike would have trouble believing that, too.

Belief in after-death communications has remained generally consistent through time. Only the official explanations change to accommodate and reflect prevailing religious, political, scientific, and psychological beliefs. Depending on when his alarm clock sounds, Rip and his skeptic brethren will claim it is a man in the machine or smart dust, the work of the devil or the touch of angels.

Millions know the truth: after-death communications are real. That these encounters challenge, even defy the laws of time and space as we understand them does not make them impossible. What is the nature of time if one can know the future before it happens? What is the nature of physical reality if unseen forces can move objects? What is the nature of human consciousness, of life itself, if we can communicate with persons who no longer inhabit this earth in earthly form? What is the nature of a love that can transcend time, space, and even death itself? A love that can bind, heal, and grow?

What is this love beyond life?

3

MORE THAN A DREAM

The dream is the small hidden door in the deepest and the most intimate sanctum of the soul. . . .

—Carl Gustav Jung

"Rita" and her father, "Dave," were always close, so when he was hospitalized for lung cancer and heart disease, she stayed in his home. One night she dreamed that her father came into her bedroom, closed the door, and gently tucked her in, neatly folding the covers around her as he had done when she was a child. Then he turned to go and, as he had done in all the years she lived at home, he closed the door behind him.

Despite the fact that she had hastily nestled under the covers the night before, Rita awoke the next morning to discover the quilt and sheets neatly arranged, just as she had seen them in her dream. Then she looked to the bedroom door. To her amazement, it was closed, again just like in the dream. However, Rita never slept with her door closed. She was thinking about her strange dream when the phone rang. It was her father's doctor calling to say that Dave had died during the night. Rita believes her dream was more than a dream, that it was her father visiting her to say goodnight one last time.

THE UNIVERSE INSIDE OUR MINDS

Dreaming is the single state of altered consciousness we all experience regularly. We do it every time we fall asleep, but no one can say for sure why or exactly how. We begin to dream before we are born, and over a lifetime we may experience tens of thousands of dreams. Of these, we will recall only a relative handful. Dreams can bring creative insight, spiritual revelation, or intellectual breakthrough. They can also draw us into worlds of terror and helplessness from which we feel powerless to escape. No wonder the act of dreaming and what Shakespeare called "the stuff of dreams" have fired mankind's curiosity and imagination.

The history of dreams and dream study begins with the dawn of human consciousness itself. Virtually no aspect of human endeavor is untouched by dreams—from the birth of world-shaking religious movements to the cheap manipulations of political campaigns and advertising agencies. We are moved, shaped, and inspired by dreams, their power and promise. The timeless quest to understand them is irresistible, for we sense that our deepest mysteries, the keys to our true selves and our universe, lie wrapped inside them.

The idea that the dream state is a conduit for communications—between the conscious and the subconscious, the human and the divine, the past and the future, the living and the dead—is as old as dreams themselves. To the ancients, dreams brought messages from gods and spirits. Whatever else we might say about the way our ancestors regarded dreams, they certainly took them seriously. The dream prophecies told in religious texts are accepted as real. The Bible includes many accounts of dreams, and half the Old Testament's Book of Daniel consists of Daniel's dreams and visions.

Just as evolving religious doctrine has shifted on matters of the paranormal, so attitudes toward dreams have undergone dramatic changes. Early Christian writers found dreams troubling. Recognizing them as a possible source of godly wisdom and guidance, they also feared them as possible vehicles for demons. Saint Jerome, who created the first Latin translation of the Bible, is thought to have deliberately included the word *dream* in prohibitions against such acts as witchcraft where no such word exists in the original Hebrew. As Dr. Robert Van de Castle points out in *Our Dreaming Mind*, these "mistranslations changed the course of Christian belief and practice regarding dreams." As he illustrates, dreams were dispatched to the "nether regions," at least theologically speaking, and not considered again until the seventeenth century.

The Romantic movement, which began late in the eighteenth century and was inspired by the dramatic changes wrought by the French Revolution, rediscovered dreams and recast them in a glowing light. With their championing of individuality, imagination, creativity, and expression, the romantics elevated the common man to the pedestal the neoclassicists reserved for heroes and gods. Artists and writers drew inspiration from nature, the mystical, the unexplained, the exotic, and the erotic. (It's not surprising that this period is often compared with the 1960s.) This period produced many serious works on dreams, some of which, Van de Castle asserts, prefigure the later theories of Freud and Jung.

While nineteenth-century romantics were reviving dreams, spiritualism grew unabated and the early scientific inquiries into the paranormal began. Coincidence? We think not. We cannot understate the seismic shifts that took place in attitudes toward God, religion, government, and science. It is impossible to appreciate the full impact of Darwin's theory of evolution on the nineteenth-century mind. As history shows repeatedly, when doctrine falters, when beliefs crumble, people seek new answers from more deeply within and from ever further beyond. Revived interest in spiritualism, for example, nearly always parallels periods of social upheaval, particularly wars. In the United States the two heydays of mediumship occurred during and immediately after the Civil War and World War I.

While a renewed interest in dreams evolved concurrently with the so-called New Age movement, relatively little has been written about dreams as vehicles for direct after-death contacts. This is curious, since our research—backed by numerous other studies on the subject—reveals that the overwhelming majority of psychic experiences, including direct after-death communications, occur during dreams. For some, every direct contact they experience is through dreams, and among those who have several different types of after-death contact, at least one dream is usually among them.

Dreams form a universe in and of themselves, in many ways. They can be viewed, interpreted, and explained in religious, historic, psychological, physiological, neurological, and psychic contexts. Fascinating as all these areas are, we are concerned here only with those dreams that are clearly paranormal. While modern dream research has focused on dreams as a medium for telepathy, clairvoyance, and precognition, in this chapter we concentrate on the most common paranormal experience: the dream visitation.

DREAM RESEARCH: OPENING THE DOOR

Dream visitations offer a litany of contrasts: shattering the darkness of sleep with stunning light, they are vivid yet ephemeral, seemingly hyper-real yet still, we remind ourselves, just dreams. Because they are unpredictable, rarely repeated, and impossible to measure, dream visitations, unlike dream telepathy, elude scientific study. The fact that they are unverifiable, except in instances where precognition or clairvoyance are factors, only adds to the difficulty of studying the phenomena. (We discuss precognitive dreams in chapter 6.)

The earliest scientific research into the paranormal aspects of dreams began in the late nineteenth century with the London-based Society for Psychical Research. The SPR documented many cases in which people learned through dreams that someone they knew had died. (We will discuss the SPR's work more fully in chapter 4.) At around the same time, Sigmund Freud was refining his psychoanalytic theories and basing them largely on dreams. Though Freud considered dreams "the royal road to the unconscious," according to Van de Castle, "[t]hrough his intense focus upon the neurotic, infantile, and sexual aspects of dreams, Freud gave dreams a bad name."[1]

The age-old idea of dreams as a medium for communications from other dimensions lost favor. Fittingly, dreams found their champion in Carl Jung. Where Freud viewed dreams as a means by which the human psyche releases repressed sexual and aggressive impulses, Jung contended that the purpose of dreaming was to communicate to—rather than repress from—the conscious mind the knowledge we need to develop as full, productive human beings. With time, Freud's dream theories have fallen by the wayside, while Jung's holistic approach to dreams and dreaming remains influential.

Technology has permitted modern science to view the dream state as a physiological phenomenon that it can observe, measure, and quantify. The discovery in 1953 of rapid eye movement (REM) and its association with active dreaming opened new vistas for dream research. Sleeping subjects could be awakened during or immediately after the REM period and questioned about their dreams. For the next several years, scientists believed that we dream only during REM sleep. We now know that important dreaming can also occur in non-REM sleep, although REM dreams are generally more intense and memorable. The REM stage is the most conducive to paranormal dreams.

In 1962 Dr. Montague Ullman, a psychiatrist, began the Dream Laboratory at the Maimonides Medical Center in Brooklyn, New York; two years later the psychologist Dr. Stanley Krippner joined him. The laboratory was soon recognized as a leading institution for dream research. Some of the Maimonides experiments tackled the question of whether dreams could be influenced telepathically. In a series of carefully controlled experiments, they demonstrated the ability of one person to telepathically transmit an image or an idea to a dreaming person who could recall it upon waking. Though statistically impressive, these findings were considered controversial.* The fact remains, however, that these experiments proved conclusively that dreams can reflect information originating from outside the dreamer's mind.

Dreams through which we gain information from outside sources, dreams in which we glimpse the future, dreams in which we communicate with spirits—all challenge the idea that our dreams are simply products of our imagination or random, involuntary neurological events. Are they *all* expressions of our subconscious minds? A release from the anxiety and fears of our waking lives? Some people do not think so.

---

*See Robert L. Van de Castle, *Our Dreaming Mind* (New York: Ballantine Books, 1994). Dr. Van de Castle, who participated in these studies as a subject, offers a fascinating firsthand account of the experiments and vigorously refutes their critics.

There are two possible ways that spirits might communicate to us through dreams. One theory states that the dream state makes our minds more receptive to outside input, such as telepathy or after-death communication. Researchers have suggested that other types of psychic experiences, such as mediumship, also occur within the context of dreams for a similar reason. Electroencephalograms (EEGs) taken while people are experiencing paranormal events frequently show the subject's brain waves in the alpha state, a condition in which the individual is relaxed yet alert. When we are sleeping, our brain waves slow even more, to what is called the theta state.

Another possibility is that spirits, having once lived and dreamed on this plane, know that while dreaming, our otherwise rational minds suspend the waking rules of logic and possibility. They may find it easier to get through to us when our logic defenses are at their ebb.

A third possibility, which dates back to the ancient Greeks, is that we are doing the visiting. While we sleep, our spirit, or astral body, separates from our physical body and travels to some psychic rendezvous. Supporting this possibility are accounts of people who during a near-death experience learned of events that occurred in physically distant locations. These out-of-body day trips may sound far-fetched. Yet descriptions of dream visitations often closely resemble descriptions of near-death experiences (see chapter 4). Could a dream be another altered state of consciousness by which we "detour" to the other side and back?

THE CLASSIC DREAM VISITATION

Our focus here is not on the how but the why, the purpose and the message of dream visitations. Are these really dreams? Or apparitions? We believe they are both. Based on our interviews and research, these are common hallmarks of a classic dream visitation.

- *Dream visitations stand out from other dreams; they are clearly significant or meaningful.* We laugh at many of our dreams because they seem so meaningless, even absurd. By contrast, we instantly recognize dream visitations as significant. Most dream visitations are spontaneous and unexpected events, initiated by those on the other side. In other instances, the dream visits appear to be answering our deeply felt emotional appeals or prayers for help. Many dream visitations seem to provide a more detailed experience of a departed loved one than other forms of direct after-death communications. For example, it is only in direct-contact dreams that we can clearly see, hear, and embrace departed loved ones again. By contrast, other visionary experiences—waking visions, near-death experiences, apparitions, and deathbed visions—usually offer only brief glimpses.

- *Dream visitations are far more vivid, persistent, and real than the usual dream.* While most dreams strike us as disorganized and disjointed, those of departed loved ones are invariably described as real, lifelike, vivid, and intense. Dream visitations do not take place in the confused "parallel world" of other dreams, where, to cite dream expert Jeremy Taylor's evocative book title, "people fly and water runs uphill." They seem like real visits because they *are* real visits. Deceased loved ones appear as they did in life, though they often seem the picture of health no matter what their physical state at death. While we soon forget most dreams, dream visitations seem to engage our waking attention and are remembered in great detail long after they have happened.

- *The message dream visitations convey is usually simple and to the point.* Unlike ordinary dreams, direct-contact dreams rarely require analysis. Even when symbols figure prominently, their meaning is nearly literal, or at least fairly obvious. Though many of these dreams are dramatic and emotional in content, their essential message is generally brief: "I love you," "Be careful," or "Watch for good news."

In June 1994, Elise Le Vaillant dreamed of her late grandmother, Frances, who had passed away in January 1992. In the dream, Elise, her grandmother, and her sister Celine were aboard a luxury liner. Pulling in to dock, the ship metamorphosed into a military vessel like a carrier. Grandmother Frances turned to Celine and exclaimed, "Your ship is coming in! Your ship is coming in!"

From the crowd on the dock emerged a handsome young man in a dark-blue uniform. As Elise and Frances watched from the deck, Celine made her way down the gangplank to the dock, where the young man took her hand. Celine then said to him, "I'm scared. I've been through a lot." "You don't have to be afraid," the young man replied. "I understand. I'll take care of you." The pair walked off together, and Elise woke with a start.

There were aspects of her dream that did not require deep analysis. Celine was over thirty and had never had a serious romantic relationship. Though attractive and accomplished, she just never seemed to meet the right person. But what did the rest of it mean?

Interestingly, Elise recognized that there was something special about her dream, so she wrote it down immediately the next morning. She did not share the dream with anyone else, least of all Celine, out of fear that it would create false hope. Four months after Elise's dream, Celine met a young man named Paul. They fell in love and a few months later announced their engagement. Paul is a Coast Guard officer whose dress uniform looks exactly like the one the man wore in Elise's dream. Exactly one year after the dream, Celine and Paul were wed.

After Elise's dream had clearly come true, she told several other family members about it. It was only then that she learned that Frances frequently used the expression "Your ship's come in" to greet any good news. As Grandmother Frances had predicted, Celine's ship had indeed come in.

- *Communication within dream visitations seems to occur telepathically.* People may awaken after a visitation with knowledge they did not have before and the sense that they received it from the spirit. Sometimes no words are spoken, but the subjects awaken feeling that information has been communicated to them telepathically. Telepathic communication is frequently mentioned by survivors of NDEs and people who have had other paranormal experiences.

  One interesting aspect is that while the subjects may remember most of the dream and even recall a specific message, they commonly emerge from such dreams with a sense that they were being told vast quantities of engaging, important information, which they now cannot recall. This is another similarity between dream visitations and near-death experiences.

- *Dream visitations serve a purpose.* Sometimes they bring a message of comfort as simple as "I love you. I'm still close to you." For example, Nelly's husband, Joe, died of cancer at age fifty-seven. One night, twenty-five years after he died, Joe made his first contact with her in a very vivid dream. (Generally speaking, most direct contacts first occur within two years of death, but they can happen anytime.)

  First Nelly saw herself and Joe in an unfamiliar church with a crowd of friends and relatives, all gathered, it seemed, to witness Joe receiving an award. She saw many loved ones she had not seen in years, some living and some deceased. Nelly sat in a pew near the altar, and at the exact moment when Joe was handed his award, she turned to see the proud faces behind her. Instead she was shocked to see the church totally empty except for one person sitting alone in the back row. The figure stood, and Nelly found herself walking arm in arm with Joe toward him. Drawing closer, Nelly realized that it was her late son, Joe, Jr., who had died years before at age fifty.

"I'm still here," Joe Jr. told his mother. The reunited family embraced lovingly, then walked out of the church. Despite the many years between Joe's death and the dream, Nelly was certain that he and their son were reaching out to her. She describes her feeling after the dream as one of "inner peace."

Other messages concern the future. They might be warnings about a future tragedy, even a death. These dreams can convey lifesaving warnings. We will examine the precognitive dream visitation in greater detail in chapter 6.

- *Dream visitations can be verifiable.* In other words, they can give us information otherwise unknown to us that can be proved or corroborated. For example, departed loved ones may communicate the whereabouts of lost items. In other instances, deceased relatives or family friends we never knew personally on earth visit us. This is especially true of children who receive dream visitations from parents and grandparents who predeceased them. When people experience clusters of after-death communications, at least one dream usually conveys a piece of otherwise irrelevant information that they can later verify.

Why are verifiable dreams so valuable? It is human nature to question the accuracy of one's perceptions. We never question other people's claims to have had a dream, even though they can offer no proof of the experience. There is no window into these dreamers' minds through which we might see, feel, or hear what they claim to have experienced. So when someone reports having had an unusually intense dream about Aunt Mildred, we usually do not quibble. Besides, what would be the point? That the dream occurred could never be proved or disproved.

The dream visitations that follow are of particular interest because in them spirits offered a specific piece of information that could be confirmed only by a third party who had not experienced the communication itself. From our study, this type of visitation, which we call a verifiable visitation, is relatively uncommon. (Of course there may be a significant number that never have the chance to be verified simply because the subject forgets or chooses not to discuss them.)

"Richard" and "Sarah" were the proud parents of two children: fifteen-year-old "Danielle" and five-year-old "Robert." Both children were bright and loving, and their parents were especially pleased by how close the siblings were despite the ten-year gap in their ages.

Like any teenager struggling to assert her independence, Danielle could be difficult at times. One afternoon, in the midst of a disagreement, Danielle taxed her father's patience to the limit. Their argument would have continued if Danielle had not left the house with her mother and two friends to run some errands at the local shopping mall. Neither she nor her father reached any resolution, and Danielle felt particularly angry with Richard for shaking his finger at her as if she were a little girl.

A few hours later, Sarah's car was hit head-on by a drunk driver, killing both her and Danielle. The two other passengers were critically injured but survived. For Richard and little Robert the loss was devastating. A conscientious parent, Richard felt it especially important to listen when Robert spoke of his mother or his sister and to help him deal with his grief.

Several months after the accident, Robert dreamed of his sister. According to Robert, Danielle greeted him and then said, "When Daddy scolded me, I was really angry with him because he kept shaking his finger at me. But I'm not angry at Daddy anymore. And I don't want him to be mad at me. Please, Robbie, tell him. Promise me you'll tell Daddy. I shouldn't have been mad at him. Tell Daddy I love him. Tell him I'm fine now. I'm with Mommy and both grandmas and grandpas, and they're taking care of me. Don't forget to give Daddy my message: I'm not angry. I love you, Robbie. I've got to go now."

Robert, certain he had seen his sister, was eager to share his happy news. When he described the dream to Richard, his father carefully explained that he had dreamed about Danielle because he missed her so much. He told Robert that was okay, but that people who died really did not come to visit us.

Robert, however, was insistent. "No, Daddy. I really saw Danielle. She looked pretty and happy. And she's with Mommy and both grandmas and grandpas."

Richard was at a loss. Now what? Little Robert was brimming with joy. Richard silently pondered which would be more damaging to his grief-stricken little boy—to firmly discourage any more talk of "visits" or just go along with Robert's little fantasy—when Robert suddenly blurted, "Danielle has a message for you, Daddy."

Richard drew a deep breath. "What did she say?" he asked softly. "Danielle said that before the accident she was mad at you because you shook your finger like this." Robert moved his index finger back and forth, precisely imitating the motion Danielle had made in his dream—the very gesture Richard had made that fateful afternoon.

Richard was struck dumb as he thought back to that day and realized that not only was the gesture correct but that the little boy had not been home at the time. And since Danielle had left the house with her mother right after the argument, she could not have spoken to Robert about it before she died. There was no way the little boy could have known this. Or at least no way except the way he now claimed to have learned it: from Danielle.

"And now she's not mad anymore," Robert continued happily. "And she said you shouldn't be mad at her because she loves you."

- *Dream visitations usually leave subjects with a feeling of well-being or peace.* A visitation may provide the answer to a question or the solution to a problem. It may change the way we look at life, and death.

Throughout their lives, neither Charles nor Lester Kenyon had been drawn to religion and neither believed in life after death. They were both well beyond retirement age when Lester died and four months later appeared to his older brother, Charles, in what Charles describes as "the most realistic dream I ever had."

"Hello, Chuck," Lester said, greeting Charles by his childhood nickname. Through the conversation, which they exchanged telepathically, the two brothers discussed everyday, mundane topics. Charles later characterized their conversation as small talk, and said, "It wasn't what he said that impressed me, but the vividness of the experience. I didn't believe it, but it happened to me. It made an impression on my mind. I felt that my brother Lester's spirit was thinking about me. If it's real, and not just a dream, it certainly makes you rethink death. If my brother is still alive somewhere, then you think, *Maybe there's less reason to fear death.* I'll say this: If it hadn't happened to me, I wouldn't have believed it. I've always been skeptical."

Three months after the visitation from his brother, Charles died suddenly of natural causes. It is tempting to speculate about whether Lester's visit had some premonitory purpose. Did Lester know Charles would die soon? Did he visit him to ease his fears of death? Given Charles's age, death might have come at any time. Most visitations are greetings, but with a purpose. Certainly Lester's visit changed Charles's attitude toward death, and perhaps that is all his brother set out to do.

DO ALL DREAM VISITATIONS FIT THE PROFILE?

No. Which brings us to further questions: How seriously should we take the messages that come to us from departed loved ones in dreams? As we will discuss in more detail in chapter 6, how should we respond to these dreams? Is there anything that we can—or should—do?

One of the more troubling dream visitations we've come across happened to my coauthor, Patricia Romanowski. We alluded to it briefly in our second book, but she analyzed it more deeply after we started this project. In September 1980, Patricia was vacationing in the Adirondacks, in upstate New York, with her future husband, Philip Bashe. They had rented a cabin on a lake, part of a large, heavily wooded property that included other cabins. The cabin had no phone, and though Patricia had given her sisters in the Bronx the owners' phone number, she had no reason to call them. Despite having suffered a massive heart attack five years earlier, her father, John, seemed to be doing as well as he ever had. True, he continued smoking cigars and having the occasional forbidden drink or steak. Still, he looked and seemed to feel fine.

In a dream Patricia saw her father standing in a dark room. It was odd because although there seemed to be darkness all around him, his face and body were brightly illuminated, as if he were standing in the spotlight on a darkened stage. As he faced her, he casually rested his right hand on a flat wooden surface, which Patricia took to be a card table or a bar. Both made sense, since her father was a compulsive gambler, and until Patricia was seven years old, her father had helped her mother run the two bars and the nightclub they owned in Wichita, Kansas.

As Patricia says, "My father in the dream was everything he was in life: handsome, assured, even kind of cocky. He was a great kidder, a lady-killer when he wanted to be, and though he was a great raconteur, when it came to really serious things, he had few words. By then, in his late fifties, between his drinking and gambling, he'd done so many crazy, irresponsible things that he sometimes found it hard to face me or my sisters and brother. So in a way, what he said in the dream didn't fully surprise me: 'I've had it. This is it. I'm checking out. I love you. Goodbye.' He turned away from me and faded into the darkness.

"I did not wake up then, whenever *then* was, but that morning over breakfast I told Phil about the dream. Since adolescence I had been doing what I now realize was lucid dreaming, so the vividness did not really impress me. Because so many people in my family are somewhat psychic, I took meaningful, or precognitive, dreams for granted. I thought everyone had them. As I recounted the dream to Phil, I was calm.

"We were eating breakfast when the woman who owned the property knocked on our door and said my sister had called and asked that I call her back immediately. I knew then that my father had died. As I later learned, he was opening his friend's bar in the Bronx when he died suddenly of a heart attack. The coroner placed the time of death at around 7:30 A.M. Although one of my sisters suspected that he had been having angina attacks for some time before, I didn't know that."

Since there is no way to be certain when the dream occurred, it is impossible to find out what kind of apparition it was. Was the John Romanowski who spoke to Patricia in her dream her father's spirit that had already crossed over? Was he a spirit in transition? Or, somehow knowing that it would soon leave his body, did his spirit come to Patricia to say goodbye? We could say that we will never know, except that Patricia fully believes that one day she will know, just not in this lifetime.

"I fully understand how someone could find a dream like that troubling. If it really was a premonition, could I have done anything to change the outcome? Could I have phoned him and said, 'Daddy, stay in bed today'? Even that would not have saved him. Some people I have shared this with are troubled by what my father said: 'I've had it. I'm checking out.' I realize that is not the soft-focus Hallmark send-off most of us imagine or would want. But that was my father.

"I think my experience points out how difficult, how like real life these experiences can be. When he turned to walk away from me, some part of me was okay with that. Again, you think about skeptics and nonbelievers saying that it must be your imagination at work. But if it had been my imagination, I would have run after him or said something to him or at least kissed him and hugged him goodbye. None of that happened, though, because it *wasn't* a dream."

Visually, the experience had several very common elements, including the loved one appearing to be bathed in light. "I think it is interesting that I did not see my father moving into light but into darkness. That he arrived on the other side in some confusion and conflict has been confirmed for me through several psychic readings. Nevertheless, I hardly needed a psychic to tell me that. My father had done a lot to make his life less fulfilling, less stable, and less happy than it should have been. Death came as something of a relief for my father, and I think he was trying to tell me that.

"The only object in the dream was the wooden surface he rested his hand on when he spoke. When I see it in my mind's eye now, it's clear that it was too high for a card table and too low for a bar. Before I knew he was dead, the fact that the surface was highly polished and not flat but slightly rounded didn't register. Now of course I realize it was a coffin. And that makes me wonder if he was not already dead when he came to me."

DREAM VISITATIONS CAN HEAL

Virtually everyone who has had a dream visitation felt that they brought peace and comfort. Many said their dream visitations also contained important messages. Yet many people ignore these messages, not understanding what they are and fearing it is their imagination at work or a bizarre coincidence when events they had dreamed come true. Few people, if any, in our research, regarded their dreams of departed loved ones as trivial. Most people would welcome more such dreams.

We recall the direct after-death communication as a dream. However, as we said earlier, it may strike us as more vivid and lifelike than a dream precisely because it is not one. All of our senses are functional in dream visitations. We not only see departed loved ones, we can often feel them, even sense the cologne or perfume they wore in their physical life. People often recall the sensation of being held, hugged, or kissed.

The effects of dream visitations are very similar to the positive results of other visionary experiences and after-death contacts, such as near-death experiences, apparitions, and readings by psychic mediums. For instance, some people believe that the dream visitation reduces their fear of death because it transforms their conception of death. What they once viewed as a dreaded, uncertain finality is now a continuation, a transformation.

Most subjects also report that the dream contacts have left them feeling less alone. Though they still grieve for their deceased loved ones, they have been given a sign that the person lives on. Dream visitations can also be opportunities for emotional healing, as in this next case.

A BROTHER'S SILENT GOODBYE

To all appearances, David DiVito was a happy, successful young man. One of eleven children from a close-knit suburban family, David was responsible and hardworking. By age thirty-four he was a married man, the proud father of a baby girl named "Tara," and a sought-after construction worker. In fact, he had built the two-story frame house in which his family lived.

Yet David also had his share of disappointment, which he took harder than anyone around him realized. His daughter, Tara, suffered from chronic kidney failure. By age one, she had already lost the use of one kidney and had undergone two serious operations. Now she was scheduled for a third, and doctors were talking to David and his wife about a kidney transplant in the near future. Sitting at her bedside constantly, David could only gaze at his little blond baby and wonder, *Why?* Her illness and David's other problems were taking their toll on his marriage.

One January morning, David's wife found him convulsing on the living room couch. She rushed to phone for help, but by the time the ambulance arrived, David was near death. At the hospital doctors pronounced him dead on arrival. The whole family was in shock, their loss made even more painful by the coroner's revelation that David had ingested a lethal quantity of tranquilizers and other prescription painkillers.

Although David was close to all of his siblings, he shared a special bond with his sister Darcy, who was four years younger. "David, me, my brother Doug, and my sister Dina—the four of us always hung out together," Darcy recalls. "David always took care of me." When Darcy speaks of her brother, there is no doubt that his death left a tremendous void in her life.

Darcy believed in an afterlife, and while she was not opposed to attending church, she describes herself as more spiritual than religious. "You don't have to go to church," she says. "God hears you." Even so, Darcy felt there were moments after David died when no one heard her, when she cried out to him, "Why can't you just come to me? Why do I have to go to a psychic?" No one answered.

Or so Darcy thought. A month after David died, Darcy had an unusual dream. "I never felt anything so real," she recalls. "This was no ordinary dream. This was unbelievably clear."

David appeared dressed casually in a blue sports shirt and neatly pressed new jeans. He was perched on a barstool, and Darcy was sitting to his left. "I felt like I was sitting right there next to him. I couldn't take my eyes off him." Behind David were three other sisters and his mother. David was pointing above his head to what Darcy describes as "pictures and images" of people he and Darcy had known. Each image appeared to be bathed in light, although each was otherwise surrounded by darkness.

Then suddenly from David's right and above him, a bright white light began glowing. Gradually, the light grew larger and intensified until it consumed the entire scene. Then, Darcy recalls, "I could see every line on David's face. He looked tired and aged, and there were tears in his eyes." Glancing up, Darcy saw that the images over his head had vanished. Then David turned to her and hugged her. They embraced tightly, and Darcy remembers not wanting to let him go, although, "I just knew he had to go back. I could feel it, although nothing was said."

When Darcy awoke, she was crying but felt comforted and reassured knowing that David continued living. "It felt so real. I could feel his embrace. Actually, I felt like I died and went out of my body,"

Darcy says, then adds that she woke up feeling exhausted and dehydrated. "The only thing that upset me was how sad and tired David looked."

A month or so later David returned in another dream. This time Darcy found herself at a funeral but could not figure out whose. David was there, but this time he looked younger. His eyes were much brighter, his skin was vibrant and smooth, and he was wearing a suit, which looked too large for him.

Suddenly Darcy saw her late paternal grandmother, Angelina, who had died more than a decade before. David was sitting next to her, but they were not speaking to each other. As in the first dream, David turned to face Darcy. She knelt by his chair and he embraced her. Again, Darcy experienced a sense of physical warmth and a feeling of love. Next her sister Dina appeared and said to Darcy, "Mommy will be so happy you got to see him." With that, the dream ended.

Darcy found it hard to understand exactly what David was trying to tell her this time. The funeral setting and the appearance of her grandmother made no sense. She instinctively knew, of course, that Angelina was there for David, but why did she also see a living family member there?

Funerals are often symbolic of transition. The presence of both living and deceased family members suggests that both David and his survivors were in a period of transition, of moving through grief to acceptance. That the adjustment was proceeding well is suggested by David's renewed and more healthy appearance in the second dream. Many psychics contend that people who take their own lives often arrive in the afterlife feeling lost and confused. Because they are solely responsible for their passing, they may suffer tremendous guilt and remorse, especially after witnessing the anguish of loved ones left behind. Clearly, Darcy's second dream indicated that David had found some peace.

Except for their vividness and hyper-real ambience, we could dismiss Darcy's dreams as the products of her profound grief. Perhaps they were. But a series of dreams that Darcy and others in her family experienced prove that they were true visitations. Other members of

Darcy's family have encountered David, and through all the direct after-death contacts runs one undeniably clear thread: that David was growing and finding contentment on the other side. In one, Darcy's sister Dale dreamed of David as a young, carefree boy. Then several months after David's passing, Darcy and her sister Dina both had similar dreams of David—the same night. In both dreams David was sitting on the edge of Dina's bed in her house. "It was as if we were just hanging out like we normally did after David would come home from work in the evening," Darcy says. In content there was little remarkable about this dream except that it occurred to both Darcy and Dina simultaneously, indicating that these were visitations.

Several more dreams occurred in the first year after David died, but one in particular stands out because it contained a verifiable piece of information. Darcy dreamed she saw a coworker named "Lisa" with David. Darcy found it funny that she would dream of David with someone he did not know in life. As Darcy pondered this in her dream, David's face dissolved and became someone else's, a stranger's.

The next morning Darcy awoke comforted but puzzled. The next day when she ran into Lisa at work, she said, "I had a dream about you."

"Me?" Lisa asked, surprised.

Darcy then explained the dream and mentioned David.

"How do you know about David?" Lisa asked, somewhat alarmed.

"David's my brother," Darcy replied softly. "He died last month."

"What? I'm so sorry; I didn't know. I didn't even know you had a brother named David. I thought you meant my boyfriend David."

"Is that him?" Darcy asked, pointing to a young man at a nearby desk.

"How did you know that?" Lisa asked in disbelief.

"Because that's the face I saw in my dream," she replied.

"Oh, Darcy. Please don't tell anyone. I don't know how you figured it out, but David and I have been having a relationship in secret. No one else knew."

Except, we should note, Darcy's brother David.

While it is unusual to have as many direct after-death contacts as

Darcy and some of her siblings have had, it is probably not as rare as we think. As we have mentioned before, there are probably countless dreams and experiences that our conscious, logical minds reject out of hand. Imagine if Darcy had been too shy or afraid of embarrassing herself to mention her dream to Lisa. Not only would she never have discovered exactly what her dream meant, she would have missed a precious opportunity to confirm that it was a real visitation.

The circumstances of David's death also contributed to the many contacts. He loved his family and they missed him immensely. We have often seen that tragic circumstances seem to enhance, facilitate, or intensify virtually any form of psychic experience. By taking his own life, David left without saying goodbye. His ongoing love for those he left behind is evidenced in his many appearances.

Darcy believes she has benefited from receiving the visits from David. "You can't stop missing someone you love that much," Darcy reflects. "I always knew definitely that there is life after death. These dream visits from David just reaffirmed it. I always feel him close to me. I do talk to him and I pray to God for him. With a more positive outlook on death, you have a more positive outlook on life."

4

TRAVERSING THE BRIDGE

Apparitions, Deathbed Visions, and the Near-Death Experience

If there is a physical body, there is also a spiritual body.

—I CORINTHIANS 15:44

Evelyn Moleta and her husband, Joe, were in their thirties when they moved with their two young children into a first-floor apartment on Tenth Street, in New York City. Their apartment was one of three in a large house; the Kwiatkowski family occupied the floor above, as they had for the past fourteen years. Evelyn and Josie Kwiatkowski soon became best of friends, and for the next thirty years, the two were almost inseparable. Almost daily Evelyn heard Josie calling her name as she descended the stairs: "Evelyn!" Then, after a brief pause, "Evelyn, Evelyn!"

By 1986, Josie, then in her early seventies, was suffering from myriad health problems, including heart disease and stomach cancer. Evelyn, now widowed, took care of her friend, visiting her often in the hospital and cooking for her and her husband, Stanley, nearly every evening. Late one afternoon about a month after Josie took a turn for the worse, Evelyn was making herself supper when her dog, Lucky, began barking persistently and running to the front door. In the same moment Evelyn clearly heard Josie's voice calling, "Evelyn." *She must be back from the hospital,* Evelyn thought. It was typical of Josie to call out Evelyn's name on her way downstairs, a sound Lucky greeted with loud, happy barks.

Evelyn rushed to the front door, but before she could open it, she again heard Josie: "Evelyn. Evelyn." *That's Josie, all right.* She never called Evelyn just once; it was always once, then twice again in quick succession. Evelyn flung open the door, fully expecting to see her friend, but no one was there. Lucky dashed out into the hall and stopped at the foot of the stairs, where he looked up eagerly. Evelyn followed and looked up, too, but there was no one. *I know I heard her,* Evelyn thought. Then she stopped. *But I didn't hear footsteps!*

Back inside her apartment, Evelyn telephoned her mother-in-law, who lived on the third floor. Had she called her name a few minutes ago? No, her mother-in-law replied, it wasn't she. Evelyn hung up not sure what to make of the incident. She knew she heard Josie; she just knew it. For the rest of the evening, she could not shake that conviction.

The next day Josie and Stanley's daughter knocked on Evelyn's door. She had bad news: Josie died yesterday.

"When did it happen?" Evelyn asked.

"My mother died yesterday afternoon at about 4:30."

"What? That's when your mother called me by name three times and Lucky barked!" Evelyn exclaimed. "But no one was there."

"Well, that must have been my mother telling you goodbye."

People everywhere have believed in ghosts, or the apparitions of spirits. (The word *ghost* is derived from the German *geist*, which means "spirit.") The sudden manifestation of a deceased person is a staple of horror familiar to the collective imagination, though in real life it is among the rarest forms of after-death communication. Nearly all cultures believe in the possible existence of ghosts, and prescribed rituals to appease potentially angry or malevolent spirits are common. Hauntings and poltergeists can be threatening, even harmful. But these cases are rare and beyond the scope of this book.

We are concerned with only those types of apparitions through which after-death communications occur. These are crisis apparitions, apparitions of the dead, deathbed visions, and near-death experiences (NDEs). We are including here the spirits seen by people in the midst of a near-death experience because of the many parallels between them and other forms of apparitions. We believe that each of these phenomena results when spirits—of both the living and the dead—traverse the bridge between dimensions.

CRISIS APPARITIONS

A crisis apparition is the manifestation of someone at or near the time of death or other crisis. While it is reasonable to consider the possibility that wish-fulfillment fantasies may produce experiences resembling apparitions, crisis apparitions rule that out. In both our research and in historical accounts, apparitions materialized to people who had absolutely no desire to imagine their loved one dead. In the most compelling, indisputable instances, the subjects do not yet know that the person they are seeing is indeed dead.

Society for Psychical Research cofounder F.W.H. Myers conducted one of the most extensive studies of apparitions. Running 1,400 pages, *Phantasms of the Living* (1886) examined 701 cases, the vast majority of them concerning spirits who manifested at or around the time of physical death. For its purposes, the SPR defined a crisis apparition as one occurring twelve hours before or after the crisis.

What makes this research so persuasive is the era in which it was conducted. In the late nineteenth century, news of a loved one's illness, accident, or death might take days or weeks to reach home. In the absence of information that would lead to concern—say news of a disaster—the spontaneous, unexpected appearance of a loved one could not be dismissed as imaginary.* Yet crisis apparitions tend to be brief and do not usually contain verifiable information, as dream visitations sometimes do. They may also occur within the context of a dream.

How common are crisis apparitions? One of Myers's colleagues, Henry Sidgwick, once estimated the odds of a crisis precipitating an

---

*In contrast, today it would be more difficult to ascertain to what degree a crisis apparition might be a projection. For example, if my uncle were flying and I heard news of his plane crash, it's possible that my anxiety might trigger a vision of him.

apparition at more than four hundred times that of any other event. Modern psychical researchers continue to note this trend, indicating that these after-death communication experiences—unlike several others—have a clear cause and a definite purpose and meaning no matter when they occur, to whom, and under what circumstances.

Several theories attempt to explain psychic experience in terms of an outer force that induces or enables a percipient (the subject or witness) to detect the presence of spirits. For example, some parapsychologists suggest that we do not literally see apparitions in the sense that our eyes perceive and our brain processes a specific combination of light waves and colors into an image. They point to cases where a percipient sees something another person present does not, and ask if it is not possible that the spirits do not manifest themselves in a visible form but instead stimulate some part of our brains to produce their image (or sound, or touch, or smell) in a form (visual, sonic, sensory, or olfactory) that we can understand as if we had perceived it. In other words, the spirits are present at that moment but in a form our common senses cannot detect. We recognize them through the sensory phenomena they induce *within* us. Just as your fax machine is not receiving actual words and letters through the telephone line but electronic signals that it "translates," so our brains translate psychic signals into a form that we recognize—the apparition.

This is an interesting theory, one that accepts the reality of discarnate survival and after-death communication. We have already discussed dreams as conduits for psychic communication, including premonitions and visitations. Clearly, something about being in the dream state—a lowering of inhibitions, a suspension of the rules of daytime logic—makes us more accepting, more open to psychic experience. No matter what our mental state—dreaming or not, fully awake, fully asleep, or in some twilight zone between, whether our brain waves are registering as alpha, beta, or theta—we must possess some physical, psychological, biochemical, electromagnetic, or otherwise yet unidentified capacity that enables us to perceive and process psychic experience. If, as seems to be the case, certain conditions are more conducive than others to such experiences, is it not possible that imminent death might be one? If it is, that would suggest that even those dying people who do not apparently experience deathbed visions—those who are comatose or deeply sedated and those whose physical condition requires medication or mechanical devices that hinder communication—may still be experiencing them.

Some psychics contend that apparitions may inhabit a "fourth dimension" in which the laws of space and time as we currently understand them are suspended. While we can agree that telepathy may play a role in the formation of apparitions, we believe, as do most of our respondents, that they really saw what they saw. The loved one they perceived was either present in this dimension or visible from another. Whatever the case, they were *here*.

CRISIS APPARITIONS OUT OF TIME

Not all apparitions appear close to the hour of death. In this next story, a distraught mother clinging to the slim hope that her son may be alive witnesses his apparition, an occurrence that seems to confirm her worst fears.

"Roy," twenty-three, was an army private stationed in Southeast Asia in 1972. The Vietnam War was beginning to wind down, and "Helen" and "Walt" were looking forward to being reunited with their son when his tour of duty ended. But just months before American forces withdrew, Roy was reported missing in action after North Vietnamese forces shot down his plane.

Roy's parents dedicated themselves to a frustrating and ultimately fruitless search for the truth. No government agency, organization, or former POW offered any information on Roy's whereabouts. At the same time, his body had not been found. Was he dead or alive? Captured or in hiding? If he were alive and being held a prisoner, where was he? How was he? When would he be set free?

There were no answers for Roy's parents. Helen in particular found the stress of not knowing, of hoping but never being sure for what, almost unbearable. One night, about five months after she received official notification that Roy was missing in action, she saw him standing at the foot of her bed. "He was dressed in his army uniform," she recalls. "One thing that struck me was how well he looked, healthy and strong. He looked so handsome in his uniform."

Helen watched and listened in amazement as Roy said, without appearing to speak, "Mom, I'm fine. It's me, Roy. Don't worry. You don't have to worry where I am. I'm here. Everything is okay."

After that, he stood silently for several more minutes. Helen asked, "Roy, where are you? Roy? Can you hear me? I love you. Tell me where you are."

"I'm here. Don't worry. I love you, Mom."

Helen opened her mouth to speak again, but Roy vanished. She had no doubt that she had seen her son. But while she found some aspects of the experience comforting, she was understandably troubled by others. On the one hand, Roy's MIA status was a glimmer of hope that he would return. On the other, the clarity of her vision and the words he spoke to her telepathically made his having died and crossed over a near certainty.

Whereas most subjects come away from an after-death communication praying that it was the real thing, Helen, like many who instantly recognize an apparition as a possible portent of death, found herself hoping she had been hallucinating or dreaming. She prayed he was alive, yet her strong personal belief in life after death led her to conclude that Roy must have died. Within a year of that visitation, Helen learned that Roy had indeed been killed.

The relatively long period between Roy's disappearance and his materialization before his mother raises the question of when he actually died. It is possible that Roy died at or around the time his plane went down, but he did not come to his mother until months later. Such delayed crisis apparitions have been known to occur, but they are relatively rare. The other possibility is that Roy had been captured and was alive for several months before he died.

Clearly, the spirits' purpose is to bring comfort and reassurance. While Patricia was working with Otis Williams, founder of the great Motown singing group the Temptations, on his autobiography, he told her about an apparition he had witnessed shortly after his long-time friend and group cofounder, Paul Williams, committed suicide in August 1973. We include it here because it is unique in two ways: First, Otis witnessed it while he was awake. Second, another group member, Eddie Kendricks, saw it too, though in another room. Williams writes in his book *Temptations*:

> I was lying in my bed one night reading. For some reason I felt compelled to look up, and standing at the foot of my bed was Paul. He said, "I'm all right where I am, Otis. I just want to let you know." And then he was gone. Talking to Eddie later, I said, "Man, you know, I saw Paul."
>
> Eddie replied, "Yeah, he came to me, too."
>
> Funny thing was, it wasn't scary at all. I believe it was Paul, perhaps not Paul as we knew him here on earth, but his spirit. And I also believe that what he said was true.[1]

Spirits rarely appear to strangers. It is love and caring that bind these two worlds. One survey found that more than 75 percent of widows and widowers have had contact with their deceased spouses. What adds to the credibility of these reported accounts is that they frequently come from people who claim to have had no other experience that might be classified as unexplained, psychic, or paranormal. In fact, often these witnesses are among the most skeptical of any claims of discarnate communications, and so typically they often disbelieve their own experiences. Usually, friends and family may dismiss them as well, sometimes with potentially harmful consequences.

Louie and Anna had been married for sixty years when she died in his arms at the age of eighty-one. For the first time in his adult life, Louie, then eighty-six, was alone. His daughter, "Marie," who lived nearby with her husband, worried about how her father would manage. After Louie mentioned to Marie that her mother had appeared to him several times, she assumed there was something wrong with him.

"Dad, you can't see dead people," Marie admonished. "You can't really see Mommy. It was just your imagination because you miss her."

Louie was taken aback but not surprised. He knew he would have said the same thing himself if he were in her place. "I saw your mother as clearly as I'm seeing you," he patiently explained. "I admit that at first I was frightened and surprised. I don't believe in things like this. That's why I never told anyone after the first time it happened. But how could I be imagining? I've seen her now three different times. She looked well. It made me feel better to know she's still with me."

Louie later shared his experiences with several other family members. They all doubted that Anna was really there and assumed that Louie's grief had spawned these harmless delusions. Marie, however, took a dimmer view. Despite the fact that Louie was perfectly capable of living independently, she concluded that he was suffering from either a complete mental breakdown or the early stages of senility, perhaps even Alzheimer's disease. She decided that it was in Louie's best interest to move him to a nursing home, whether he wanted to go or not. Fortunately for Louie, one nephew believed him. He told Marie of his own paranormal experiences and convinced her that what Louie reported was an extremely common, even normal occurrence. Marie agreed not to force her father to leave his home but still maintained he was "seeing things." Louie knew he was seeing something, too: his wife, Anna.

Apparitions can occur any time, any place. Their messages may be simple or complex, highly emotional or surprisingly practical. Take the case of Shirley and Sol. When Sol died suddenly of a heart attack in his fifties, his wife, Shirley, was not only distraught but in desperate financial straits. Sol had been the family's sole provider and, as head of the household, the one who handled its business. Shirley's ignorance of financial matters now threatened her security. She knew that she was entitled to pension money Sol had earned years ago as a government employee, but claiming it meant facing a dauntingly complicated application and dealing with a bureaucracy. As she stared at the papers already piled high on her desk, she felt helpless and overwhelmed.

One day as she sat agonizing over the work ahead, Sol appeared.

Although she did not see the apparition speaking, she clearly heard Sol's voice: "Shirley."

"Sol?"

"Yes." *He sounds wonderful,* Shirley thought. Before she knew it, Sol began leading her through filling out the pension forms. In a concerned tone, he said, "Here's what you do. This is how you fill out the papers to get the money."

Over the next several minutes, Sol directed Shirley on how to complete the forms, told her where to take them, and even gave her the name of a person to call in that office—every piece of information Shirley needed to collect the funds. Sol's apparition remained visible the whole time, but once she had finished, he vanished. The papers were letter perfect and the check was processed quickly. Shirley later confided to a relative that Sol had helped her out. Although she outlived her husband by many years, that was the only time Shirley was aware of Sol's presence.

DEATHBED VISIONS

An elderly woman dying of cancer and unable to speak because of a respirator tube ignores the family gathered at her bedside and instead smiles and appears to be grasping at an invisible something dangling before her eyes.

A seventy-five-year-old man appears engrossed in a friendly card game. He shuffles and deals to four other players, fans his cards, picks some up, lays some down. He makes small talk with his buddies, smiles at unheard jokes, and stops once or twice to say hello to other friends and relatives as they enter the room. The only things that seem to be missing are the cards and the friends. Or so it would appear to the son and daughter-in-law at his deathbed.

What is going on? Although loved ones who witnessed these scenes may have been alarmed or confused, they need not have been. If our loved ones can return as apparitions in our dreams and waking hours, why wouldn't they be near in our time of greatest need: the hour of death. What the survivors observed was one of the longest studied and most frequently reported forms of after-death communication: the deathbed vision. Simply, a deathbed vision occurs when a person who is dying, or close to death, reports having visions of deceased loved ones. There is good reason to believe that the spirits are actually present.

The Classic Deathbed Vision

During a typical deathbed vision, the dying person seems to be seeing things. Most visions are of departed loved ones, and they are often surrounded by or emanating light. It is not unusual for deathbed visions to include religious figures such as angels, the Virgin Mary, Krishna, Yama (the Hindu god of death), or Jesus, among others. When the deathbed vision includes a deceased person, it is virtually always someone who was close, such as a child, parent, spouse, sibling, or grandparent. Deathbed visions are typically short, lasting five minutes or less. Some, however, seem to continue for quite some time. Most occur within minutes or hours of death. Some are experienced days before. In very rare instances, weeks or months may pass between the vision and the death, but those instances may not be deathbed visions per se but apparitions or precognitive experiences.

Invariably, the dying report that their deceased loved ones arrived to ease the transition to the other side. Most of those who have had deathbed visions were happy they had the experience and said it made them less fearful of death. Typically, the dying person describes the experience as one of peace and beauty. It is conceivable that there is even more to the deathbed vision, but the brevity of the experience and the short time between it and the subject's death preclude further detailed studies like those on near-death experiences. It is important to remember that deathbed visions happen to people who die; there are relatively few instances of people living for long periods after a deathbed vision.

Research has found that deathbed visions occur to both those who have religious beliefs about an afterlife and those who do not. Some deathbed visions seem to help ease depression and pain. Many visions reported are vivid, and colors are bright or intense. Rarely have there been reports of hell-like, negative deathbed visions, although some dying people do express fears that they will be met at death by someone with whom they had difficulty in this life, such as an abusive parent.

What Do Deathbed Visions Reveal About Life Beyond?

For centuries, people regarded deathbed visions as proof of life after death. In fact, before the recent interest in near-death experiences, deathbed visions were equally well known and accepted. And when people witnessed their loved ones passing, they saw things most of us never see. Some who have been present during a deathbed vision have also seen a form of apparition, often described as energy forms, mist, or "something cloudy," just when the patient reported the deathbed vision.

In 1858 the writer Louisa May Alcott, then twenty-five years old, wrote about her twenty-three-year-old sister Elizabeth's worsening illness and subsequent death from scarlet fever. Louisa and her mother had untiringly nursed the "thin and emaciated" Beth in the Alcott family's Concord home. In Alcott's diary entry for March 14, 1858, she wrote:

> My dear Beth died at three this morning, after two years of patient pain. Saturday she slept, and at midnight became unconscious, quietly breathing her life away till three; then with one last look of the beautiful eyes, she was gone.
>
> A curious thing happened, and I will tell it here, for Dr. G. said it was a fact. A few moments after the last breath came, as Mother and I sat silently watching the shadow fall on the dear little face, I saw a light mist rise from the body and float up and vanish in the air. Mother's eyes followed mine, and when I said, "What did you see?" she described the same light mist. Dr. G. said it was the life departing visibly.[2]

Had Louisa May Alcott and her mother witnessed Beth's soul leaving her body? Yes. What is even more remarkable, however, is that Dr.

G.'s response suggests he had seen this phenomenon many times before. As our loved ones pass behind closed doors, what else are we missing?

Why Deathbed Visions Are Not Hallucinations

In 1926 SPR cofounder Dr. William Barrett published *Deathbed Visions: The Psychical Experience of the Dying*, the first systemic study of this phenomenon. Barrett became interested in deathbed visions when his wife, an obstetrical surgeon, told him about a patient of hers who was hemorrhaging to death following the delivery of a healthy baby. The woman talked about seeing her dead father and sister in a very beautiful place.

Hallucination? Wishful thinking? Anoxia? So skeptics might argue. However, these possibilities are ruled out by a single fact: out of concern for her health, she was never told that her sister had died several weeks before. When virtually all personal news traveled by post (a process that could take days, even weeks), it was possible to keep word of a family member's death secret. Obviously, that kind of scenario is far less common today. However, we did find two cases in which shortly before her death a woman revealed knowledge of things she could not have otherwise known.

"Myrtle," who was more than ninety, had been bedridden for several months, weakened by congestive heart failure. Her memory was poor, she often felt confused, and in the past year her physical condition had deteriorated markedly. Because of this, her widowed daughter, "Meg," in whose home she lived, was careful not to excite or upset her. The only people Myrtle saw daily were Meg and a part-time private-duty nurse.

When Myrtle's eldest son, "Chuck," died, her family agreed not to mention it unless she asked, which seemed improbable. Chuck's home was hundreds of miles away, so the fact that Myrtle had not seen him would not necessarily worry her or arouse her suspicion. In fact, it had been many months since Myrtle had seen or mentioned Chuck. Six weeks after Chuck died, Myrtle's health declined; her heart grew weaker, and she suffered severe edema and difficulty breathing. Not only was she unable to recognize her loved ones, she rarely acknowledged them. Her doctor predicted that it would be only a short while before death, weeks at most. All anyone could do until then was make her comfortable.

Several loved ones were with Myrtle when she lifted her head from the pillow and pointed at the air before her. In a weak but audible voice, she called out, "Jeremiah!"—her late husband—then "Rachel"—her late mother. After drawing another labored breath, she said, "Chuck. Chuck. I'm coming. You look so handsome with that light around you. Oh, what a beautiful light."

Those gathered, including assorted children, spouses, and grandchildren, were stunned. No one had told Myrtle of her son's death. Almost equally remarkable was Myrtle's expression. For the first time in months, she was smiling peacefully, as if oblivious of her physical suffering. She immediately closed her eyes and fell into a deep sleep. Several days later she passed on.

We know that certain altered states of consciousness, such as dreaming and dying, seem to open the psychic channels. Although not a deathbed vision per se, Ida Cohen's case suggests that organic brain disease and degeneration might also facilitate some forms of direct after-death communications. Ida, age ninety-six, seemed to be living her last years in her own world. She was practically deaf, and advanced hardening of the arteries made her incoherent much of the time. She rarely recognized or spoke to her children and grandchildren, who visited every weekend.

Russian-born, Ida had spoken English perfectly since coming to America. For the past few years, however, she seemed to have forgotten English, and the rare word she did utter was Yiddish. Now even her command of Yiddish was slipping. Day after day, she sat propped in her wheelchair, staring out the window, softly murmuring to herself. Despite all this, her family remembered her as the loving, once-tireless mother of six they knew, and continued to visit faithfully.

During this time, Ida's son Lou was stricken with cancer, news his siblings determined it best not to tell Ida. When he died, they kept that secret too. Before visiting her, they all agreed that in her presence none would betray the truth. Given her mental deterioration, they were certain she would never suspect.

The first time they visited after Lou's funeral, the family found her sitting at her window, silently rocking back and forth. As usual, each greeted her with a gentle kiss on the cheek, not expecting her to recognize or say anything to them. To their surprise, however, Ida suddenly turned from the window and in a firm, clear voice and in perfect English said, "You don't have to tell me. I know. My Lou is dead. I know. Lou is dead." She turned her gaze back to the window, slipping back into the dark, confused silence from which she never emerged. Until the day she died shortly thereafter, no one ever heard her speak English again.

No Strangers on the Other Side

During deathbed visions dying people not only learn and reveal information they did not previously possess, they also seem to recognize and can identify people, usually relatives, they never knew in this life.

"Sammy" was only ten years old when he was diagnosed with metastatic cancer. Due to an inoperable spinal tumor, his prognosis was grim. For several weeks the child remained in the hospital, where his parents kept a constant vigil at his bedside. Heavy painkilling medication left him drifting in and out of consciousness. As the days passed, Sammy grew so weak that he could no longer communicate even in his rare lucid moments.

One day Sammy suddenly raised his head slightly and blinked. Slowly his hand rose, and as he pointed toward the foot of his bed, he said, "Grandma 'Martha.' Grandpa 'Willie.'" With those words, Sammy fell into a coma and soon died.

"Sammy looked like he was smiling," said his mother, recalling her son's last words. But what did he see? And what did it mean? Martha and Will were Sammy's maternal grandparents, but both were dead long before his birth. He had never known them in life, and whenever they were spoken of, they were always called Grandma and Grandpa. His parents doubted that he even knew their given names.

Considering the facts, a deathbed vision seems the most likely explanation. But Sammy's parents had no way of knowing for certain until several months later, when they visited a psychic medium. During their reading, the medium claimed that Sammy's spirit said that when he died his grandparents met him, that they were there in the hospital room that day and took him by the hand at the moment of death so that the transition would not frighten him. Further confirming the integrity of the communication, the medium stated that Sammy's grandmother's name was Martha.

The implication of deathbed visions that include such verifiable information is obvious: they are real. Granted, few deathbed visions contain information that can be verified or tested by those left behind, but that does not mean that *only* those incidents can be assumed to be true. Most deathbed visions so closely fit a basic pattern that it makes more sense to infer the reality of all from the proven truth of a few than to assert that only verifiable cases "count."

Deathbed Visions in Hospice Care

Daniel Alessandro is chief financial officer and vice president of an international corporation. At night he volunteers his time to hospice care, where he has witnessed and comforted people through deathbed visions and dying. In our conversation, Daniel expressed views and opinions we have also heard voiced by open-minded nurses, doctors, and medical workers. But Daniel's experience as a hospice worker differs significantly from that of someone working in a hospital. The decision to begin hospice care occurs only after the individual and his or her loved ones have accepted the inevitability of death. Unlike a hospital, where desperate, heroic measures often prolong or postpone death, the hospice mission is to care for and comfort the dying, not "rescue" them from death.

Daniel is one among many we have spoken to who has no doubt

that deathbed visions are real.* "You'll see dying patients in hospice reaching out. They see the souls of the departed coming. That's why, statistically, so many dying people fall out of bed. That's why some have to be held down. Where are they going to? They're getting up to go to the light. The moment of death that we often witness is that period when they're between this physical world and the other side. Their soul has not detached completely from the body, but they still have some idea that they are going somewhere; they hear it and see it."

Of course, publicly stating that he believes in deathbed visions puts Daniel somewhat at odds with the official medical position. As we have mentioned before, the SPR undertook the study of deathbed visions back in the 1890s. The most important study done after that was the work of Karlis Osis. Between 1959 and 1969 he surveyed more than six hundred American physicians and nurses who reported on the deathbed visions of their patients. Osis and Erlendur Haraldsson continued their research in two more studies, including one in India. What makes their work significant is the research they conducted to determine "the relationship between deathbed visions and such factors as the patient's age, sex, medical condition, cultural background, stress, and conception of an afterlife." Osis and Haraldsson concluded that "[deathbed visions] are relatively independent of age, sex, religion, and socioeconomic status."[3]

In fact, deathbed visions occur to people who fully expect—and are fully expected—to recover.

In 1959 Osis randomly surveyed five thousand doctors and five thousand nurses. Six hundred forty responded, and Osis discovered that their descriptions of deathbed visions they had witnessed fit a discernible pattern that included sudden elevation in mood; visions of angels, deceased loved ones, or religious figures greeting them and

---

*In addition to formal interviews, we've spoken to dozens of people who work closely with the dying. We've been surprised to learn that their estimates of the frequency of deathbed visions vary dramatically. For example, we found one man who had been with over a thousand people in their last moments. Although he believes that deathbed visions are real, he did not recall having witnessed more than a handful. This he attributed to the greatly weakened physical state of the dying and their often being under heavy sedation.

encouraging them to come along; and visions of beautiful, other-worldly, heavenlike places. At that time, hospital staff wrote off such incidents as the result of oxygen deprivation, psychoactive medication (tranquilizers, painkillers, sedatives), or some death-related diminution in brain function. However, Osis realized that these types of "hallucinations" were not what one would expect from someone who was oxygen deprived or drugged.

Attitudes have begun to change. "I think more and more doctors are coming to see that there *is* something more there," Daniel opines. "I have a responsibility to comfort the dying person. You have some people in the medical field who don't believe in anything, and they can look at something and just totally deny that it's happening. But for every doctor who says no to deathbed and predeath visions, I can find a doctor who totally agrees."

THE LOST ART OF DYING

"Dying people look at me all the time, as if to ask, 'What's going on?'" Daniel says. "They are seeing things and knowing things that no one else can see or know. For example, Michael was in the last stages of amyotrophic lateral sclerosis, ALS, or Lou Gehrig's disease. His wife told me that she thought he was close to passing on. When I got to him, he was thrashing about. I knew right away what was going on. His wife was crying, 'No, no, no.' She didn't really want him to pass on. Michael said, 'I have to go, but I can't. I can't leave.'"

When Michael's wife stepped out of the room, Daniel moved closer to Michael. The man looked unconscious but was actually aware. Kneeling beside the dying man, Daniel took his hand and said, "Michael, this is Daniel. I know you know I am here. I know you've been out of your body and you're scared. You're seeing things going around you and you're wondering what's going on. It's okay. It's the beginning of what you're going to feel."

"Then all of a sudden Michael became calm," Daniel says. "Because now he had the reassurance and he was no longer scared about what was happening."

JOEL MARTIN AND PATRICIA ROMANOWSKI

Daniel, like many who view death in a spiritual context, believes that our culture fails to teach us how to approach our last earthly act: dying. Daniel's theory and technique may sound novel, but they are not new. Ancient religious texts describe what awaits the spirit after death and counsel us how to respond. Today—thanks to modern medicine, Madison Avenue, and the art of euphemism—we have become a youth-obsessed, pain-defying, death-denying society. It is entirely conceivable that with enough luck and good timing, we can live our entire lives without ever witnessing a single death other than our own. "It is difficult to accept death in this society *because* it is unfamiliar," Elisabeth Kübler-Ross writes. "In spite of the fact that it happens all the time, we never see it."[4]

Is it any wonder that when our time—or a loved one's—arrives, we feel so unprepared?

In human history, this "death-free" existence is a relatively recent and novel state of affairs. Before World War II most people died at home, making it rare not to have witnessed a deathbed vision. Today, the situation is completely opposite. One means through which we have returned to earlier times is hospice care. You will notice that these are the circumstances in which most of the deathbed visions we recount occurred.

Before World War II, most people learned what they knew about death from watching a loved one die. Their attitudes toward death, in both its physical and spiritual aspects, were more realistic than our own. Few then questioned that at the moment of death, their loved ones were not in the presence of caring spirits or God. Through witnessing the deathbed visions of others, seeing their peace and happiness, those people knew firsthand what we today glean largely from books like this: that death need not be an emotionally painful experience for the dying.

THE SPIRITUAL JOURNEY

When our great-grandparents' time came, they and their loved ones took comfort in prayer and religious ritual. The power of prayer and religious ritual, which we discuss more fully in chapter 10, cannot be overstated. It is also interesting to note that the deathbed is often the scene of other paranormal activity besides the deathbed vision. Daniel told us of John, an African American and a Baptist, who was in his early seventies when cancer ravaged his body. Thin and frail, John lay at the threshold of death as Daniel held his hand. John's daughter, who planned to remain at her father's side through the night, told Daniel that her mother had passed away two years earlier and her sister had died in an accident a year before that. Now, Daniel realized, John's tenacity started to make sense.

"Your dad doesn't want to leave you alone," Daniel told her. "It's really important that you speak to him and tell him that it's okay to move on." He suggested she read to her father the Twenty-third Psalm: "The Lord is my shepherd. . . ." The hours passed slowly, then around three in the morning John's daughter heard her late mother's voice saying, "John. John, it's time. Come." Startled, she felt a chill, then saw her father open his eyes and stare straight ahead. She immediately began reading the psalm aloud. As she read it a third time, John breathed a peaceful sigh and passed on.

The prevalence of religious figures and symbols in deathbed visions might suggest they are merely projections, wish-fulfilling hallucinations. But Daniel offered another instance—one of many we've learned of—that turns that theory on its head.

Bernie was an orthodox Jew who had dedicated his life to the centuries-old Judaic and Talmudic traditions. That meant that he observed the strict dietary laws and was devout in prayer and study. Like virtually all Jews, he did not recognize Jesus Christ, who was born a Jew, as the messiah. When Daniel met Bernie, Bernie was in his mid-fifties and in the final stages of brain cancer. One day, with his daughter at his bedside, Bernie suddenly opened his eyes, and staring into the air he cried, "Isn't it beautiful? Isn't it beautiful?"

"What is he talking about?" she asked Daniel.

Mindful not to offend the family's religious beliefs, Daniel answered only, "Well, he just sees things right now."

Just then Bernie, who had been drifting in and out of consciousness, exclaimed, "Isn't he beautiful? It's the Christ!"

Bernie's daughter became visibly upset. It was inconceivable, even offensive, to her that her orthodox Jewish father would see Jesus. Daniel tried to comfort her, saying, "He's just passing through; don't worry about it," but it clearly bothered her. "Even I always thought a dying person's religious beliefs would affect what they see, until Bernie," Daniel reflects. "Then I was totally amazed."

What might account for this? As we know from people who have had near-death experiences, the other side is a place of intense spirituality. Whatever their religious beliefs, millions who have returned from an NDE speak of the light they encountered as an all-encompassing, sentient being who radiates and enfolds them in love. As Dr. Moody and others have pointed out, some interpret this light to be Christ or another religious figure, but many do not. They return to their bodies with a sense that God is, or is part of, or is the source of, that all-inclusive light. From that point of view, there would seem nothing contradictory about a person of one faith seeing figures or symbols of another.

In this and several other aspects, the relationship between the deathbed vision and the near-death experience bears closer examination. We believe that the parallels between the two reinforce the legitimacy of each. As you will see, many elements common to both appear in other forms of after-death communication. Most important, though, is the fact that apparitions are a key part of the NDE. For a moment, let us look at a classic near-death experience in detail.

THE NEAR-DEATH EXPERIENCE: DETOUR THROUGH THE OTHER SIDE

That our deceased loved ones are able to return to us, however briefly, proves that a bridge of consciousness, of love, of light, connects this life and the next. In the near-death experience, people who are physically dead begin the journey to the afterlife but do not complete it. Certain elements of the classic NDE—the appearance of spirits in unusually bright light, the sense that they are communicating to us telepathically—typify other types of apparitions, including visitations.

As we mentioned earlier, before the advent of modern medical technology, people had far fewer opportunities to undergo physical death and live to tell about it. Still, events that are indisputably NDEs are mentioned in, among other writings, those of Plato, the Bible, the *Tibetan Book of the Dead*, and subsequent secular accounts, including one dating back to the eighth century. During the late nineteenth century, psychical research pioneers, such as Sir William Barrett (author of the previously mentioned deathbed visions study), Edmund Gurney, and James Hyslop of the Society for Psychical Research, in London, gathered some information on what we now term the NDE.

The so-called classic NDE features some or all of the following events, usually in this order: a sense of ineffability about the experience, feeling that it is literally beyond description; realizing that one is physically dead; being overcome by a sense of peacefulness and quiet; hearing a constant monotone noise or unusual music; entering a dark tunnel; becoming aware of being separated from one's physical body; being met by spirit presences, usually predeceased loved ones; perceiving an ever-growing, increasingly brilliant clear or white light that one senses to be a living force; witnessing a review of one's life; and reaching a point at which one is either told to or chooses to return to one's body.

For many of those who have glimpsed the other side, the near-death experience is a positive, transforming event. In a British study conducted by Dr. Peter Fenwick, approximately a third of the respondents reported feeling they were more psychically adept and more socially conscious after their NDE. About 38 percent felt they were more spiritual, and half were firmly convinced that there is life after death. We should also note that not all NDEs are positive; 15 percent reported experiencing fear, and 10 percent felt a sense of loss as a result.

Judging by the results, it is clear that if the spirits who come to us in apparitions, deathbed visions, and within the context of an NDE have a purpose, it is to comfort us during the transition. Still, it is important to remember that people who live to recount their NDEs are still among us. So while people recall their relief or happiness at encountering a deceased loved one during the NDE, the message they often receive is to turn back, that it is not yet their time to die.

The comfort subjects derive from these experiences takes on additional significance when we consider why today so many people have "come back." On the surface, the answer is simple: medical technology rescues the dying in numbers unimaginable even twenty years ago. However, we believe there is more to it. The millions who acknowledge and share their NDEs can be viewed as emissaries—messengers who have revolutionized our thinking on death and dying. Rather than learning about how it feels to die from a religious tome, we may actually know—even be—someone who has been there, done that—almost. Thanks to these travelers, even those of us who have not chanced across the bridge of light have some idea of what may await us, so that we may regard our own future journey with a sense of peace.

Chuck Antku is one such traveler. Six years before Dr. Moody made *near-death experience* a household term, U.S. Army First Lieutenant Chuck Antku experienced something so profound, it changed his life forever. Then he was just twenty-three and a long, long way from home, serving in the mountainous central highlands of Vietnam.

"One day we were out on patrol and got caught in an ambush. In the first ten or fifteen seconds, ten of the thirty-one men were killed. Eventually all but two were either killed or wounded. During the battle I was shot through my right shoulder, then shot through my left shoulder. And I was badly injured elsewhere, as well. There was so much horror—screaming and crying. It was an insane situation.

"Suddenly, there were a couple of loud explosions. I got hit with either hand grenades or rockets. There's no way of ever telling. I'm very sure it was a rocket. The explosion was right next to me—within a foot or two—and it was very large. The pain was unbearable. I remember just lying back down, closing my eyes and saying to myself, 'That's it. It's over.' I'd given up, which was probably the hardest thing to do. The fact of the matter was, I was hurting in so many places. I just didn't want to hurt anymore.

"As I laid there, there was a ringing that went with the explosion, and right after it a vibration. As the vibration became more intense, I think I was withdrawing into myself so I didn't feel all the pain in my body. As the vibration began, I saw a golden light. Then as the vibration became more intense, the light also became more intense. The next thing I remember is that the pain started to go away, until the pain was completely gone. And within my mind, I was no longer on the battlefield.

"The next thing I knew, I saw what I can only describe as a tunnel of light, a bright light and line of four or five people standing in front of me. And my late paternal grandmother was one of the people I saw."

Chuck's grandmother, Goldie Meyer, had died two years earlier of natural causes at the age of ninety-three. Chuck had been especially close to her; during his first ten years, she had lived in the same house as Chuck's family. He was happy to see her. She looked just as she had before she passed, small with her gray hair up in a neat bun. Of Hungarian ancestry, Goldie had what Chuck describes as "a real old European look."

"I didn't recognize who the other people were, but I did focus on my grandmother," Chuck recalls. "There was light around her and the others, and it was kind of misty. I sensed that there were other people there, but I had no contact with them."

Chuck and his grandmother began to communicate telepathically. "I said to her, 'I've had enough. I want to be with you.' My grandmother's answer was, 'It's *not* over. You *have* to go back. You've got other things to do.'

"I argued with my grandmother, telepathically, saying, 'I don't want to go back to that. It's not going to be any better. I don't want to go back. I've had enough. I want to stay with you.' But I was given the message from her: 'You can't. That's just not your decision. It's not over. You can't leave earth. You have to go back.' She kind of laid down the law."

Before Chuck returned to his body, he spent some time in an out-of-body state. "When I went back, I was above the battlefield, seeing everyone else there. I was kind of like hovering and then slowly coming back into my body. I saw myself lying there with everyone around me. It was like looking at a big picture as you would see it all from above the trees, if you were hovering in a helicopter. It was a horrible sight. There was a lot of smoke. We had walked through an area that had been napalmed before we were hit. So I saw the charred hillside, the charred trees, and I could see other people lying around me. There were dead soldiers from both sides, Americans and North Vietnamese.

"Despite all the horror, it was the most peaceful and calm sensation I ever experienced. So I went from the worst and most painful situation I'd ever been in to where the pain was actually gone. Then, suddenly, there was another explosion that kind of brought me out of it. The explosions were continuous—rockets and hand grenades from both sides. That's when I opened my eyes and said to myself, 'Boy, you *are* back.' And the pain returned immediately."

Looking back, Chuck is absolutely certain he glimpsed the other side. "There's no doubt in my mind that I did experience this. It wasn't as if I'd fallen asleep. It doesn't seem possible that the pain could have gone away the way it did if I'd just been dreaming."

It would be several more hours before what was left of Chuck's company could fight their way to him and the other injured men. Hours later, a military helicopter arrived and began evacuating the wounded and dying. The process took hours, and Chuck, who had been hit early that afternoon, received no medical attention until he was finally flown out near nightfall. Chuck lost a massive amount of blood, suffered excruciating pain, and was near death. As a result of his injuries, he lost a finger and partial use of his left hand. Both eardrums had been blown out, and in addition to his bullet wounds, shrapnel had torn through his legs, chest, and the back of his head. After he recovered, he was discharged and returned home to the States.

Today Chuck Antku is married, a father and a grandfather. He holds a high-ranking position with a federal government agency. He has also managed a rock group and written for television and film. Chuck's near-death experience profoundly changed his way of thinking and he has used it to help others facing death. "I'll share it with anybody," he tells us, "because it's real."

MULTIPHENOMENAL APPARITIONS AND VISITATIONS

One challenge in organizing our research was classifying cases that included several different phenomena. While deathbed visions, near-death experiences, and other forms of apparitional experience tend to follow common patterns, that is not always the case. The following accounts challenge our conception of what comprises a deathbed vision, a dream visitation, or a crisis apparition and prove the reality of these experiences.

Not all apparitions we would classify as deathbed visions appear at the deathbed, which is another point against their being biochemically induced hallucinations or the brain's physiological response to the stresses of physical death. Fran Butterfield was practically the personification of the word *spry*. A registered nurse, she worked full-time caring for patients until she retired at the age of seventy-six. Several years later, in her early eighties, she married for the second time.

"My grandmother's mind was always very clear. She was very alert and with it," her granddaughter Elizabeth told us. "She definitely was not prone to hallucinations or senility just because she was elderly." Physically, Fran was in remarkable shape for her age. So when Fran complained of sudden, intense leg pain, her family rushed her to the hospital. There she was diagnosed with sciatica, a painful but not dangerous condition caused by the inflammation of nerves running from the lower spine through the legs. Her doctor prescribed a course of anti-inflammatory medication to relieve the discomfort and admitted her for observation and tests, just to be on the safe side.

Fran was waiting in the emergency room for a nurse to return with the injection. Suddenly the curtains around the examining table parted and Fran's late father emerged. William Butterfield, who had been dead more than forty years, appeared not as the elderly man he was when he died but as he had been when Fran was a young girl: tall, slender, and handsome, with dark brown hair and a full beard and mustache. Her father was wearing a familiar long black coat, tie, and shirt.

"Fannie," he said, addressing her by her childhood name, "why don't you come with me? Why don't you come home with me?"

"Papa! What are you doing here?" Fran asked.

"Come on, Fannie. Come with me," he replied.

"Papa, I'm coming—" Fran blurted, then, realizing what she'd said, quickly covered her mouth and shaking her head vigorously cried, "No! No, Papa. No. I don't want to go now!"

At that moment, her father vanished and the nurse appeared. "You're not going to believe this," Fran confided to the nurse, "but my late father was just here. I saw him."

"That happens a lot," the nurse said matter-of-factly. "It's not uncommon. Don't worry about it."

Later that day, when Elizabeth stopped by the hospital to visit, Fran said, "You're going to think I'm crazy. But I just saw my father. He was really there, standing there as solid as you are. I was surprised because I thought that if I'd see anyone, it would be my mother. She died when I was very young, and I'd always prayed to her. I'm a little frightened. I don't want to die. I'm not ready to go yet. I'm going to fight all the way." Then, with characteristic spunk, she added, "Besides, I have a blanket I have to finish crocheting."

Elizabeth had to laugh. "Oh, I don't think it's meant for right now. I don't think you're going to pass just yet. Let's just concentrate on you getting better." Elizabeth patted her grandmother's hand affectionately, and Fran's mood brightened immediately.

"Oh yes, you're right, dear," she replied before moving to happier subjects. As ever, Fran's mind was sharp as the proverbial tack, and Elizabeth was certain that her great-grandfather's appearance at Fran's bedside was not a hallucination.

Fran recovered quickly and returned home, but less than a month later the pain returned, this time accompanied by dizziness and light-headedness. While hospitalized for treatment, observation, and a series of tests, Fran confided to Elizabeth, "I saw my father again, dear. And this time I also saw the Blessed Mother, the Virgin Mary."

"They're watching over you," Elizabeth replied, trying to disguise her own certainty of what the apparitions portended. The test results confirmed what Elizabeth had sensed all along: except for the discomfort of the sciatica, Fran had no serious health problems. Being realistic, however, Elizabeth had to remind herself that Fran was in her mid-nineties and that death could come anytime.

Less than a week after the last vision Fran reported, she died of a heart attack. Initially written off as due to natural causes and advanced age, Fran's death was later discovered to have been the result of hospital error. She had accidentally received and suffered an adverse reaction to another patient's medication, resulting in complications that led to her death.

While the family was understandably outraged over the cause of Fran's death, her repeated deathbed visions have provided Elizabeth a small measure of comfort. "It must have been her time to go," she says philosophically. "That would explain the visions."

5

"TELEGRAMS" FROM THE OTHER SIDE

Signs and Synchronicities

It is one of the commonest of mistakes to consider that the limit of our power of perception is also the limit of all there is to perceive.

—C. W. LEADBEATER

"Every time I feel sad or wish my brother was here to hug me, no matter where I am, I hear his favorite song on the radio."

"On several occasions, I've smelled cinnamon rolls heating in the microwave around breakfast time. That was my wife's favorite breakfast treat. I knew it was her, because I haven't had those rolls in the house since she died. I know it's her."

"I had an angel-wing begonia that I'd gotten shortly after my mother died. Something about the plant—its large, ruffled, gray-tinged leaves, the deep-rose blossoms—reminded me of her. After the first year it never bloomed again until fifteen years later. I came home from the doctor after learning I'd miscarried my child. I was thinking about how much I still missed my mother. Then I noticed that the plant was in bloom."

A simple event—the discovery of a long-lost object, hearing a special song, catching a whiff of a familiar scent, feeling a familiar hug or a kiss—can have a profoundly comforting effect when it comes to us from a departed loved one. We have heard thousands of stories from people who have sound reason to believe that these are not random events to which they have attached some meaning but genuine messages from the other side.

Our skeptical, acceptable catchall explanation for these phenomenons is chance. But *do* things happen purely by chance? And what does that mean anyway? These are interesting, probably unanswerable questions but crucial to any discussion of after-death communications, especially those involving signs and patterns of synchronicity. One reason subjects have difficulty coping with and understanding their direct after-death communications is that Western culture predisposes us to disbelieve experiences that are unique, unusual, or hard to categorize. Just as we are culturally programmed to suspend our disbelief toward certain subjects (established religious claims of miracles) or in certain settings (at the theater), so we are socially predisposed to suspend belief in others.

When direct after-death communications take the form of signs, their meaning is clear and precise. What distinguishes signs that suggest direct after-death communications from random events or coincidence is their timing and their inherent significance. For most people we talked with, the timing of a sign or an event was its most compelling, convincing aspect. There is no apparent reason, no recognizable cause behind the effect. In other words, no other possible explanation for the scent of cinnamon rolls, the blooming plant, or the song on the radio. The overwhelming majority of people we surveyed believed that the synchronous events and signs emanated from or were caused by someone close to them on the other side. And that they were produced, caused, or manifested for the purpose of being witnessed by them.

Carl Jung proposed a theory of synchronicity (or acausal meaningful coincidence) in an attempt to explain the appearance of events that are related but whose causal relationship is unknown. Or perhaps it would be more accurate to say that these events are inexplicable by the laws of physics and time we assume to be true today. For example, your mother's favorite vase topples to the floor at the precise moment of her death, a thousand miles away. Or on the anniversary of your grandmother's death, you find in a thrift shop a copy of her favorite Stengelware flowerpot—the one you broke when you were ten and could never replace.

The idea of synchronicity is generally accepted in Eastern religion and philosophy as part of a natural order. To Western minds, however, the idea of related events that seem to occur spontaneously can mean only one thing: coincidence, chance, or pure luck. That the universe may contain—even be governed by—unnamed forces whose operation defies our sense of logic is literally unthinkable. Still, we need to break away from automatically assuming that just because we cannot explain or understand something, it cannot be real.

Other theories proposed to explain synchronicity are derived from recent discoveries in physics, neurology, and other nonparapsychological fields. Fascinating as these are, we will limit our discussion of synchronicity to how it applies to direct after-death communications. We know that our brains are constantly exposed to millions of pieces of information—sounds, sights, scents, tactile sensations, tastes—yet we selectively focus on a mere fraction of these. One theory of how loved ones communicate to us through synchronous events is that they do not *cause* these events. Instead they somehow direct our attention—attention we might easily have focused elsewhere—to a number of random, inherently meaningless occurrences. The meaning then is not in what happens but in our noticing it among the hundreds of other things on which we could have focused.

That may work sometimes, but what does one make of an instance where our attention is drawn to something meaningful and extremely unlikely, such as a flower blooming through the snow? In a case like that, you must consider that a loved one somehow manipulated events or your perception of them on this side. But how?

It is too easy to dismiss *any* unexplainable occurrence as simple coincidence or chance. The first thing many people will say when discussing their direct-contact experience is "Maybe it was a coincidence, but . . ." Well, maybe it was a coincidence that the moment after viewing your late daughter's favorite film, *The Wizard of Oz*, you glanced outside *and* saw a rainbow. If you live in an area where your cable system airs the film four times a week, *and* you keep your television on constantly, *and* you live in a sunny, humid climate where a constant moisture level makes the daily appearance of a rainbow likely, then coincidence may explain it all.

But suppose you do not own a television or a VCR, *and* on the anniversary of your late daughter's death you are visiting her best friend, *and* the movie comes on, *and* you see a rainbow outside the window, *and* it is a snowy Christmas day in Vermont. One need not be a statistician or meteorologist to conclude that the possibility of all these events occurring *all together* under these particular circumstances is extremely low. However, for argument's sake, let us say that this could be a mega-coincidence. After all, anything is possible. The problem is that while everything is possible, significantly fewer things are *probable*. With each related element you add to the case, the probability diminishes exponentially. When assessing any direct after-death communication experience, but especially those that suggest synchronicity, the relationship, or the meaning, linking the individual elements is key.

The most important factor—and the one that we believe points to many synchronous experiences originating from loved ones on the other side—is to whom they relate. Interestingly, although we each have several deceased loved ones we would consider close, synchronistic experiences involve only one person at a time. We have yet to encounter anyone who smelled Dad's famous barbecue sauce while hearing Aunt Edna's favorite Glenn Miller song on the radio at the same moment their late nephew Skippy's portrait crashed to the floor. If beloved spirits are all around us, as many mediums and psychically adept people believe, why aren't such "party-line" contacts more common? Instead, when synchronistic experiences involve more than one element, all of them inevitably relate to a single person. This redundancy confirms, often repeatedly, that the source is genuine.

Their timing, location, content, and meaning are not random; the pieces fit. Not only do the pieces fit, but more often than not the recipient instantly understands their significance and to whom they "belong." Further, they usually involve someone close to the subject.

DISCRETE OCCURRENCES AND CLUSTERS

Synchronistic experiences can be classified as either repetitive or dynamic events. Examples typical of repetitive synchronistic events are songs and scents associated with the departed loved one. Our dear friend and editor, the late George Coleman, told us that whenever he felt extremely lonely or despondent, a particular song would come over the radio. This began shortly after his father died when he was a young man and continued until shortly before he died in 1994.

Repetitive events are often subtle and involve a single element. What marks them as synchronistic, transdimensional communications are their circumstances and their association with the deceased, which is usually immediately apparent to the subject. Another common repetitive synchronicity involves the deceased's name. Molly Martinek was only fourteen when she died following surgery to correct a congenital heart defect. We told her story in *Our Children Forever* and have remained in touch with her parents, Dennis and Suzy. They tell us that after Molly's passing, they noticed that the then-uncommon name Molly would appear to them unexpectedly, sometimes several times a day, in songs they heard, movies on television, pages of magazines to which they happened to open. Both parents allow that coincidence might account for some of these occurrences, but they note that the name would often appear after one or both had thought about or prayed to Molly, and on special occasions such as her birthday and the anniversary of her passing. We have heard of similar instances from dozens of people with whom we spoke.

In 1987 I became close friends with Father John Papallo, a Roman Catholic priest and member of the Capuchin Franciscan Order. Like most who knew him, I found in Father John a rare depth of compassion, love, and charity. He was the Catholic chaplain at the Kings Park Psychiatric Center on Long Island, and he worked tirelessly to help others. Father John and I had many conversations on topics ranging from current political events to the paranormal. He took no position on the subject of psychic phenomena, but firmly believed it belonged in the spiritual as opposed to the scientific or psychological realm. Privately he confided to me that he did believe in miracles and in things that seemed to involve phenomena neither science nor religion could explain. One day he said, "God knows our needs, and He is always there for us when we are most in need."

In April 1989 I attended a dinner to raise funds for Father John's current project, a group home for troubled and homeless young men.

An accomplished singer who had trained for a career in opera before entering the priesthood, Father John was known for his beautiful voice. That evening he sang a moving version of the old Frankie Laine hit "I Believe" that no one present will ever forget.

Barely two weeks later, on the night of May 1, 1989, the car Father John was riding in skidded across a winding, rain-soaked road and collided head-on with another vehicle. Father John and the young, pregnant mother at the wheel of the other car were killed. Though only forty-six, Father John had had an immeasurable impact on the lives of all who knew him. His loss to us personally and to the community at large was inestimable.

When I returned from his funeral, I turned the radio to an all-news station. As I did, I overshot the station I was seeking and, to my surprise, heard the song "I Believe." When it ended, a new song began and the signal faded into static. The following day, my radio tuned to a station that plays popular standards, I again heard "I Believe." Later that day, another station, again "I Believe." Hearing the song three times in twenty-four hours seemed much more than mere coincidence.

A week or so later, as I pondered some troubling personal matters, Father John came to mind. Half-seriously, I prayed, "Father John, can you hear me? Can you let me know if you do?" I switched on the radio, turned the dial, and there it was: "I Believe." And so it has been for the past seven years, in times of crisis, or around Christmas or birthdays, Father John's song somehow finds its way to me. In addition, Father John has come through in other ways, as detailed in our second book. As if that were not proof enough, one day in June 1996, my coauthor, Patricia, arrived to deliver a chapter of this manuscript. The moment she walked in the door, "I Believe" began playing on the radio; the chapter was this one. We both looked at each other and shrugged. Perhaps Father John was letting us know that we were on the right track.

MESSAGES DELIVERED BY NATURE

Dynamic synchronistic events are compelling and indisputable because they are made up of two or more incidents related to a single person. Events that involve the cooperation of nature and other forces beyond human control can be very persuasive.

Betty and Joe Cassidy were in their late sixties when their son Hugh died at the age of thirty-eight following a long illness. As Betty tells us, "The day I buried my son, several of us remained at his grave. We were talking when suddenly this beautiful monarch butterfly came by. We were all so moved by it. The butterfly is a sign of rebirth. The next day, I went back to the cemetery to say a prayer. There was the butterfly again.

"About a month later, we went to empty out the cottage Hugh lived in. He had a little end table in the living room. On it we found the most beautiful monarch butterfly lying dead. I made the association between my son and the butterfly at his grave and now in his cottage. Logically, the butterfly should not even have got into the cottage. It was a joy to see this beautiful monarch butterfly. It was a sign from Hugh. I kept the butterfly in a Tiffany box."

Several years ago I interviewed a Long Island county court judge named Stuart Namm. He appeared on both my local radio and television talk shows, and I found him candid and gracious. After he stepped down from the bench, Namm and his wife, Lenore, retired to North Carolina. In April 1996, I was shocked to read in *Newsday* that Lenore had died suddenly, of a heart attack, in her husband's arms. She was sixty-one. According to the lengthy obituary piece, the grief-stricken judge told a reporter that his wife had loved to count the flocks of pelicans as they flew overhead on a nearby beach. She would also predict when a lone pelican trailing the flock would appear. Inevitably, they would prove her correct.

Following his wife's funeral, Namm walked to the marsh behind his home. There he spotted a lone pelican, something he had never seen there before. As he watched, the bird took flight and passed directly over him. "It was like a sign to me," Namm later told a reporter, "that my wife was at peace."

SENSORY CONTACTS

In addition to seeing and hearing spirits, it is also possible to feel them touching, holding, or kissing us. Another related phenomenon is known as thermodynamic effect, or psychic wind. This is a breeze or gust of wind that the subject feels, which appears to have no discernible physical cause. It often occurs at the moment of another person's physical death.

"Mort" had been extremely ill for some time. Although only in his late forties, a serious heart condition and rheumatoid arthritis had rendered him almost completely bedridden. "Ruth," his devoted wife, spent most of her time in the upstairs bedroom with Mort. One day she went downstairs for a cup of tea. It was a warm July day, but the house remained comfortably cool inside, so the windows were opened only an inch or two to allow in fresh air. Sitting at the kitchen table, Ruth felt a strong rush of wind pass through the room. At first she thought a storm might be brewing, but outside it was bright and clear. She then realized that the windows were not open wide enough to let in that much of a breeze, even if there had been one outside, which, judging from the still trees near the window, there was not. A few moments later Ruth went upstairs where, to her shock, she found Mort dead.

Frances was eighty-four when she married Bill Nelson, a widower. Their relationship was passionate and loving. They married on Valentine's Day, and Bill often surprised his new bride with a single red rose. Shortly after they married, Bill planted a rosebush outside their bedroom window, where Frances could admire the beautiful flowers.

Sadly, this perfect couple had been married just two years when Bill died of cancer. His funeral happened to fall on their anniversary— Valentine's Day. It was bitterly cold that day, and when Frances approached the house after the funeral, she looked at the rosebush and thought of Bill. To her amazement, she saw a single bud. She was immediately impressed with the feeling that it was a sign from him. Later that day, her granddaughter, a medical student, noticed the rosebud too. "But that's impossible, Grandma," she said. "It can't bloom this time of year and in this weather."

Several weeks later, Frances was praying for Bill, as she did every night. Suddenly she looked up in the darkened bedroom and saw him standing a few feet away. As she explains, "I could see him as clearly as if he were alive." Bill approached her, then bent down and gently kissed her on the cheek. "I would have stayed with you if I could," he said softly. "But it was my time to go. But we'll be together again. I have to go now." With that, his image faded and vanished.

In the time since Bill's death, Frances's granddaughter has given her three roses, two red and one pink. Months after they were picked, they remain perfectly preserved, with soft, bright petals and a scent as rich as if they were picked yesterday.

"Those roses never died—just like our love," Frances says. "Bill sent those roses to me."

THE ODOR OF SANCTITY AND OTHER SCENTS

The power of scents to attract or to repel, to calm or to agitate is well known. From ancient times, mankind has treasured that which smelled beautiful and gone to extremes to eliminate or at least cover up odors that offend. We use different scents for a range of purposes daily, for everything from banishing normal body odors to manipulating our moods. Every pleasurable experience—from eating to lovemaking—is enhanced or diminished by what we smell.

When scent forms a direct after-death communication, however, its purpose and our response to it are quite different. We have all had the experience of being transported back in time by a particular scent—perhaps the smell of an ex-lover's cologne, a favorite dish cooking, even the childhood aromas of Play-Doh and crayons. What more clearly evokes long-gone school days than the scent of chalk, white paste, or mimeograph fluid? Or early experiments in adulthood, like cigarette smoke, alcohol, or perfume? Savvy real estate agents advise sellers to be sure apple pie is baking when potential buyers visit, and many of our most common emotional reference points are scents: the scents of a new baby, fresh-baked bread, a spring rain, autumn leaves.

We found that the most illuminating observation on the subject came from the late Pop artist Andy Warhol. A self-confessed scent addict, Warhol would wear a particular perfume or cologne for a short period of time, then switch to another. He saved a bottle of every scent he had ever worn. This way, as he wrote in *The Philosophy of Andy Warhol (From A to B & Back Again)*, every time he encountered a fragrance again, he could recall a particular time and place. "Of the five senses, smell has the closest thing to the full power of the past," Warhol wrote. "Seeing, hearing, touching, tasting are just not as powerful as smelling if you want your whole being to go back for a second to something."[1]

When we perceive a scent during a direct after-death communication, its purpose is the same: to take us back to a time, place, or experience we shared with the deceased loved one. These are usually among the most fleeting but pleasant and intense contacts. How those on the other side create these phenomena is unknown. We have encountered hundreds of psychic readings in which a spirit alludes to or describes having sent a fragrance in the past. Usually subjects can confirm these events, which we believe indicates that those on the other side can cause these aromas to manifest. Whether we are normally detecting a scent that our loved one somehow produced here or whether our loved one has psychically prompted our brain to perceive a scent as if it did exist is unknown.

As you will see, scent manifestations are often perceived by groups of people, and while this seems to rule out the "brain manipulation" theory, it might be possible for the spirit to cause more than one person to sense the same thing simultaneously. Precisely how spirits cause this phenomenon to occur does not even matter. The particular scent chosen, the timing of our perceiving it, and its significance to the subject and the deceased leave little doubt that these are deliberate after-death communications from the other side. While these are among the rarest of psychic experiences, they are extremely evocative and comforting.

"Kevin" and "Bridget" were not just grandson and grandmother but best friends. Kevin grew up in the same two-family house as his widowed grandmother. He was so devoted to her that after he married and had children of his own, he invited Bridget, then more than eighty, to live with him so that he could take care of her. Bridget's last years were filled with happiness and the joy of being surrounded by grandchildren and great-grandchildren. She died at the age of eighty-eight, of natural causes, in her sleep.

A devout Roman Catholic, Bridget prayed daily to the Virgin Mary. On a dresser near her bed stood a statue of Our Lady of Mount Carmel, a representation of the Virgin Mary given to her years earlier by a priest. It was perhaps her most treasured possession, and after she died, Kevin placed it in his own bedroom, on a night table next to his bed.

The chilly March morning after Bridget died, Kevin was wakened by the overpowering scent of roses. There were none in the room, none in the house, none outside. Getting out of bed, Kevin sniffed all around the room and noticed that the scent intensified as he moved closer to the statue. There was no question about it: the scent was emanating from the statue.

In the history of the Catholic Church, the scent of roses is associated with what is known as the odor of sanctity. Briefly, the odor of sanctity is a sweet, pleasant, usually floral smell that has been detected in the presence of saints and other holy persons. Of all flowers, the rose is most closely associated with romantic love, but it is also a symbol of Christ's love and is associated with mystics, saints, and the Virgin Mary.

Another odor that subjects frequently encounter is cigarette or pipe smoke. Sometimes the scent arrives as a brief greeting; other times it engages our attention for something more important.

John Hay remembered his father as a spiritual though not necessarily religious man. "He was a good soul, a nice man," John recalls. "He loved life. He was one of those upbeat people that everybody liked being around. He told me years ago when I was a kid that he had a dream that told him when he was going to die. I asked him, 'When will that happen?' He answered, 'In the month of May, in my seventy-seventh year.' He used to tease about it, and it became a joke in our family. Well, sure enough, he had a heart attack in his seventy-seventh year, and it was in the month of May."

About six months after John's father passed on, John was driving with his wife and six-year-old son. "All of a sudden, the car filled with the smell of tobacco smoke. It was the cherry blend pipe tobacco that my father smoked all the time," John says. He kept driving, thinking for a moment he must be imagining it. Finally, when John could no longer ignore the smell, he asked his wife, "Do you smell anything unusual in the car?" "Yes, I smell cherry blend tobacco," she replied without hesitation.

They were soon stopped at a large intersection where the red light held for upwards of two minutes. John, who practices meditation daily, recalls, "I put myself into a very calm frame of mind. I closed my eyes and opened my mind. Suddenly a message was impressed upon me: 'Get in touch with your mother right away. Call your mother. She's having an emergency.' It was a thought that I was impressed with, not a voice."

Five minutes later John was home, dialing his mother. He could tell by the way she answered the phone that she was panicked. She said she sensed that something was seriously wrong but could not figure out what. She was disoriented, and as she spoke to John, he could hear that she was beginning to lose consciousness. He hung up and immediately called his sister, who lived next door to their mother. She in turn called for an ambulance, and their mother was rushed to a nearby hospital where doctors discovered a blockage in one of her carotid arteries, threatening a full-blown stroke. Doctors informed John that his mother almost certainly would have died within hours had she not undergone emergency surgery.

Obviously, John's father captured his son's attention with the familiar scent his son associated with him. But that is only half of the story. It was John's willingness and ability to open himself up to the communication and then have the faith to act that saved his mother's life. Later, in chapter 10, we will discuss meditation and other means of facilitating direct after-death communications from this side.

SIGNS

"Nick," a forty-one-year-old college professor, found it impossible to accept the death of his older brother, "Stan." The two brothers had been close all their lives, and three years after Stan's death Nick still had not recovered. One day Nick fell into a deep depression, due in part to his grief over Stan and in part to other personal and professional problems. As tears welled in his eyes, Nick cried, "How I wish I'd have his help now. Oh, Stan, if you can hear me now——" Nick's voice trailed off in heavy sobs.

Nick doesn't recall how long he sat there, his mind lost in a fog of grief and sadness. When he happened to glance at the clock, he jumped up. *Oh my God, I'll be late for class!* he thought and began to rush about the house gathering his things. As he grabbed a textbook he needed for that day's class, he knocked an adjacent book from the shelf. Reaching to pick it up, he noticed that a postcard Stan had sent to him from Europe a few months before he died had fallen from between its pages. Nick had completely forgotten about the card. Turning it over and reading his brother's happy note, Nick's eyes fell upon Stan's signature, and he felt a distinct chill.

"I was never a believer in things like that——the supernatural, life after death," Nick explains. "I was always too logical. Coincidence was a better explanation, I thought. But when that happened with the postcard, I felt so strange. For those few moments, I felt like Stan was there with me again, right there. I don't think that incident was a coincidence. I can't explain it, but I just know that it was something——somehow——that my brother caused.

"Did it solve all my problems? No, of course not. But did it help? That one small thing, at that moment, was an experience that helped me beyond words. It may sound silly, but it was of immense comfort to me."

PSYCHOKINETIC PHENOMENA

Strictly speaking, psychokinesis is the ability to influence material objects through the power of pure thought. The most famous psychokinetic occurrences are probably those demonstrated by Israeli psychic Uri Geller in the 1970s. Psychokinesis has been studied closely in controlled settings, and there is evidence that people can learn to manipulate objects without physically touching them. When we speak of psychokinesis in the context of direct after-death communications, we are referring to the unexplained movement of physical objects. We consider these to be psychokinetic because we believe that in direct after-death communications it is the mind, or the consciousness, of the deceased that causes the movement.

Direct after-death communications that involve psychokinesis can be quite startling. They occur when we are awake and fully conscious, and are often accompanied by sudden noise or movement. Perhaps because many of the phenomena people witness with psychokinetic communications—banging, knocks, objects that fall or seem to fly through the air—are closely associated in the common imagination with hauntings, poltergeists, and other, less welcome spirit encounters, it takes some subjects a while to "warm up" to this form of communication. The one thing we can say about these communications is that they certainly get people's attention. They also resist logical explanation.

A few nights before Christmas, Eleanor Salch was in her bedroom getting dressed when she heard a knock on her door. Assuming it was one of her three adult sons who lived at home, she called out, "Just a minute. I'm getting dressed."

No one answered, and Eleanor assumed that whoever it was went away. A few moments later, there came a knock more forceful than the first. "Hold on a second! I'll be right there," Eleanor snapped. Once she was dressed, she opened her door to find no one. She marched into the living room, where her three sons were watching television. "Who was knocking on my door?" she demanded.

"What do you mean, who was knocking on your door?" one of them answered. "We're just sitting here, watching TV."

"Come on," Eleanor persisted. "Which one of you knocked on my door two minutes ago?"

"None of us, Mom," a second son replied. "Nobody knocked on your door."

At that instant Eleanor was impressed with the thought that her late husband, Eddie, had knocked. After all, this was the family's first

Christmas without him. While she took some comfort in the thought, she quickly told herself, *That's ridiculous. Wishful thinking.*

Two nights later, as the family finished decorating their Christmas tree, Eleanor found herself thinking about the knocks. Try as she might, she could not put the episode out of her mind. "Remember what happened two nights ago when there was a knock on my door?" she mused aloud to her sons. "I wonder if it was Daddy trying to give us a message for Christmastime. I wish we had some way of knowing if that was Dad's spirit knocking at the door."

At that very second, a fragile glass ornament flew off the tree and landed two feet away on the linoleum floor. Miraculously, the German-made antique, a wedding gift from Eddie's mother, did not crack. The significance of the incident was immediately clear to Eleanor. Every Christmas she would admonish Eddie about the special ornaments. "Be careful with those," she would say sharply. "I'll kill you if you break one of those!"

Every year, Eddie would promise to be careful, but inevitably he'd laconically announce, "Oh well, I broke one."

"What do you mean, you broke an ornament? How can you act like it's no big deal?" Eleanor would shout. Their bickering over the ornaments became as much a family tradition as decorating the tree. Of course, the two always made up afterward, and over the years these yuletide spats became a running family joke.

This Christmas, however, Eddie was taking very special care. Eleanor has no doubt that her husband was announcing his presence.

Eileen Deger was lying in her darkened bedroom one night a few months after her mother died of breast cancer. She tossed and turned, but sleep eluded her. At one point, she opened her eyes and was shocked to see a shapeless, lightly glowing fog move through her room. She sat up, rubbed her eyes, and looked again. Something was definitely there, but it vanished when she turned on the light. Eileen had a very strong feeling that it was a sign from her mother.

Sometime later Eileen found her thoughts drifting to her mother's last weeks. Though the two had been extremely close, her mother could not bring herself to discuss her imminent death. As Eileen sat at her vanity, putting on her makeup, she recalled her mother saying shortly before she died: "The worst sound is the noise of the dirt hitting the top of the coffin." As Eileen heard those words in her mind, she heard a crash, then the sound of dirt being thrown against hard wood. She turned to see that a pot of philodendron had suddenly been flung to the bare floor wood from a shelf. It sounded just like dirt raining down on a coffin.

To Eileen, this was absolutely a sign from her mother. Those who have studied psychokinesis would suggest another possibility: that Eileen concentrated so intensely on her mother's words that her own psychic energy caused the pot to fall. While that explanation cannot be dismissed completely, it raises an interesting question. If, as we know, the human mind can generate psychokinetic phenomena, why aren't there more of them?

To play the cynic for a moment, consider who would be more motivated to experience or produce such startling phenomena than the bereaved? Even if only one in a thousand of the deeply grieved managed—consciously or unconsciously—to produce some psychokinetic event, it stands to reason that reports of this form of paranormal activity would be far more common than they are. Yet it remains uncommon, compared to dream visitations, for instance. We believe that the rarity of such events in direct after-death communications supports their origination with loved ones on the other side. If *all* psychokinetic events were produced by subjects, it seems reasonable to assume there would be millions of times more than there are.

The following case involved psychokinesis, but under such complex circumstances that one can only conclude that several direct contacts occurred. Mary Jasen was a pretty woman with dark hair, large brown eyes, and an energetic warmth that drew people to her. She enjoyed life fully and had a rich, loving marriage with Len, a physician who was eighteen years her senior.

Shortly after their first wedding anniversary, Mary was diagnosed with breast cancer, which initially responded to surgery and courses of radiation and chemotherapy. Throughout, Mary was optimistic but a realist. Breast cancer had claimed her mother's life years earlier. When, two years later, Mary's doctor sadly informed her that the cancer had spread to her lymph nodes, lungs, and bones, she accepted the news stoically. Never one to give up, she looked ahead with courage and honesty. A devout Roman Catholic, she believed in an afterlife, and as her disease progressed to its final stages, she openly discussed her feelings about death with family and close friends.

One day shortly before Mary succumbed to cancer, she told a close friend named Christina that she would "come back" to her after she left this physical world. Christina, who had known Mary for years, never doubted her friend's determination. If anyone would find a way back, it was Mary. Still, she had to ask, "How will I know it's you?"

"You'll know it's me because I'll make a racket. I'll bang on the refrigerator to get your attention. You'll hear me knocking. That's how you'll know it's me."

"But why the refrigerator?" Christina asked.

"You know I love food. The refrigerator is my favorite place," Mary answered with a hearty laugh. "Oh, one more thing: Don't tell anyone. It'll be our secret code. That way, when it does happen, you'll know it's really me." Several months later, at the age of forty-five, Mary passed on at home, with her husband by her side.

Christina, deeply saddened by the loss of her friend, waited for Mary's message. As months passed with no news from Mary, Christina began to feel let down. Had Mary moved on and forgotten her promise? Did she cross over to find there was no way to communicate back? Was it possible that there was nothing beyond this life?

For five years after Mary's death, Christina pondered these questions, though as months turned to years, she eventually accepted that she would never hear from Mary again. Then one night, Christina had a vivid dream in which she saw Mary and Len eating at a picnic table. It was a bright, warm summer day, and Christina was struck by how healthy, how alive Mary appeared. Mary turned to face Christina and playfully scolded, saying that her loved ones on earth need not worry about her; she was fine on the other side. In an instant, the dream vanished.

Shortly after that, Christina was visiting Len, and the subject turned to Mary. When Len mentioned how much he still missed his late wife, Christina decided to tell him of her dream. Len listened as Christina described the dream scene in great detail. After a moment, he said, "That sounds just like where we often had lunch. Mary would meet me on my lunch hour, and we'd eat at a picnic table on the hospital grounds." Christina never knew that. Nor had she ever been to the picnic area at the hospital where Len worked. However, she was pleasantly surprised and reassured by his answer. Perhaps this meant that her dream was a genuine visit from Mary.

"Since you shared that, now I'll tell you about the strangest thing that just happened to me," Len said. "I was sitting alone in my kitchen the other evening. Suddenly, I heard what sounded like someone throwing rocks at the kitchen window. At first I thought it was kids in the neighborhood. I was afraid they'd break the window, so I went outside to look around. There was no one there. So I went back inside. Then I heard it again: *bang bang*.

"Then it dawned on me: The windows were covered by screens! How could I have heard a sharp banging noise against a screen? I couldn't have. I sat in the kitchen pondering the source of the noise, when it started again. I tried listening very closely so I could figure out where it was coming from. I'd been mistaken. The noise wasn't coming from the windows. It was someone banging on the refrigerator door!"

Christina almost blurted out that she knew, but Len was so engrossed in telling her his story, she bit her tongue. "I was startled!" Len continued. "But then, instantly, something—I don't know what—gave me the overwhelming feeling that it was Mary! So I said, 'Okay, Mary. Hello. I hear you. I hear you. I know it's you.'

"I don't know why I felt it was Mary. I just knew it. As soon as I spoke to her aloud, the banging noises stopped. I smiled to myself. *What an odd way to let me know she was around*, I thought. But I was pleased. I really felt that Mary was close. It didn't frighten me, for some reason. If anything, it was strangely comforting." When Christina told Len of Mary's promise, he was incredulous. Now he was certain beyond doubt that he had heard from Mary.

This case not only raises many questions but suggests some possible answers. First, the questions. Why didn't Mary return exactly as she had promised Christina—by banging on a refrigerator in Christina's presence? Why did she make her presence known only to Len, who didn't know about her promise? Unlike Christina, he was not expecting to hear from her. The third question is, Why didn't Mary knock on Christina's refrigerator? Why did she bang in Len's presence but not Christina's? No one but Mary knows, yet we can examine the results of this event and conclude the following: the genuineness of this contact is proved by both its specificity and the cross-corroboration that results from its being split between two people, one who knew what to expect, one who did not.

For example, if Mary had banged on the refrigerator in Christina's presence alone, that would not necessarily mean it was not a valid communication. Given the promise between the two women, Christina and most people who believe in the possibility of paranormal events might conclude that by communicating back in that predetermined code, Mary—and Mary alone—was the source of the noise. But by communicating in the code to someone who knew nothing of the promise, Mary ensured a high degree of cross-corroboration. It is interesting that once Len realized the noise emanated from the refrigerator, he sensed that it was Mary. The day this occurred was not a special anniversary, nor did Len have any more reason on that particular day to think of his late wife than he had on any of the other 1,500-plus days since her death. Len's feeling so certain that he was in his wife's presence is a hallmark of true direct after-death communications. Most subjects falter when they attempt to describe the feeling, but they all say that they "know" it is true.

It is also interesting that Christina had dreamed of Mary shortly before the banging incident. Had she not mentioned her dream—which contained verifiable information Christina could not have known before speaking with Len—one wonders if Len would have confided in her about his experience. If he had not told her about the banging, Christina might never have had occasion to reveal the promise. So while Len might have gone on feeling he had experienced a direct contact with Mary, he would not have had the same certainty.

Finally, there are the elements of Christina's dream, which only Len could confirm. In essence, Mary sent a message to Christina that only Len could confirm and then sent a message to Len that only Christina could confirm.

ELECTRICAL DISTURBANCES

Electrical disturbances or interruptions are frequently reported as direct after-death communications from the other side, often occurring soon after a loved one's passing. Are the spirits somehow able to manipulate electromagnetic fields? Can the spirits influence electrical equipment to communicate their messages?

When we physically die, our soul or essence survives, most likely as a form of energy. Since energy operates according to electromagnetic principles, it is not unreasonable to think that the spirit can manipulate or interfere with electrically powered devices and systems. It has long been a theory that psychic phenomena occur through some form of energy, although exactly what type is not yet known. This was the premise behind Thomas Edison's interdimensional telephone (see Appendix I).

A similar theory would account for so-called phone calls from the dead. These are instances in which a telephone rings, usually a short while after a loved one's death. When the phone is answered, one hears static and the departed loved one's name comes to mind or their voice is actually heard. We will discuss this form of direct after-death communication in chapter 7.

One of the most convincing cases we came across is the story of Irene Wolfe, which involved a series of events encompassing several different phenomena. Her story shows how direct after-death communications not only help us to deal with grief and find resolution but open us up to future contacts.

Irene, a thirty-two-year-old mother of three, was finding the holiday season unusually depressing. Three months earlier, the authorities had sent her husband to prison for stealing from his place of employment. Irene had no choice but to move with her children into her childhood home with her widowed mother.

"My life had come to a crashing halt. I was wallowing in my own lack of self-worth. I'd reached rock-bottom," Irene says of this period. "I always hated New Year's Eve anyway, because it's one of those holidays that can either make you happy or very depressed. Well, my situation didn't help me that year."

Even in happy years, the holidays always brought bittersweet reminders of her father, Joe, who had succumbed to cancer when Irene was sixteen. This year, though, Irene felt his loss even more acutely. Perhaps it was suddenly finding herself a single parent, or the fact she was back in her childhood home. Whatever it was, Irene could not resist the pull of her oldest memories, not all of them sweet.

"I never felt emotionally close to my father," Irene recalls. "He was a perfectionist and strict. I didn't feel I could live up to his expectations. It's hard enough to be sixteen, so to lose a parent at that age is tough. I'd always looked for my father's approval—his love and acceptance. It did not come easy. He did not show his feelings easily. The way he expressed his feelings was in the things he did for us."

One special thing that Joe did faithfully for his family every holiday season was string beautiful multicolored strands of Christmas lights across the house, and Irene always felt special when he asked her to help. As Irene thought back to the wintry days in years past when she and her father had climbed ladders to string the lights, she felt both her father's love and her loss.

Shortly before Christmas, Irene decided she would decorate the house herself. Maybe it would cheer her up. After hours of arranging the dozens of light strands just so, she flipped the switch. Nothing. She climbed up and down the ladder countless times, checking connections, unscrewing each of the hundreds of bulbs and examining it individually, replacing any that looked worn. Hours later, she checked the household wiring to the outside outlets. Still, nothing wrong. She finally gave up in frustration, angrily reasoning that since nothing else was going right this year, why should the lights work?

That New Year's Eve, Irene and her younger sister, Sally, sat in the darkened living room, watching a Barbra Streisand concert special. At ten minutes before midnight, one of them mentioned that it was about time to start channel hopping so they could catch the live telecast from Times Square before the famous ball dropped. For some reason, though, that old tradition did not seem so important tonight. Just then Streisand introduced "Papa, Can You Hear Me?" from her film *Yentl.* Before she sang, Streisand lighted a candle, which, she explained, was in memory of all the fathers who had died, including her own.

As Streisand spoke, Irene recalled how she never heard that song without thinking of her father and the close relationship they never had. Irene turned to Sally and mused, "You know, I wonder if Daddy knows what is going on in my life. I wonder if he is aware of what we are going through right now. If he could just know or see—or be with us. I just wish I knew."

That very moment—just as Streisand sang the first notes of the song—the darkened kitchen was washed in a soft, colorful glow. Sally and Irene hurried to the kitchen. They found no lights on there, but outside the window the Christmas lights blinked and twinkled wildly. What was even more unusual about it was that they began blinking instantly; usually they had to warm up for several minutes first.

Irene and Sally rushed to awaken their mother. "Ma, you've got to see this!" Irene cried. "You're not going to believe it. The Christmas lights are on!"

"You're kidding," her mother replied. As Sally and Irene breathlessly explained what had happened, the three made their way to the front window. Gazing out the window, they felt Joe's presence and began to cry.

"Thank you, Daddy," Irene whispered.

Years later, Irene told us, "At that moment I knew my father was hugging me. It was his way of saying, 'I'm here.' I think my father knew that I needed him. What better way to show me he was there than with something we always did together? What better way to reach me? It could have been anything, but he chose the lights.

"I think my father knew that I needed him. I feel that my father, like others in the hereafter, always knows what's going on here on earth. When I'm going through a hard time, I know those on the other side are right there. I've always felt that way. I always believed in life after death. Deep down inside, I always knew there was something."

As seemingly miraculous and inspiring as the incident was for Irene and her family, she is the first to admit that such a communication is not a solution to anything. "That was such a powerful event," Irene recalls. "I needed that so much. I'd gone through a lot. Even after that, though, it was a good two or three years before things got better. Still, the experience showed me that there is hope. And I felt that I still had two parents—one on each side."

Since then, over a decade has passed without Irene hearing again from her father "that vividly," as she puts it. About six years later, however, the death of her brother Joe prompted another after-death contact. One night about a month after Joe died, Irene awoke from a lifelike dream. In it, she saw herself standing before her bathroom mirror. When she looked at her reflection, she saw that she had been crying. "The dream was so real," Irene remembers, "that I could feel tears on my face."

When Irene looked around, she saw Joe standing close by. He put his arms around her and said, "Don't worry. I'm all right."

"I felt him hug me," Irene says. "It was a strong hug. That was the amazing thing: I felt the hug. He looked fine, like he did the last time I saw him before he died.

"Before this, I would go to mass every Sunday. I had a belief in God and I knew there was an afterlife. But I didn't believe it as strongly or as unconditionally as I do today. I look at everything as God's will. There's a purpose for everything. God doesn't make mistakes. I've come back to the fold. I came home and the doors were open."

Like most recipients of direct after-death communications, Irene found that the experiences changed her attitudes toward life and faith, before and after death. But for Irene, they also led to spiritual fulfillment through involvement with the Catholic Church. A month after Joe's appearance in her dream, Irene began working for a Catholic youth ministry. In 1993 she traveled to Denver, Colorado, to join a crowd of 375,000 there to witness Pope John Paul II's papal visit. "I really believe that was another turning point in my life," Irene says. "I was looking for answers out there. I know my father was there. I know my brother was there. I felt dead friends and acquaintances. They were all there."

Irene is now married to Tim, whom she met when she began working in the youth ministry. Today they are both youth ministers, helping teenagers through difficult times. "I tell people not to be afraid of communications from the other side. Don't feel foolish. Even to this day, I will talk about my experiences because I feel it's very important to know that our deceased loved ones are very much aware of our grief. They are aware of our pain. They have all the emotions they had on earth. They have their arms around us."

6

SEEING TOMORROW

Precognition

Miracles do not happen in contradiction to nature, but only in contradiction to that which is known to us in nature.

—SAINT AUGUSTINE

On a typically perfect L.A. Saturday morning, the sun shone brightly and the glistening Pacific beaches beckoned. But Hollywood agent Rowland Perkins had an important meeting to attend. Business before pleasure, he reminded himself as he drove through his Beverly Hills neighborhood to the freeway.

Rowland had not gone more than a mile when he distinctly heard a male voice loudly command, "Go see your father." Although certain he was alone, Rowland reflexively turned toward the front passenger seat, from which the voice seemed to emanate. No one was there. Still, as Rowland recalls, "When I heard the voice, I didn't even question it. It seemed very natural for me to go. It's funny to me now that I didn't question. It happened so quickly. In a strange way, it didn't feel strange to me. I didn't cry out, 'Oh my God!' and leap up. I literally turned the car around, went out over the canyon, and drove to my parents' home in Westwood. When I arrived, they wondered what I was doing there. I answered, 'Just thought I'd come by and see how you guys were doing.' I didn't even tell them about the meeting, which I phoned ahead and begged out of."

Rowland spent the next three hours with his father, Jack. During their conversation, the elder Perkins casually remarked, "I know you and your brother will, but you've got to promise me you'll take really good care of your mother if anything should ever happen to me."

"Don't be silly," Rowland replied. "You don't even have to ask."

"I know I don't have to ask that, but I did," Jack answered contentedly.

Later that afternoon, Rowland returned home. Around midnight his mother phoned in panic. "Your father," she cried urgently, "something is wrong!"

"I jumped in my car; I lived only about fifteen minutes away. However, by the time I got to my parents' house, a doctor was there and my father had died," Rowland says. "I knew he had problems on and off with kidney stones. Otherwise, he was in good health. Doctors said that my father tried to pass a kidney stone and the pain was so excruciating it caused a fatal heart attack. It was sudden and totally unexpected."

Clearly, the voice Rowland heard had conveyed a special message. Although he still can't even begin to guess whose voice he heard, Rowland is grateful that it spoke to him. "Although I've never been deeply into the metaphysical, I would say I'm open to the subject. I finally concluded that the incident meant that someone was giving me the opportunity to see my father one last time," he says. "I was really at peace with myself because it was as if that experience was ordained to happen."

WHEN THE FUTURE IS NOW

Rowland is one of millions for whom an after-death communication has contained information about or offered some preparation for future events. Some messages are extremely precise and detailed, while others feel like hunches. They can be amusing, mundane, or profound. They can compel us to perform small, seemingly insignificant acts without fully understanding why. Or they may warn of imminent, life-threatening danger. Whatever their message, however they arrive, future-oriented direct contacts present us with the opportunity to see, prepare for, or even change events that have not yet occurred. No other form of after-death communication can be as readily verified or as easily accepted as a glimpse of the future that comes to pass.*

There are two related but distinct forms of psychic phenomena involving knowledge of future events. One is precognition, the experience of gaining direct, often very specific information about a future event. Precognition is by far the most common form of psychic or paranormal experience. As we have seen, it can arise in the midst of a dream, where most precognitive experiences occur. It may also come upon one suddenly, as a waking vision. Sometimes it is as simple as a thought that bursts into one's consciousness. People who experience precognitive episodes have the sense that they know something but are unable to explain precisely how they know it. (The related phenomenon of retrocognition, or the knowledge of things past, is much rarer. We will discuss it in greater detail in chapter 9.)

While premonition also involves knowledge of a future event, it is much less specific. People who have premonitions will describe the sensation in words such as *hunch, sense,* or *feeling.* Whereas a precognitive experience is clear and explicit (for example, Abraham Lincoln's dream of attending his own funeral), the person who has a premonition will simply feel that something is not quite right or sense an uneasiness about someone or something. Or they may feel compelled to act, as Rowland Perkins did, to heed some warning or comply with a command whose source or purpose is not fully clear at the time.

Many documented cases suggest that at various times, groups of people—most strangers to one another, some continents apart—have altered their behavior in response to individual premonitions about the same object or event. Perhaps the most famous instance is that of the *Titanic,* which was carrying less than 60 percent of its passenger capacity when it sank after hitting an iceberg in April 1912. In the week before the ship sailed, many passengers, including J. P. Morgan,

---

*Because numerous examples of premonition and precognition appear throughout the book, our focus here will be on the possible how and why of these seemingly impossible events.

canceled their reservations.* A study of U.S. railroad accidents in the early 1950s found a similar pattern of mass cancellations and reduced passenger counts on a number of trains involved in accidents hours, days, or weeks later.

The group premonition phenomenon has been discovered at work in a number of natural disasters as well. The most famous was a 1966 landslide in Wales that killed more than a hundred children when it buried a school in coal waste. More than two hundred people later reported their premonitions of impending disaster, ranging from a vague uneasiness to sensations of choking and clear visions of children screaming and black clouds. A few people had even predicted the exact date of the landslide.

Though rare, group premonitions and precognitions are invaluable since they are so easily and convincingly verified. An individual's isolated verified precognition might be dismissed as coincidence or luck. However, when many people seem to have independently, simultaneously shared such an experience, something other than chance must be at work. Examining group incidents has so far not revealed how precognitive experiences originate, but it does provide rich opportunities for establishing that the human ability to see into the future—though weak, limited, and often ignored—is absolutely real.

CRISIS ALERTS

The majority of premonitive and precognitive experiences are isolated instances. One common type of premonition occurs at or near the moment of another's death. This is not a crisis apparition; there is no materialization, we see nothing in the visual sense. This crisis alert is a psychically received message that causes a subject to know, inexplicably and suddenly, that something terrible has occurred or that

---

*Interestingly, in 1898 Morgan Robertson wrote *Futility*, a novel about an "unsinkable" luxury liner christened the *Titan*. The dozens of parallels between the fictional *Titan* and the doomed *Titanic* are amazing. For example, both sank in the month of April after hitting an iceberg; the *Titan* measured 800 feet in length, the *Titanic*, 882.5 feet. Was Robertson's novel the premonition of a distant event?

someone has died. Crisis alerts differ from other types of premonitions and precognitions in that there is little or no time lapse between the subject's knowledge of an event and its actual occurrence.

These events feature several key elements that may help us to understand how the deceased communicate to us. Although contemporary science has yet to explain exactly what these messages consist of or how they travel, some transmission of information occurs. Even if you totally discount the concept of life after death or after-death communications, you cannot deny the countless accounts of crisis alerts occurring between people on *this* side. Accounts of mothers inexplicably knowing that their children—out of sight, thousands of miles away—have been hurt or killed are legion. These verifiable events confirm the existence of psychic connections linking all of us, both in this life and beyond.

A Brother's Unspoken Love

Johnny Peck was Laura's half-brother, her father's son from a previous marriage. Although Johnny lived with his own mother, he and Laura saw each other when he visited their father every other weekend. During their late teens Laura and Johnny became very close, but as a young adult Johnny distanced himself from her and other family members.

"After being close with Johnny for a period, I lost touch with him," Laura recalls. "Johnny was homosexual, but he never came out and told me he was gay. I had suspected it for a while, but it was not something I asked him. It didn't matter, you know. He was still my brother."

Johnny was working as a nurse in New York City, and Laura lived about an hour away, in suburban Long Island. On the day of her wedding, Johnny failed to show up. "He never called me after the wedding to explain why," Laura says. "I didn't know at the time that he had AIDS, so I guess he was embarrassed or confused. Part of me was a little angry that he didn't give me the courtesy of a phone call. I was also angry that he didn't want me to see him while he was ill."

Until that point, Johnny had hidden from his father the fact that he was gay. "He did eventually tell my father, after he found out he was sick with AIDS. Surprisingly, my father took it very well. Johnny was his firstborn son, and he stuck with him throughout the whole time he was sick."

But Johnny made it clear to everyone else, including Laura, that he did not want them to see him. Deeply hurt, Laura tried to understand her half-brother's feelings but could not help regretting his decision. "I think he thought that by asking that my sisters and I not visit him, he was protecting us. He didn't feel that I was capable of dealing with his illness. I should have said I didn't care what he said. I know it would have been a difficult situation for me, but it was something I should have pushed. Then another part of me respected his wishes."

Johnny's last months followed a course familiar to anyone who has dealt with AIDS: drug regimens that seem to work and then falter, periods of relatively good health shattered by sudden setbacks. Though Johnny had lost a tremendous amount of weight and grew weaker, he was not, as Laura says, "at death's door. I knew Johnny was going to die eventually; there's no cure for AIDS. But my father never gave me any indication that he was almost gone or ready to die. It wasn't as if anyone thought he could die any minute."

Laura took her seat on the 7:12 A.M. Long Island Railroad train as she did every weekday morning. As the train sped toward Manhattan, Laura gazed out the window at the hazy mist hanging in the cold air.

"Unexplainably, I started to get this sinking feeling. It just came out of nowhere. It's so hard to describe. It wasn't a feeling of horror. It was more like extreme sadness and disappointment that all of a sudden overwhelmed me," Laura says. "But there was no reason for it. I knew it was connected to my brother, and I remember looking out the window and saying to myself, 'Johnny just died.'"

Laura glanced at her watch. It was 7:30.

"I knew that as soon as I got to the office, I had to call my mother. It wasn't to confirm what I felt. It was to let her know what I already knew."

On any other workday, Laura's mother would have been at her own office by a few minutes past nine. For some strange reason—which neither Laura nor her mother or father ever questioned—Laura was certain her mother would be home when she called. She was right.

"Hi, Mom. Is everything okay?"

"No. Your brother passed away," Laura's mother replied sadly.

"Yeah, I know that already. What time did Johnny die?"

Laura's mother explained that her father had gotten the call at 7:30, which meant that Johnny died shortly before that.

"I think my brother wanted to let me know that he was gone," Laura says today, reflecting on her experience. "Maybe by giving me that feeling, it was his way of saying goodbye. I think that was his way of getting in touch with me just one last time. Maybe it was easier for both of us to say goodbye like that rather than to face each other, given how he felt about the condition he was in. One strange thing was that it never dawned on my mother to ask how I knew that Johnny had died. My family is not into psychic phenomena, yet no one thought my premonition was strange."

Like many people to whom a loved one has reached out at the moment of physical death, Laura views the incident as having a greater importance to her life. "It gave me a sense of completion. If I'd never gotten that sensation, I would always have wondered, *Did he think of me?* Perhaps I would have carried guilt throughout my life, wondering if I should have done more to make the relationship between us closer, especially toward the end. I've accepted Johnny's passing because of the premonition. I think it was normal. I knew it happened for a reason."

Troubling Warnings

In Laura's case, her premonition brought comfort and reassurance of Johnny's love. For some people, however, premonitions can be confusing, frightening experiences. "Diane" was a thirty-one-year-old woman who had experienced several premonitions. These usually took the form of an overwhelming feeling of anxiety, and while she never knew until later whom or what the premonition concerned, inevitably tragedy followed.

She was at her chiropractor's office for her regular Wednesday evening appointment when she suddenly bolted up from the treatment table crying, "I've got to leave! I've got to go!"

"What's wrong?" the startled doctor asked.

"I've got to get out of here!" she replied, her voice quivering. She hurriedly dressed and ran out the door. The doctor and his receptionist were left to wonder what might possibly have prompted such bizarre behavior in a woman they knew to be happy, stable, and friendly.

About half an hour later, Diane called the office. "I'm sorry I had to leave so abruptly," she explained. She sounded calmer yet still spoke with an insistence that struck the doctor as uncharacteristic. "I suddenly got violently ill. I felt like I was overwhelmed with a terrible panic attack and very nauseous."

"Do you know what's wrong?" "Dr. Reed" asked. "Is there some reason for this?"

"Well, I've had this same feeling several other times in the past. It's always revolved around something terrible, like serious injury or illness, or death. Please don't think I'm crazy. But the feeling is not going away. I feel so sick to my stomach. I know something bad is going to happen. I just don't know what yet. I'm sorry, I can't come back to your office tonight. I'll call you tomorrow."

The following morning, as promised, Diane called Dr. Reed. Choking back tears, she explained that after she spoke with him the night before, she got word that her brother-in-law, a police officer, was killed in the line of duty. The incident occurred approximately one hour after she fled Dr. Reed's office.

While Diane's inability to understand her premonition left her powerless to alter future events, some people seem to be given such opportunities but cannot realize them. It's impossible to know how often people experience premonitions and precognitions, what type they are, and how they deal with them. For many, the very idea of receiving knowledge of the future is fraught with fear and anxiety.

Best to leave it alone, many say, best to let fate run its course. Other times, people will try to change the outcome they have foreseen but be prevented from doing so by circumstances beyond their control.

CAN PRECOGNITION HELP US TO CHANGE THE FUTURE?

Richard III foresaw his defeat and death in battle. Calpurnia dreamed of the death of her husband, Julius Caesar. During World War I, a young soldier named Adolf Hitler dreamed he'd been buried in an avalanche and awoke to move his position only minutes before several men sleeping near him were covered by mounds of dirt. In American history, arguably the most famous precognitive dream is the one President Abraham Lincoln had of his own funeral only days before John Wilkes Booth assassinated him in 1865.

History is filled with precognitive experiences. In 1947, on the eve of a welterweight title fight with Jimmy Doyle, the boxer Sugar Ray Robinson had a frightening dream. In it he saw himself hitting his opponent, then looking down at him lying on the canvas, "his blank eyes staring up at me." As he recounted this dream in his autobiography, Robinson saw that "Doyle wasn't moving a muscle and in the crowd I could hear people yelling, 'He's dead! He's dead!'" Robinson was so badly shaken by the dream that he tried to call off the fight. He failed; his trainer and promoter assured him, "Dreams don't come true."

Robinson reluctantly went ahead with the bout. He and Doyle fought through seven rounds. Then in round eight, Robinson knocked out Doyle with a left hook to the jaw. Doyle went down, hit his head on the ring floor, and Robinson found himself reliving his dream for real. Doyle died the next day.

Was the dream merely a reflection of Robinson's own fear and anxiety on the eve of a fight, or was it something more? Was this a precognitive dream of a tragic future event? Was it a warning from the other side? Was the dream "sent" to him by loved ones of Doyle's? Was it Doyle's time to cross over? Dreams like Robinson's, and the precognitive experiences of millions of others, challenge the premise that only our own thoughts, feelings, and knowledge inform our dreams.

Like so many psychic phenomena, precognition as it occurs in real life has defied controlled study. However, the many impressive results of controlled experiments in which subjects correctly predicted a range of events—from the correct faces of cards to numbers randomly generated by computer—indicate that we do possess precognitive ability. Studies that examined large numbers of spontaneous precognitive experiences agree.

Dr. Louisa E. Rhine, at the Duke University Parapsychology Laboratory, analyzed thousands of precognitive experiences, and her findings generally conform to those of others who have studied the phenomenon before and since. She found, for example, that about two-thirds of the precognitions took place in dreams, and that 60 percent of those were extremely realistic and detailed. She also found that precognition experienced when we are awake is more convincing than that in dreams. When she examined nearly two hundred cases of people who had tried to intervene to avoid the events they dreamed, once she ruled out all other possible factors (such as vague or nonspecific warnings, the actions of others that might have contributed to the result, and so on), she found only three who had been successful in their intervention.

Does that mean, then, that our efforts to avert an unfortunate outcome (and, interestingly, precognitions of shocking or tragic events outnumber those of happy, welcome events by four to one) are in vain? No. The literature is full of cases where people use precognitive dreams and experiences to avert disaster. For example, a mother might dream that her young child hurts himself playing with a particular toy, so she takes the toy away. One might argue that perhaps it was a toy that should have been taken away in any case. Or that, with the toy now removed, there's no way of knowing whether it would have hurt the child. There is, however, a considerable body of evidence suggesting that sometimes such precognitions do give us an opportunity to prevent an undesirable outcome.

In a case cited by Dr. Louisa E. Rhine, a mother dreamed that a storm shook her home so violently that a heavy chandelier over her baby's crib fell and killed the child. She awoke her husband, who dismissed her dream, pointing out that the weather was calm. Undeterred, the mother moved the baby from its crib and was sleeping with the baby at her side when a storm descended, causing the chandelier to crash into the crib, exactly where the baby's head would have been.

Cases such as these leave us to wonder what we mean when we speak of the future, of fate, of time. We must remember that time as we understand it is an invention, a fantasy, an order we impose on a phenomenon that may not even exist. Seconds, hours, days, and years, patterned after recurring natural events, create the illusion that time continues in one direction from one point to the next—past to present to future. Our everyday lives operate under the assumption that events unfold in this chronological order. How then can a person know what will occur in the future if it has not yet occurred? How can we know what lies ahead if the future is, by this definition, unknowable?

However, some argue that the future is not by definition unknowable, that fate is not immune to our efforts to change it. A good deal of what occurs in our lives follows the basic rule of cause and effect. We switch on the light, the room grows brighter; we drop a cup, coffee spills all over the floor. Therefore, conscientious parents do all they can to protect their children. The mother who forbids her child from playing on a busy street is not said to be in any way altering the future. She is simply acting on common sense. The mother who leaves her child unsupervised to play on that same busy street would be said to be "tempting fate." That raises the next question: Is fate at work when a car strikes a careless parent's child?

Without consciously thinking about it, we predict and shape our futures thousands of times each day through our decisions and our actions. Yet when we examine our assumptions about what will occur given a certain set of circumstances, we also recognize that those assumptions are based on what is *most likely* to occur, not what we *positively know* will happen. For instance, we know that if you drop a cup of coffee, it will spill out. Some coffee may splash on you and the cup may break, *but you will not absolutely know that these events will take place until they do.* There is a very good chance the cup will break, but then again, it may not. Precognition is distinguished from the vast realm of the possible in that the specificity of its information foretells *only* the outcome that *actually occurs.*

So while a great deal about the future can be assumed or expected, it is never totally predictable based on what we know and observe. Most precognition and premonition concern matters far more complex and significant than spilt coffee, yet the same principles apply. Granted, in the case of the baby sleeping under the chandelier, other factors might have influenced its mother's decision to have the baby sleep somewhere else. Nevertheless, her emotional, motivating response to the precognitive aspect is what compelled her to act. There is reason to believe that the emotional "nudge" prompting us to act comes from the other side.

It is tempting to wonder, If some precognitive events give information that makes it possible for the subject, or receiver, to avert disaster, why don't they all? It does not seem fair that the mother who moved her baby from its crib received sufficient specific information in time to act to change the predicted outcome while someone else, like Diane, was helpless in the face of an impending threat she could not even identify.

WHY DOES THE FUTURE COME TO US?

Given all the limitations and frustrations of these communications, one wonders, What is the purpose of precognition? What are its sources? Do we, as some believe, simply absorb far more information than we are consciously aware of? Is information a form of energy that can be transferred from one sentient being to another, including loved ones on the other side? There is sufficient evidence to support any of these possibilities. We must also keep in mind that possible or apparent causes are not necessarily a one-size-fits-all proposition. Given how widely precognitive and premonitive experiences vary in content, meaning, apparent purpose, and the subject's ability to act on the information they convey, it seems safest to view each of these experiences as unique. Why they occur, what they mean, what they tell us about life before *and* after death depends more on the other circumstances of the case—the people involved, when, where, and how it happened, and the outcome—than on *how* the message was received.

If we take the case of the mother who saved her baby from the falling chandelier, it is entirely possible that her dream incorporated information she did not know she had (perhaps she had unknowingly heard a storm forecast). Another school of thought holds, somewhat unconvincingly we believe, that through a form of psychokinesis, the mother unconsciously caused the chandelier to fall after she removed the baby.

Of course, anything is possible. However, given the specificity of the dream (Why not dream the storm blew in a window? Or caused a tree to fall on the house?), another source of intelligence seems the most logical source. If we accept that this mother's premonition originated in another intelligence, it would have to be one capable of working outside the limitations imposed by time and space as we understand them. More important, though, it would seem to be an intelligence with some emotional connection to the child or the mother.

WARNINGS?

It is sometimes difficult to determine the origin of a dream premonition. Is it a communication from the spirit world? A manifestation of our own thoughts and fears? A telepathic message that originates—consciously or unconsciously—in the mind of another?

These were the questions that ran through "Candy's" mind when she awoke following an intensely disturbing dream. In it, Candy saw the interior of a human heart. "I felt like I was traveling inside the heart," Candy recalls. "Like in that old science fiction movie *Fantastic Voyage*, where they shrink down some doctors and a submarine and inject them into a dying man's bloodstream. I was not just looking inside the heart; I was actually there. The main arteries were bulging as if they were blocked and on the verge of bursting. Suddenly a male voice communicated to me telepathically: 'Don't feel bad. There's nothing you or anyone else can do. It's his time.'"

Candy had a strong sense that the unusual dream was a premonition about someone she knew. But who? Since the vision gave no indication of who might be involved, she spent the rest of the day agonizing, praying it would not come true. "I felt very helpless and confused," she recalls. "I kept running through my mind, thinking of anyone to whom it could apply. My father had a history of heart problems; a few years before, he'd had bypass surgery. My brother is very young, but he'd been under a lot of stress at work. I just didn't know, and it was driving me crazy."

That evening she learned that a friend's husband had died that afternoon of a heart attack. Candy wondered why the dream message came to her and not to his wife. Since there was nothing anyone could have done to prevent the tragedy, why had the message come at all?

Similar questions preyed on "Maxine's" mind back in 1968. Like most other Americans, she watched the evening news; like many of them, she too had a personal interest in the Vietnam War beyond the casualty counts and the antiwar protests. For her, it was her only grandson, twenty-two-year-old "Tony," who was stationed in Southeast Asia. About a year ago, just as Tony completed the first year of his two-year commitment to the army, Maxine had begun counting the days until his return.

A devout Roman Catholic, Maxine walked to church every day. There, clutching her rosary beads, she prayed for Tony's safe return. As the war intensified, she began to light candles for him as well. Her prayers appeared to have been answered in February 1968, when Tony came home.

Less than a month after Tony's homecoming, Maxine experienced a dream in which she clearly heard a voice say, "Don't be so happy. One walks in and one walks out." The message was repeated two more times before Maxine awoke with a start. She sensed that there was something more to the dream, but every time she tried to recall it more fully, it seemed to slip away. The cryptic warning was all she remembered and all she thought about for the next few weeks.

Two months after Tony returned, his father, "Joseph"—Maxine's only son—suffered a stroke. For a week and a half, the family anguished over his grim prognosis. Then Joseph inexplicably began to rally. However, a month later, at 10:30 A.M. on May 11, 1968, Joseph died suddenly. Unbeknownst to him, at that exact moment, Tony was getting married. Tony did not learn of his father's death until hours later.

With this odd turn of events, Maxine finally understood the meaning of her premonition: Tony, or his new bride, "walked in," Joseph "walked out." When she spoke of it years later, she was convinced that someone on the other side was trying to prepare her for the events of that spring, both the joyous and the tragic.

Maxine's, Candy's, and Rowland's experiences exemplify one theory about premonitions: that they are intended to prepare us to deal with traumatic events. Another theory is that, as we mentioned earlier, our notion of time is flawed, that in fact what we call the future is knowable and occurring all the time. We are simply not conditioned to recognize it under normal circumstances. Or perhaps they are not messages but lessons in the inevitability and acceptance of things we cannot change, here or beyond.

A RESCUE FROM THE OTHER SIDE

This is not to say that those on the other side can never help us avert disaster; they can. But usually, these warnings arrive so near to the event, they may not be true precognitions. They are worth considering, though, since a warning heeded may result in a fate averted.

"Ava's" sons, "Kurt" and "Bryan," were everything to her. Especially after her husband, "Simon," died, the boys drew even closer to her. In a cruel twist of fate, Kurt, the younger son, died at age thirty-six of a brain tumor, followed less than two years later by his brother, Bryan, dead at forty-one of a heart attack.

Ava was alone. "Why my sons?" she wailed. "Why would God take them both so young?" She had no answers, but she prayed and held fast to her faith. Her two widowed daughters-in-law remained close as well. Still, the unfairness of it all haunted Ava, and many nights she cried herself to sleep.

One night while sleeping, Ava distinctly heard a man's voice calling, but she could not make out what he was saying. Though the voice grew louder, she kept sleeping until his words became clear: "Fire! Fire! Fire!"

Thinking she was dreaming, Ava shifted under the covers and fell back to sleep. Suddenly she heard, "Ma! Wake up! Fire! Ma! Wake up! Fire!" *That's Bryan!* Ava thought, sitting up in bed. But why? Ava made her way to the kitchen. There the unmistakable odor of smoldering plastic and a heavy, choking smoke startled her. Now fully awake, she took just seconds to see that the toaster's cord was smoking and hot to the touch. With trembling hands, Ava yanked the cord from the socket and doused it with several pots of water.

Later, sitting at her kitchen table as the smoke cleared, Ava realized how close she had come to dying. And how her son had reached out from the other side to save her.

PREMONITIONS THAT PREDICT OTHER
PARANORMAL EVENTS

If precognition can foretell future events, can those events include the paranormal experiences of others? Are dreams truly gateways to other dimensions that allow us to see things imperceptible to us in our waking state?

We tend to think of deathbed visions as perceptible only to the dying. In this remarkable case, a woman not only saw her grandmother's deathbed vision but did so before it occurred. "Amy" had lived with her grandmother "Margaret" since childhood. Every morning Amy walked through Margaret's living quarters to take her dog, "Brandy," outside through the back door. Every single morning began with Amy calling "Good morning" to her beloved grandmother.

One night when Amy was about thirty, she had an unusual dream. In it, she was watching herself go through her morning routine, but she was both in the dream and outside it. She had the sense that she was watching a film of herself walking through the house with Brandy and passing her grandmother's bedroom, just as she had done for years.

Yet something was markedly different about the morning in her dream. When she reached her grandmother's apartment, she heard Margaret calling from her bed to many loved ones. Amy recognized most of the names. Some had died in recent years, while others had passed decades before, in some cases twenty, thirty, forty years before her birth.

Amy could clearly see the people gathered around or sitting on Margaret's bed. She recognized Margaret's late husband, "Tony," Amy's grandfather; her son, "Joe," who was Amy's father; "Charlie" and "Joe," Margaret's late brothers; her mother, "Rosa," and father, "John." Some, like her father, Amy had known herself; others she knew from seeing family photographs and hearing relatives talk about them. In all, Amy guessed there were about twenty people in Margaret's room. Amy was struck by how often Margaret called to her younger brother, Charlie, who had died twenty years before. Brandy sniffed each person and wagged her tail happily, seeming very comfortable in their presence, although Amy thought it odd that no one acknowledged her or Brandy.

Suddenly, Amy awoke. The dream remained crystal clear in her mind, so real and yet so peculiar. What did it mean? She surmised that the dream portended a future death, most likely her grand-mother's. But, she reassured herself, Margaret was in relatively good health for her age. Sure, she was regaining her strength from a recent bout with the flu, but who wasn't this year? She was doing so well, there was no doubt she'd be up and about in just a few days.

Amy dressed, then led Brandy down the stairs to Margaret's apart-ment. Right outside her grandmother's door she heard her call out, "Tony . . . Charlie . . . Joe . . . Patrick . . . Mother . . . Father . . ." Amy quietly peered into the room. There she saw Margaret lying in her bed and pointing to persons unseen at the foot of her bed, oblivious of Amy and Brandy. Suddenly Brandy began to jump up and sniff the air as if she were greeting people. "Brandy!" Amy admonished in a firm but quiet voice. "Let's go out!" But Brandy would not obey. She seemed as engrossed in the invisible goings-on as Margaret. Finally, Amy had to literally push the dog through the house and out into the yard. When they came back ten minutes later, Margaret was sleeping peacefully.

For the next several days Amy thought about her dream and what she witnessed in her grandmother's bedroom. She desperately wanted to ask her grandmother whom she was pointing to and why. She also wanted to tell her grandmother about her dream, but she decided against it, worried that it might upset her. However, as she turned it over in her mind, Amy could not dismiss that day's events as pure coincidence. Secretly, she feared that the deathbed vision predicted in her dream was being realized, that there was no turning back and nothing she could do to stop it.

Amy took some small comfort in the fact that Margaret never mentioned the deathbed vision and in fact seemed very calm and happy. The only thing unusual in Margaret's behavior over the next couple of days was that she seemed preoccupied. Three days after Amy's dream, Margaret passed suddenly from a heart attack.

Amy's experience raises some intriguing questions about deathbed visions, precognitive dreams, and the psychic sensitivity of animals. As we know, the deathbed vision is an age-old, widely documented phenomenon. And it is common to experience one in the context of a dream. What we find most fascinating about Amy's experience is that she accurately dreamed a deathbed visitation that was not her own.

If precognitive dreams do occur, one could simply classify Margaret's future deathbed vision as a future event like any other. After all, we seem to have the capacity to precognitively dream all kinds of things. Why wouldn't a paranormal experience like a deathbed vision be "predreamable"? Since we cannot say with certainty what makes these phenomena possible, it is only logical to conclude that nothing about them can be considered impossible. In terms of how Amy experienced the dream and how closely the subsequent reality followed her dream, it was clearly a precognitive experience.

Amy dreamed of and Margaret later called out to relatives of whom Amy had no personal knowledge. Even if Amy carried in her subconscious or deep memory a name she might have heard as a very young child, as some skeptics might argue, that still would not diminish the odds against Amy later hearing her grandmother call out to the same combination of names she heard in her dream. Whenever a psychic incident contains more than a few factual elements, the chances of total concurrence diminish exponentially with each new element. In other words, say Amy dreamed and Margaret called out eight names. Given that Amy does not believe she had conscious knowledge of all the names involved, the chance that Margaret would have spoken a name Amy did not dream is even greater. Or, put another way, Margaret's long life included many more loved ones than she named. How was it, then, that Margaret called out *only* to names Amy recognized from her dream?

Another question is why Amy clearly saw the deathbed visitors in her dream but did not see them the next morning. Perhaps because of their distinct, limited purpose, deathbed visions can be seen only by those they arrive to comfort.

Whether or not Brandy had some psychic sense of the spirits' presence in Margaret's room, at the least Brandy behaved exactly as Amy dreamed that she would. Brandy barked and wagged her tail in the exact location that Amy had seen the spirits in her dream. Reports of animals responding to paranormal activity are extremely common.

RESPONDING TO PRECOGNITION

What should you do if you believe you have received a precognitive message? It is difficult to say. Much depends on the content of the message—whom it concerns, whether or not the events predicted can be altered—and, most important, how compelled you feel to act, if that is an option. For example, a message from your late father about your kid riding his bike on a busy street would probably be more compelling than a dream of your long-suffering, hundred-year-old grandfather's funeral. You can ground your child, take away the bike, or forbid riding in the street, thereby eliminating the possibility that he will be hit by a car while riding his bike today. But you can do nothing to prevent your grandfather's imminent death. This issue is especially troubling for parents, many of whom normally dream of anxiety-provoking, even terrifying situations involving their children.

One woman we spoke with wondered about a dream she had had twice. In it, she and her six-year-old daughter were walking along a pier. Suddenly her daughter vanished. Then she looked down and saw her lying underwater, silently sinking without a struggle. Although hundreds of people crowded the pier, no one seemed to notice her desperate cries for help. Then she realized that she could not move, and when she opened her mouth to scream for help, no sound came out. There the dream ended.

Might this be a premonition? It is hard to say. The woman, who has had other verified precognitive dreams, reports that those dreams were very different from this one. She notes that the "classic nightmare" muteness and paralysis did not occur in the precognitive dreams. Also, everything in those dreams unfolded normally; they were "clear." This dream about her daughter, however, was foggy, dreamy, and unrealistic. For example, she does not know how her daughter gets into the water; she just suddenly appears there. She does not struggle or cry out; she just slips under.

We should also note that this woman is very knowledgeable and concerned about matters of children's health and safety, to a degree friends and family consider excessive. Her daughter is her only child, and she often finds herself thinking about how her little girl is growing more independent and venturing into a world she realizes she cannot control. Knowing herself as she does, this woman feels that this dream reflects her anxieties and conflicts about her daughter growing up.

The panic she experienced in the dream evaporated upon waking, while with her other precognitive dreams, it lingered for days and weeks after. While she does not regard this as a premonition, she has enrolled her daughter in swimming lessons. She also told us that if she ever finds herself and her daughter on the pier in her dream, they will leave immediately.

Whether you should act in response to a precognitive experience is a question only you can answer. As we have seen, true precognition very often speaks quite loudly and clearly for itself. In cases where a deceased loved one issues a warning or an instruction, the subject has a very definite sense of what must be done and often follows through.

Dr. Louisa E. Rhine concluded that one should always respond as one sees fit. If the experience provokes a compelling sense of urgency, if you truly feel you have no choice but to intervene, then do so. But bear in mind that studies of people who have acted to change events suggest that the actions of one person rarely make all the difference. The events foretold through precognition are like anything else that happens in life—the culmination of dozens, hundreds, thousands of words, thoughts, and deeds, not to mention chemistry, physics, and chance. Even if you do intervene successfully, it is possible that you will never know for sure that it was your action that changed the course of events. This is why we should not feel remorse or guilt if we fail to avert an event we have precognitive knowledge of. As we have seen, many precognitive or premonitory experiences are intended to prepare us to cope with, not prevent, future events.

Precognitive communications remind us of both the power and the limitations of love and intervention from the other side. It is difficult to understand why our loved ones—who by coming through to us seem to possess superhuman abilities to transcend time, space, and death—cannot do more. But we must remember that the ability to communicate from the other side may be perfectly normal, even quite simple, but seem exceptional to us given how we understand the universe. (Think back to Rip Van Winkle and that computer we talked about in chapter 2.) Perhaps what we speak of as the future is not a monolithic entity but a constellation of different phenomena, each with its own laws. Just as water can be ice, rain, snow, or vapor, it may be that some parts of the future are foreseeable, while others are not; some amenable to human intervention, while others are fixed, fated.

That we cannot answer these larger questions should not dissuade us from heeding or responding to precognitive communications. Simply because many fail to deliver a chance to cheat death or head off disaster is not cause to view them as meaningless or without purpose. In accepting these messages, we give ourselves opportunities for healing and understanding in the midst of tragedy and loss, at the times we need them most. What greater gift could someone who loves us bestow?

"DADDY CAME TO SAY GOOD MORNING"

Eternal Family Ties

So that he seemed not to relinquish life, but to leave one home for another.

—CORNELIUS NEPOS

Clearly, direct after-death communication experiences are usually isolated events or a series of events witnessed by or involving only one person. Why is this? One reason may be that our relatively limited capacity to perceive and accept such phenomena make them seem rarer than they are. Another reason may be that the spirit chooses to reach out to only one person among several.

These patterns seem to fall by the wayside when it comes to bereaved families, particularly those with children. As you'll see, for some families, direct after-death contacts are numerous, involve several different phenomena, and serve many purposes. For example, a widowed mother might have a precognitive dream about future employment, while her child is mysteriously helped in finding a lost toy. Where young children have lost parents, we often see more playful exchanges, with no more practical purpose than the games of peekaboo and catch they enjoyed before. There is no greater, more binding love than that between parent and child, and through direct after-death communications, we know that death does not diminish or break this bond.

These cases are interesting for another reason: they involve children. Children's direct after-death communication experiences are very common, although they can be a source of concern for adults who do not understand them. We have found that even the very young experience what appears to be contact with spirits, usually those of departed relatives. The similarities between their experiences suggest that these are not just kids' imaginations run wild. As we learned in researching *Our Children Forever*, which concerned the psychic and mediumistic experiences of bereaved parents, children's psychic experiences offer insight into a range of phenomena, including near-death experiences and after-death communication.

Until the age of ten, most children do not understand what death really means. Before age six, they believe death is reversible, and few children of any age can conceive of life without a parent. The pervasive cultural taboo against frank, honest discussion of death extends to children with a vengeance. In fact, world-renowned child-rearing expert Penelope Leach dubbed death "the Great Unmentionable."

Children are, of course, naturally curious about everything. When we fail to help them understand death in terms appropriate to their understanding, the picture gets filled in anyway by the cheap, distorted, and unrealistic images of death permeating the media. What passes for so-called children's entertainment is a virtual carnival of misleading, frightening, even dangerous ideas about death. From the allegedly "romantic" reviving kiss Disney's animated Snow White receives (in her coffin, no less) to the gut-spewing antics of video game warriors, every possible variation on death—from the sublime to the nauseating—parades before our children's eyes. Few families devote even four hours a year to any meaningful discussion of death. Consider that the average American child spends four hours watching television *every single day*, much of it flooding their minds with distorted depictions of dying and death.

Given all this, one would imagine that children's accounts of their near-death experiences and direct contacts would reflect their intellectual conceptions—both realistic and fantastic—of death. Oddly enough, they do not. For one thing, among children old enough to report the incident, the spirits don't seem to engage in the kind of wild, fantastic behavior you would expect from a child who was actively fantasizing.

Indeed, the stuff of most kids' television and video programming is far more "imaginative" than what the kids say occurs during their contacts. Grandpa's spirit doesn't perform tricks; Aunt Ellen doesn't magically grow bigger, then smaller. No one gets slimed. If anything, children's direct-contact experiences tend to be mundane, brief, fleeting, and sporadic. Surely if a child really set her active imagination to work, these direct contacts would be very different: more enduring, more common, more exciting, more fun, more entertaining.

Children's experiences deserve careful attention for other reasons. Unlike adults, they are less likely to be influenced by religious or cultural concepts of the afterlife. Their ignorance of the taboos against paranormal experience frees them from the inhibitions more sophisticated, mature people feel. If anything, most children's ideas about death, once they've reached middle-school age, tend toward the morbid. If we look at how the media presents death and spirits, more often than not the images are designed to instill fear and terror. Yet when children allegedly "imagine" contact with the dead, they do not tell tales of gory corpses, ghoulish scenes, and eerie sounds.

There are serious researchers and therapists who no longer assume that imaginary playmates are simply figments of the imagination. Many well-known adults have written of being accompanied in their early years by protective spirits, among them Helen Keller and the great psychic medium Eileen Garrett. If you were to assert that most kids are living in an altered state of consciousness, few parents would disagree. If only for reasons related to emotional and cognitive development, children inhabit a reality that is, at least in comparison to our bustling, logic-driven adult lives, "alternate." This means that there is less rather than more reason to question the accounts of children.

THE DEATH OF A FRIEND

Stephen Kaplan and I met in the early 1970s, when he taught a college course with the offbeat title "Vampires, Werewolves and Other Creatures of the Night." Stephen got a lot of media attention after the State University of New York at Stony Brook dropped the controversial course. We met when he appeared on my radio talk show, where we debated the origins of legends and discussed myriad paranormal topics. Even when we disagreed, which we often did, I liked and respected him, and we soon became fast friends.

Stephen was, by his own admission, flamboyant and eccentric. Beneath that, however, he possessed an amazing intellect and was a genuine scholar. He was also highly ethical, and though he did believe in certain instances of paranormal phenomena, he was always quick to point out anything that was less than genuine. Over the years he developed an international reputation as a parapsychologist and lecturer. Among his many professional endeavors, his legacy will surely include his tireless pursuit of truth in the case of the best-selling book and motion picture *The Amityville Horror*. Through more than two decades of tireless investigation, Stephen proved it a hoax. Unlike others determined to disprove paranormal phenomena, Stephen pursued his subject out of a conviction that genuine psychic events will gain greater credibility only when frauds are exposed.

Stephen and I began our friendship with the same strong feelings about discarnate survival and the possibility of transdimensional communications: we were skeptics. Nevertheless, as we each pursued our individual research and occasionally worked together, our attitudes evolved. Stephen was often very helpful to me in designing experiments to test self-proclaimed psychics. In more than two decades of long conversations, Stephen proved both a devoted friend and a sharp devil's advocate. Sitting back in his squeaky office chair, his phone and his fax machine almost perpetually busy, Stephen thrived on exchanging and debating ideas.

On the evening of June 9, 1995, Stephen's wife, Roxanne, called to tell me that he had died. When the couple's two young daughters, Jennifer, ten, and Victoria, seven, returned from a neighborhood shopping trip, they found their fifty-four-year-old father dead on the living room couch. A massive heart attack had stricken him while he slept. He and I had spoken at length just the night before, and he sounded fine. While he had a long history of cardiac and related health problems, we all believed that he was improving.

After I hung up from talking to Roxanne, I thought back to the last several times I had spoken with Stephen. In one of our conversations shortly before he died, he said, "Well, Joel, it'll be the ultimate experiment. When one of us passes, let's see if we can send messages from the other side to the survivor." I agreed, never thinking we would be trying to keep our promise for many years to come.

On June 12 I delivered the eulogy at his funeral. It was a gloomy, rainy day. Of course, I would miss my friend, but the thought of his family having to go on without him saddened me even more. As I have learned from personal experience, the deepest conviction in life after death cannot dull or soften grief's sting. I soon discovered, however, that Stephen was never very far away.

That evening, depressed and drained, I fell into an uneasy sleep. Within what seemed like only moments, I felt someone's big, strong arms wrap around me from behind in a bear hug. I could not turn to see who or what was holding me, but I sensed it was someone much larger than I. Though I did not know who it was, I felt safe. Soon I received the impression that the person embracing me was Stephen. "Is that you, Stephen?" I asked. We exchanged no words; I did not hear his voice. Nevertheless, I felt that I knew it was he, that he had told me so telepathically. In the next instant, I was awake, calmer than before. I was confident that the message was from Stephen and that he was reassuring me that life did continue on the other side. Our experiment was a success.

However, it did not end there. About a month later I had another vivid dream about Stephen. This time I clearly saw him sitting at an office conference table in a large mobile home or trailer. Seated around the table with me were several people I recognized, all family members, friends, and colleagues of Stephen. He appeared exactly as he had in life, speaking with great excitement and conviction about new ideas for paranormal research projects and media appearances. He looked healthier and younger, free of any trace of the physical illnesses that plagued him.

When I awoke, I was disappointed that I could not recall exactly what Stephen had said. Still it was very comforting, though I had to wonder why, in the presence of my dear, departed friend, I had been so fixated on the location of the dream. For some odd reason, my thoughts kept returning to the trailer, to the idea that we were conducting a business meeting in a trailer. *How odd*, I thought. I concluded that even in a genuine visitation experience, some aspects may be purely imaginary, beyond our comprehension, or just goofy. This, I reasoned, must have been one of them.

Several weeks after that dream, I received a surprise offer to write and appear in a network television special about the paranormal. I happily accepted the job and traveled to Los Angeles, where I stayed for several months. A few days after my arrival, I attended a meeting of executives and other key people involved in the project. The meeting was to take place at a production company office on the lot of a major Hollywood studio. On the appointed day, I was directed to the production company's office: inside the same trailer I had seen in my dream of Stephen.

This went well beyond coincidence. I had been party to literally hundreds of production meetings for various projects through the years. This was my first and only meeting in a trailer. Further, although I could not recall exactly what Stephen said in the dream meeting, I knew that the subject was media and the paranormal. Why didn't he talk to me about what life was like beyond the veil? Or discuss his family? Or talk about any of a hundred different topics? Clearly, then, this dream had something of a precognitive element, but I also like to think that this was Stephen's way—his new, transdimensional way—of sending congratulations.

I was not the only recipient of Stephen's messages from the other side; Roxanne and Stephen's daughters have also "been in touch." After Stephen's funeral, about a dozen people returned to the Kaplan home. People were chatting when the phone rang. Seven-year-old Vicky picked up the receiver and asked, "Hello? Hello? Hello? Who's there?" When no one replied she suddenly blurted out, "It must be Daddy."

Skeptics would point out that the only reason Vicky assumed the call came from her father was that he had just died. However, this phone call was just the latest in a series that began the day after his death. Vicky was not the only person in the household to have answered a ringing phone to find no one there. "From the day after he died, on the days before his wake, on the day of the wake, and the funeral—a three-day period—the phone was going crazy," Roxanne recalls. "It happened no less than five different times in the three days immediately after Stephen died. Each time the phone just rang with no one at the other end, and it did not disconnect, so eventually we just hung up. Once I thought I heard someone sigh.

"If the calls came on Stephen's phone line, I could understand it," she continues. "Everyone gets calls like that. However, these were calls on our private phone, which we have not listed under the name Kaplan. That had never happened before his death, not on that private line. And this is very important: we thought that if Stephen were trying to contact us from the other side, his favorite thing was the phone. It would make sense, because he lived half his life on it."

What the Kaplans reported is a surprisingly common occurrence often known as "phone calls from the departed." Even to those who fully accept the possibility of life after death, imagining the deceased placing a call seems quite a stretch. However, if we think for a moment about how telecommunications works and assume that some form of energy facilitates or comprises after-death communications, it is not so unfathomable. It takes only a minuscule charge of electricity to make a telephone ring.

In rare cases, subjects claim that they answered a ringing phone and heard the voice of a close departed loved one speaking—anything from a few words to a lengthy conversation—then fading or vanishing. People have also reported having normal telephone conversations with persons who—unbeknownst to them—were physically dead at the time.

In *Love, Janis*, Laura Joplin presents a sensitive account of her older sister, the late blues-rock singer Janis Joplin. She recounts several instances of people close to Janis receiving after-death communications, including phone calls from the dead:

The day after Janis died, [record producer] Paul [Rothchild] ran into [friend] Bobby Neuwirth. Each commented on the haggard look of the other. "What's wrong?" "The telephone keeps ringing, and it's Janis. She says, 'It's okay, man. This is a good place. I'm in good shape. Don't worry about a thing.'" "Wow! I don't believe it! The same thing's been happening to me."[1]

We have come across many people who answered the phone and found no one there but just knew or sensed the departed loved one was at the other end. Often these calls involve a degree of synchronicity; for example, one might be praying for the departed before the phone rings. While these phone calls most often occur shortly before or after death and are generally unpredictable and sporadic, some people report receiving these mystery calls on such special occasions as birthdays, holidays, and anniversaries, or in situations where they function as a warning.

Each time they answered a call that seemed to have no caller, both Vicky and Jenny would say, "Oh, it's Daddy again." They have since reported various contacts from their late father. Two days after Stephen died, Jenny was looking into the bathroom mirror, brushing her teeth, when she saw her father standing behind her, wiping a tear from his eye. When she told Roxanne what she had seen, her mother naturally wondered aloud whether she had imagined it. Jenny replied no. Months later, in our interviews for this book, I posed the same question, but Jenny would have none of it.

"No, it's not my imagination," she replied firmly with a trace of indignation. "Just because I'm thinking about my father doesn't mean that I can just suddenly say, 'I'm going to see him right there.'"

Vicky and Jenny's contacts continued, but they incorporated an element of precognition that eliminates the "wishful thinking" explanation. For example, in August 1995 Jenny was washing her hands in the bathroom sink when she felt someone tap her on the shoulder. She looked up to see Stephen. "Next month. First day. Very good news," he said, then vanished.

Jenny told Roxanne what had happened, and they waited. Stephen's financial affairs were not yet entirely settled, and the sudden plunge into widowhood had left Roxanne feeling anxious. Delays in processing the insurance, social security, and pension claims resulted in an uncertain cash flow. On September first, just as Stephen had predicted, an unexpected and much needed check arrived in the mail.

Shortly afterwards, Vicky glimpsed her father standing in a doorway. Stephen folded his arms and seemed to be staring intently in the direction of the family's pet cat, Cookie. The cat had cancer and after treatment was believed to be holding her own. The family knew Cookie probably would not survive the year but had no reason to think her death was imminent. Yet the day following Stephen's appearance, Cookie suffered a fatal convulsion. "Cookie missed Stephen terribly when he died," Roxanne says. "The poor thing would sit by the door waiting for him. Cookie really was Stephen's cat, and he was waiting for her to cross over."

Stephen also may be around helping with the more mundane aspects of parenthood. On the day of Jenny's birthday party, about nine months after Stephen died, she became upset when she could not find a toy called "The Littlest Pet Shop." No one recalled having seen it around for months.

"Stephen was always good at finding their toys," Roxanne recalls. "When they would come to me and ask, I'd say, 'Forget it. I'm not looking in that huge pile of toys in your room.' Or I'd take a quick look, lose my patience, and then they would go to Stephen. When they asked for his help, he'd always reply, 'The Great Daddy will find it for you,' and usually he did. When I'd ask him how he did it, he'd say, 'Oh, I have my secret ways.' He would make a great mystery out of it, and the kids would think he was the great finder of lost toys."

On Jenny's birthday, she desperately pleaded to her father, "Daddy, please help me find my Little Pet Shop toy. Please." A short time later, she and Vicky rushed up to Roxanne and, jumping up and down, explained that they had found the toy on top of a bookcase they had searched several times before.

Stuck to the toy was a sticker of a dove, a symbol that holds a special meaning for the Kaplan family. The sticker had belonged to Vicky, but now it appeared inexplicably on Jenny's toy.

After Stephen's passing, Roxanne felt that both girls would benefit from joining a children's bereavement support group. Crises such as death are more difficult for children than we imagine. Because they lack the skills to express their feelings, support groups that bring together children in a similar situation can be very helpful.

At one session, Vicky and Jenny's group was encouraged to write a message to their loved one who had passed on. Vicky wrote, "Daddy, please make contact with me. I love you."

The next morning, as the girls were getting ready for school, Vicky suddenly remembered that Roxanne had forgotten to give her money she needed for an upcoming school trip, and today was the deadline for payment. As Roxanne recalls, "I took my purse and pulled out a handful of dollar bills, and I started to count them. And there, right across the top of a dollar bill, written in marker, was the signature 'Stephen.'"

Vicky gazed at the bill, then broke into a smile. "Daddy answered me! Daddy answered me!"

Did he? "We and several people I showed it to agreed it looked like Stephen's handwriting," Roxanne says. But where did the dollar bill come from? Was it possible it had been lying around since before Stephen died? No. "This was change from something I bought just the night before. I hadn't seen it then because it was in a stack of dollar bills. When the clerk gave me my change, I just stuffed it in my purse."

Perhaps because of their parents' professional interest in the paranormal, Jenny and Vicky were more open to their experiences. Unfortunately, not everyone they encountered was. "We brought up our experiences with Daddy in the bereavement group," Jenny says. "I don't think the two women who were group leaders truly believed that those things really happened to us. When the other kids started telling what happened to them, I don't think the ladies believed them either.

"One boy told about how he was riding in a car and thinking about his mother, who died in a car crash. He felt a nudge on his back, but no one was there. Another time, he said, he saw her spirit. But the group leaders told everybody not to laugh or comment about what anybody else said. It doesn't really matter to me what they think. I *know* my experiences were real. And Vicky feels the same way."

Ironically, despite Stephen's many contacts with his daughters, he seems to have forgotten Roxanne. In one unusual synchronistic experience she felt compelled to purchase a magazine she had no interest in—the sci-fi movie publication *Fangoria*—only to discover her husband's name listed in it. Beyond that, Stephen has been silent.

"People always say that after someone dies, they see the person because their mind makes them see it. I'm a skeptic myself because I haven't seen Stephen, and it hurts my feelings. Steve and I had been in parapsychology research for years. Just as Houdini had a secret coded message for his wife—which she long tried to get through mediums—Steve and I had a deal that whichever one of us went first would come back and make contact if possible. We didn't have a specific message like the Houdinis did, but we had silly nicknames and words that nobody else knew. Yet I have not had anything happen from him."

Roxanne admits there have been a few signs from him, but these are not what she expected. This is common. How wonderfully reassuring it would be if our loved ones always came through with the one indisputable message or sign that no one else could know, one we could never doubt. Yet that rarely happens, even when people painstakingly plan how contact will be manifested, as with Mary Jasen's refrigerator-banging. Is it because our loved ones are somehow unable to carry through with our earthly plans? Or is there a purpose behind their not making it too easy for us? Or are there signs and messages everywhere, like a forest we do not realize that we live in until we throw open the shutters? When we have specific expectations about a direct-contact experience, we leave ourselves open to disappointment.

It is very important for us to let go of expectations and disappointment; we do not know what the departed can and cannot do. Many people we spoke with admitted to feeling angry or jealous because a deceased loved one communicated to someone else. Lovers are puzzled when the communications seem intended for a distant aunt. Mothers cry to hear that their late child's cousins regularly see and talk to him, and wish for just one small sign. If most of these people felt free to be so honest, they would probably say, "It's bad enough that they died, but now they're ignoring me."

Are they really? Our powers of perception are limited, our attention often scattered. Who can say how many signs, contacts, and messages escape our notice? You may ask, Wouldn't our loved one make sure that we noticed? It would be nice to think so, but that may not be the case. In families where three of four surviving members have clear direct contacts, the fourth who seems left out is often the person who is the truest believer, the one who never questioned that communication would occur. Considering the fact that direct contacts usually take their subjects by surprise, it may be that those who are most certain about after-death communications subconsciously deny or block them. This probably is not so for Roxanne Kaplan, because she has experienced signs and witnessed her daughters' contacts.

Acceptance takes work, but we must remember that eternity offers us plenty of time and many opportunities for communication. Even I wonder why Stephen has gone to such trouble to reach me. Why isn't Roxanne having vivid, detailed, premonitory dreams about him? We will never know. Still, we must not forget that when Stephen reaches out to touch one of us, he touches all of us.

"EVERYTHING IS OKAY"

Rick and Mary Vitro were newlyweds living out the American Dream. Rick, a computer engineer, and Mary, a business consultant, had recently moved from New York to Clearwater, Florida, where they built a home and began a promising life together. They had been friends for many years before their marriage; in fact, they first met in a New York City club in 1981, when Mary and her best friend, Jill Kameny, were having a girls' night out. Then, however, it was Rick and Jill who fell in love and married. After they divorced, the three remained friends, and later Mary and Rick fell in love and married in 1988.

A year later, Mary gave birth to their only child, Douglas, but the family's happiness would prove short-lived. Throughout the previous year, Rick had suffered a series of unexplained chronic health problems. In January 1990 he developed a near-fatal case of pneumonia and was diagnosed with AIDS. Although he survived that initial crisis, over the next twenty-two months, until he died in late October 1991, the Vitros' lives were never the same. Mary balanced the demands of full-time care-giver and full-time mother with courage and humor. Doug was an incredibly even-tempered, joyful baby. "He was my sunshine, my anchor, my sanity," Mary says of her son. "I know that through it all, someone was looking out for us. Neither I nor Doug nor Rick's ex-wife Jill contracted the virus. We were all so lucky."

For people who have dealt with AIDS, Mary knows how lucky she and Rick were in other ways, too. He had access to the best care and treatment. Rick's parents moved from New York to be nearby, and his mother in particular was a constant source of support. Mary had a large network of family members and close friends. Nevertheless, nothing could change the fact that Rick was dying, and by late summer 1991 his condition had declined precipitously.

"I had always wished that things could have been like in the movie *My Life*, where the father knows that he's dying, so he makes videotapes for and writes letters to his baby boy. Rick couldn't do that. I know that he loved Doug with all his heart. But from the moment he learned that he had AIDS, he seemed to make sure that he didn't fall in love with him, and that's a difference. At first he would say, 'I have a new son. I can't die.' But as it became clearer that the disease was gaining hold, I think the thought of dying won out over everything else.

"Although I knew that Rick wanted to die at home, it reached a point where he had to be hospitalized. The morning we left for the hospital, I asked him if he wanted to go in and say goodbye to

Dougie. But he just couldn't do that. Now I see that he tried to do those things in other ways."

A few days after Rick entered the hospital, his best friend, Bill, came down from New York to stay. "I think that when Rick knew that Bill was here, he felt that he could let go. I came home from the hospital one day and had a conversation with my mother, who died in 1972, when I was just fourteen. Her picture is on the mantel, and I remember looking at it and saying to her, aloud, 'Please don't let him suffer anymore.' It was not a prayer, exactly, because she was really here. I felt that I could reach out and touch her.

"The last time I saw Rick, he seemed to have lost awareness about where he was and what he was doing. But right before I left to go home for the night, I was sitting next to his bed and resting my head on his pillow. He said, 'You know, I really love you.' That was the last time we ever spoke. We never talked about what would happen after he died, such as how he would try to contact us. Still, Rick was Catholic, and subconsciously, I think no matter how far you may stray, once you have those ideas about life after death, they really don't go away. By then he knew of my own psychic experiences with my deceased parents and a very impressive psychic reading I had. He knew what I believed, and he never put it down. When we talked about his dying, he would often say to me, 'I will miss you a lot.'"

On the morning of October 24, 1991, Dougie came running into Mary's bedroom screaming, "Mommy, you have to wake up! You have to wake up! You have to wake up!" Then, as Mary recalls, "He said it was because 'Daddy . . . something.' I forget exactly what he said, but Daddy was definitely part of it. He was not really crying, but he was very alarmed, very upset. I got up.

"Looking back, I know that I knew something was wrong. I knew that I needed to call the hospital. I think Rick was visiting everybody because his mother, Peggy, had a sense, too, that something was wrong. Still, I just couldn't bring myself to call. When I did, they said he was holding his own, but about twenty minutes later I got the call to hurry to the hospital, that Rick was dying. When I got there, he was dead.

"The first unusual thing happened as Bill and I were leaving the hospital. I was quite familiar with all the hospital procedures. Whenever a dead body had to be removed from a room, they would announce a special code over the PA system for that floor. Everyone would go around and make sure no patients or visitors were in the hallways, and they would close all the patients' doors until they removed the body. Rick had been on the third floor of this very modern building, with no windows you could really open. From *outside* the building I heard that code. At the time, I knew it was Rick, but much later I realized that having heard that was physically impossible for me."

Back home, she tried to explain Rick's death to their two-year-old son. "We took a walk, and he did not seem to want to talk about it. I felt that Rick was with us then." Mary, Doug, and her in-laws flew up to New York, where Rick's funeral was held. She was staying at her sister's house on Long Island when she looked out into the garden and saw Rick sitting on a glider near a hedge. "He looked like his usual self. The only other thing I really remember about those days around the funeral was that I kept feeling like I should call him at home because he would be there.

"One night about two weeks after Rick died, I suddenly smelled toast cooking. It was so odd; I hadn't used the toaster oven all day. Then I looked at the clock——it was eleven, the time that Rick made himself toast and we had tea together almost every night. I walked into the kitchen, and I could smell it so distinctly. I had to look in the toaster oven to make sure it was off. The first time it happened, it was, like, Wow. It was very awe-inspiring but also very reassuring. I think that because I had a few very good psychic readings, I knew it was possible. I did not doubt for a minute that it was Rick." Several times, she has smelled his cologne, and objects she has misplaced seem miraculously to turn up in plain sight. "I know it is Rick."

While most of Mary's direct after-death communications have been positive and reassuring, a few have not. "For a while after he died, I would be in the shower in the master bath when I would hear his voice saying, 'I'm dying.' I felt his presence. However, I also wondered whether I was either projecting what I know he felt or if his emotions then were so intense that they somehow lingered here for a while. I know that's one theory about what ghosts are made up of: sort of emotional fingerprints. Whatever it was, after a few times, I just could not bring myself to use that shower for many months."

From a very early age, Doug showed signs of being intellectually gifted and was always advanced in his verbal skills. Mary believes that one reason Doug, who is now nearly eight years old, has done so well is that the family allows him to express his grief and to talk openly about his father. Because Mary had not been allowed to grieve for her own mother as a young teenager, she knew how important it was for Doug.

Doug also engaged in a behavior we have heard of from several other parents of grieving children: talking on a toy telephone to the person they miss. Doug had many long, detailed conversations with his dad. Whether Rick was actually talking to his son through the phone no one knows. A good friend of the family we spoke with recalled noticing that whenever Doug said he was talking to his father, it seemed more like a real conversation than it would when he claimed to be talking to his grandmother or one of his aunts. For example, the pauses, during which Doug was presumably listening to his father speak, were realistically long, not the fast-paced "Hi-how-are-you?-I'm-fine" typical of a one-sided play conversation. Yet even if he were not talking to Rick, Doug was never admonished or discouraged from this healing play.

When Doug was around three, he told Mary that Daddy had come to see him and told him that he was sorry he could not be with him at Christmas. Then he gave Doug a special present, a red Porsche Matchbox car. Doug could not have known that Rick had spoken of a red Porsche as his dream car. When Mary saw the car, she asked neighbors if anyone had given Doug the car or if he might have inadvertently taken it from a playmate. No one had ever seen the car before. It seemed to have materialized out of thin air.

One night about six months after Rick's death, Mary had an unusually intense dream about him. "It seemed to me that he had come just to let me know that things were okay. It felt like a visitation, but I didn't give it too much credence. So many seemingly paranormal things had been happening that I think I was sort of saying to myself, 'Enough already. Maybe it's your imagination, Mary Kay.' But a few minutes later, I saw something that made me think again."

Mikka, the family's Siberian Husky, was standing in Mary's bedroom doorway and appeared to be greeting someone. Mikka cocked her head, her ears and tail were up, and she subtly shifted her weight from paw to paw in the dance of anticipation Mary saw only when Mikka recognized someone she loved. No one was there, of course, but Mikka persisted in looking out the doorway and across the living room to Doug's bedroom. Mary called "Mikka!" sharply, but the dog did not respond. Clearly, something had her attention.

Within seconds, Doug came bounding out of his room and happily announced, "Daddy was here!"

"No, Doug," Mary replied. "You must have seen Daddy in a dream."

"No," Doug insisted. "Daddy came by to say good morning and that he loves me and everything is okay." Hearing those words and seeing Mikka, Mary knew that Rick had come home.

Rick's appearances sometimes serve a practical purpose. One night Mary dreamed that she was in a huge auditorium or Broadway theater with her sister, brother-in-law, son, and some other people. She went to the ladies' room, and as she stepped down, she suddenly found herself in her garage. Rick was there, on his hands and knees, trying to peer under the washing machine. "You really need to clean under the washer," he said. He repeated it, then Mary woke up.

"The next morning, I cleaned under the washer, but I found nothing. In fact, I did not even know what I was looking for. Probably over a year before Rick died, he had lost a religious medal and chain. We found the medal, but the chain, which was a gift from his mother, had not shown up, and we gave up on ever finding it. I didn't realize then that was what he was referring to. Several months later, a neighbor took the machine apart after I told him it wasn't working properly. He found the gold chain caught on a piece of metal near the drainpipe. That's what Rick was trying to tell me in the dream."

Mary and Jill have remained best friends and visit each other often. For Jill, who was unable to have a child with Rick, Doug is very special, and she is happy and proud to be his Aunt Jill. Several times when they have been together, Mary says they have been certain of Rick's presence. "And Doug knows that his father is up in heaven, looking out for him. He often says so. Although I know that it's difficult for him when, for example, the other kids in his class make things for Father's Day, or the daddies come to school to talk about their jobs, he really does all right. We know Daddy is still here."

WHAT LISA SAID

After-death communications flow constantly, yet we miss many. Through psychic readings and direct after-death communication experiences, we have learned that spirits often mention attempting and failing to "get through." A great misunderstanding about discarnate survival and communication is that death transforms us into omnipotent, omniscient beings. We are conditioned to believe that if someone on the other side wants to contact us, nothing can stop them. That is right, to a point. Nothing can stop them—except us and our distractions, our logic, our denial, and our fear. Earlier we touched on some reasons why one person may receive many messages and another none at all. Later, in chapter 10, we will go into greater detail about how we can help facilitate direct contacts from this side. Here let us look at how our everyday lives affect our perception of direct after-death communications.

Fear—of disbelief, ridicule, being ostracized, confronting the unknown—takes a heavy toll on people's confidence in their direct-contact experiences. Virtually everyone we have ever talked to has said they initially felt very alone or that they were the only people in the world to whom this had ever happened. Until very recently, most chose to keep their experience and their feelings secret. Yes, the subject has come out of the closet, but we estimate that the number of people openly addressing the subject still represents a very small percentage of those who have communicated with a deceased loved one.

We found a direct correlation between the number and intensity of direct-contact experiences and the subject's family structure. People who have close emotional bonds with loved ones on this side are more likely to perceive contacts. They are also more likely to have a greater number of contact experiences and be more confident in their belief that the communication was real. We can hazard some guesses about why this is so, based on what we have seen.

People who can talk about their direct after-death communication experiences are more apt to believe they are real. When they can discuss them with others who have had similar experiences—particularly if they involve the same deceased loved one—they become more accepting of the phenomenon and are more likely to witness future incidents. A close family or group of friends can provide instant cross-corroboration, enriching and illuminating one another's experiences. We believe that the vast majority of messages from the other side are like the proverbial tree that falls in the woods. If one person heard it from a distance, they might suppose that a tree fell. Yet if two, three, or four others heard the same tree falling, making the same sound, at roughly the same time, there would be no doubt.

When families experience and share a series of direct after-death communications, they discover things many other subjects do not. For instance, they may find that the deceased loved one has come to two or more of them with essentially the same message, as Rick did with Mary, Doug, and Mikka. Or that in one contact the spirit reveals something about a previous or future communication with a third person. Each contact in a cluster illuminates the others. It is almost as if the departed wanted to be sure that we do not miss a thing.

In contrast, consider the death of a person who is single, married without children, or from a small or scattered family. The person might attempt dozens of contacts, but how many would be noticed? How many would share their experiences with someone else who might have received a message from the same person? Especially today, when so many family members live miles apart and extended families lose touch, it is easy to see how countless potentially confirmable, multiepisode clusters might go unnoticed.

One family's multicontact experience began the evening Lisa Oberman died. A car had struck Lisa a week before, on her thirteenth birthday, and for several days after, she lay comatose on life support until her death. That evening her father, Alex, had what he describes as a "very real dream. It was nighttime, and there was a tremendous number of children—black, white, Asian. They were all playing and running around. I was standing there observing them. Finally I see Lisa. I said, 'That's my daughter.' I felt a tremendous love. You cannot physically feel this kind of love. It was something that you cannot explain. I went over to her. Her face was shining and bright. She was playing with all the children. They took off their jackets and ran around. When I woke up, I knew who it was. These were all souls of children who had passed on."

Within days of Alex's dream, his wife and daughter each separately received similar messages from Lisa. Her twenty-one-year-old sister, Linda, experienced a vivid dream in which, she tells us, "Lisa looked well and happy. I could see her dark hair and blue eyes. She said to me, 'I'm fine. Don't worry.'" Linda found the dream of her little sister comforting. What she did not know until later was that her mother, Carmen, also received a message from Lisa. Yet unlike in Alex's and Linda's experiences, Lisa conveyed her message to her mother telepathically. Suddenly Carmen was impressed with the thought, "I'm fine, Mom. Don't worry. I have to go."

Telepathically, Carmen responded, "What are you doing? Where are you now?"

"We go to school here. We're learning. But everything is different here, because when you want something, all you have to do is think about it." Subsequently Lisa impressed her father with the following, nearly identical message: "Don't worry. I'm all right. Everything here is different. When you think of something, it's here. I'm fine. I have to go now."

"It was a message that was unmistakable," Alex says. "It was not *my* thought or imagination. It was Lisa's thought coming to me."

Bear in mind that none of the three shared their experiences before the series was complete. If these communications were figments of the family's imaginations, as skeptics might argue, you would proba-bly find greater variation among them. If you asked parents what they would expect to hear from a deceased child, "I love you" and "I miss you" would top the list. Yet they appear nowhere here.

Another message survivors of children who suffer serious, painful physical injury and a prolonged death long to hear is "I didn't suffer" or "I was in no pain." Nothing like that; only "I'm okay." Lisa was doing all she could to ensure not only that her message to her family got through but that they could believe it.

"THEY TOLD ME THINGS"

Direct after-death communications can serve many purposes, but probably the most valuable is helping the loved ones left behind to cope and go on with their lives. For Terry and her husband, Ronnie, it appears that he had been laying the foundation for his future commu-nications for decades. While his attempts to comfort his family from the other side were welcome and effective, Ronnie's story shows how powerful, and limited, direct after-death communications can be.

Ronnie and Terry's story began in 1960, when most people were not as free in discussing their psychic experiences as we are today. That year, when Terry was nineteen and her boyfriend Ronnie was twenty-two, he shared a prediction with her: "I'm going to die young." Not long after, he was in a serious car accident. Later he described to her how within moments of the crash he had an out-of-body experience. In the 1960s they had not yet coined the term *near-death experience*, but Ronnie's account of leaving his body fits the classic NDE pattern.

Terry and Ronnie were married in 1961, and eventually they raised a family of five children. Over the years, Ronnie had many more psy-chic experiences. One day, when he was nearly fifty years old, he heard a voice tell him that he was going to die soon. He told Terry he thought it was God's voice. Terry disagreed; she thought it most likely came from a deceased loved one, perhaps as a warning. Within two years of hearing the voice, Ronnie began complaining of a persistent pain in his side. Despite his wife's pleas, Ronnie delayed seeking medical care. "He was putting it off," Terry recalls. "He would say, 'After the baby is born,' or 'After this wedding.'"

When the pain became unbearable, Ronnie saw a doctor, who diagnosed advanced colon cancer. Ronnie submitted to surgery and chemotherapy, but his prognosis was poor and doctors held out little hope. Terry was badly shaken, sad that Ronnie had to suffer but also angry that he had neglected to see a physician sooner.

"I think because he believed he'd heard God's voice, he accepted the fact that he was sick," Terry says. "Maybe that's why he didn't do anything about it sooner. In his mind, this was his destiny. Ronnie felt I was in denial. I was praying for miracles. He was thinking that he had to keep fighting to stay alive—for me. Ronnie would have died at home, but I wanted him to live, so I rushed him back to the hospital."

One morning, just before Terry went to visit her gravely ill husband in the hospital, a close relative shared a vivid dream he had the night before. In it Ronnie's late father appeared to him with a message. "Don't worry," he told Terry. "Grandpa was here. He's coming for Ronnie. I saw Grandpa in my room, sitting there. All the kids were there. Grandpa was watching them, so I know he's coming for Ronnie."

Terry listened attentively. A practicing Catholic, she wondered if her husband, a convert to the faith, truly understood the communication between those on earth and the spirits of the deceased. Later that day, Terry asked Ronnie if he believed that such contact was possible. His answer surprised her: "Shhh. I'm talking to them now." Ronnie lay in his hospital bed, eyes closed, apparently engrossed in an exchange he alone saw and heard. When he opened his eyes, she asked, "What did they say to you?"

"They told me things," was all he would say.

She then told him that a relative "had dreamed about your father." She thought this might prompt her husband to open up.

"Yes," Ronnie replied. "And my grandmother too."

"So Ronnie knew," Terry says now. "He'd communicated with the spirits. The souls were real close. My relative's dream was confirmed by my husband's experience."

About two weeks after Ronnie's deathbed vision, he seemed to be dying. "Oh my God, Ronnie. I don't think we're going to make it today," Terry told her husband. A short time later, he lapsed into a coma, and the following day, he died. He was fifty-three.

"I wonder if he waited for me to say verbally I knew he was dying. Then he could let go. At that point, I told him, 'It's okay if you want to leave,'" Terry says, explaining how hard that was for her to do. "I struggled all my life, but that was okay. As long as my children and my family were healthy and safe, everything was okay. But now, my husband wasn't healthy. My husband wasn't here anymore. And you have people telling you that God took him because He has something for him to do. What a crock! A real crock. I was crazy when Ronnie died. Because my life was very involved in the Church, this was as if my best friend—God—took my husband, and then to tell me that it's because he has to do something . . .

"We were married just short of thirty-two years. When I got home from the hospital that day, my mother said I wasn't supposed to cry. She told me to be strong. I felt like someone put their hand in me and ripped my heart out and now there was this big hole. And she told me, 'Don't cry. Be strong.'

"I went out to the backyard, and I *knew* Ronnie was standing next to me. Then suddenly I felt someone touching my head, patting my head. Ronnie used to tap me on the head like I was a little girl. Actually, it used to annoy me. He was six feet tall. I'm five-feet-one. So there I was being patted on the head. I felt like he was hanging on my shoulder. And I said, 'Oh my God, Ronnie's here! He's here!' That was a comfort.

"The day we came home from the funeral, my sixteen-month-old grandson ran into the bedroom. I still had Ronnie's hospital bed in there, and the bedroom door was open. My little grandson put his arms out and said, 'Gampa, Gampa,' and ran to the bed as if he were hugging someone. Yet there was nothing there. At least *we* saw nothing. My grandson must have seen Ronnie.

"Within two weeks after Ronnie died, I felt him touching my face. I felt his hand on me. I felt him kiss me and smelled flowers. It was a nice smell. Sweet, almost like the scent of a bouquet. It was a soft, lovely perfume. But the windows were locked, and there wasn't any cologne or perfume around. The next morning a friend who was staying with me came downstairs. She sat on the couch and said, 'You've got to stop crying.' 'I can't help it,' I answered.

"Then she said, 'I dreamt of Ronnie and I told him, "You have to do something. Terry has to stop crying; she is always crying."' My friend then told me that in her dream, Ronnie said, 'I know she is always crying. We're trying. We put flowers in her hair, but she keeps crying.' I immediately made the connection. That was what I was feeling when I smelled the flowers. My friend did not know anything about the smell of the flowers or the feeling or sensing of my husband near me and touching me."

These and other experiences convinced Terry she needed to learn more about after-death communications. "I wanted to know, What is going on? Is this happening because I'm going crazy or I'm in some emotional state? A psychic told me that what I was experiencing was real. She said my husband's spirit was there but also told me that I did have to let go. She said that he had to leave. I really did not want to let go. But, of course, you have to."

For the next several months after that, there were no signs or messages from Ronnie, though Terry fervently hoped for them. Then one night Terry had a dream that she interprets as a nonpsychic event, not a communication from her husband. "In the dream we were at an airport, and I was leaving Ronnie there. I had to go home to get something. I interpreted the dream to mean that I was letting go. I had a huge empty satchel with me. I felt that was my new life."

Although intellectually Terry knew that she had to go on, as time passed she grew concerned, wondering how Ronnie was doing in his new life. She prayed to him, "Please come to me and let me know how you are." Then she had a very vivid dream. "There was a fence with slats in it. All I could see were his feet. He wouldn't let me see his face, but I knew it was him. 'I want to see you. You've come all this way and I can't see you?' I asked. 'No, you can't come in here,' Ronnie replied.

"'Yes, I can, because I want to see how you are.' And that's what I did. I went through the fence. He wasn't well. He was leaning on me. Then he brought me to a mountain. I could see down into a huge valley. There were many, many pine trees. Ronnie said to me, 'I live down there. I live on the land.'

"Several weeks later, my nephew told me that he had a dream in which he was walking in the woods and came upon Ronnie. His uncle told him not to worry, because he was now living in a log cabin, and he was living on the land. My dream was just like my nephew's; one confirmed the other. It was Ronnie."

Terry and her family have had many other contacts with Ronnie, fewer as time goes by. Terry has experienced both direct after-death communications and communicating to her husband through a psychic medium. We asked her to describe the value of each experience.

"I went to a psychic medium because it was another way to contact Ronnie. Yet when I think about it now, what I experienced between myself and my husband's spirit was far greater than going to a medium. Both types of experience had a value for me through that terrible grieving period. The psychic's reading helped me gain a lot of strength, and it helped me to focus again on living. The personal experience with Ronnie—well, what could compare with that?"

Terry is quick to point out what the experience cannot do. "How do you describe having just buried someone? I looked into that grave that was forever, that was going down to hell, for all you know. And you say, 'What the hell was it all for?' It didn't make any sense. But the experience—the after-death contact—tells you: Don't think it ends there in the grave. Understand that the true you, the vital part of what and who you are goes on. It might not be visible, but you go on.

"You know there is a connection, and you actually feel their presence. You feel their touch. They let you know they're kissing you. They send electricity through you. You might not be seeing them, but there is life beyond this one. When I die, and I have to leave this world, I am going to where I will still be able to communicate with my children. Even if I'm not touching and holding them, I will see them. I will be confident that they are okay. And if they're not, I will do what I have to do to help them. Because they do help you from the other side.

"I don't pray to my husband, I talk to him. For instance, when I need help here. My prayers, my requests, are to God. Ronnie's helped me from the other side. He helped me find the job I have now; he helped get our children's lives in order. There has been a lot of help. But that's the kind of father he was. No, he hasn't let go at all."

"SOMETIMES"

Jimmy Norcott was only thirty-five years old when he succumbed to melanoma, a virulent form of skin cancer that had metastasized throughout his body. Happily married to Regina, he was the father of two: Courtney, ten, and Matthew, five.

"Leaving Courtney and Matthew was very hard for him," his widow, Regina, says. "So I know that Jimmy must be around them all the time. Courtney has said that she feels his presence. And Courtney is not the type of child to tell you something if it hasn't happened. I asked her if she'd seen him—his spirit. She just looked, smiled, and said, 'Sometimes.'

"For example, Jimmy wanted to buy Courtney a pair of Rollerblades. He told her that when she gave away the dolls she didn't want to the church, so they could go to needy children, he would buy her the skates. But he died before he could buy her the Rollerblades, in November." In December, about a month after their father's death, Courtney and Matthew attended the annual Christmas party held at the firehouse where Jimmy had served. The family had attended the party every year and took comfort in being surrounded by friends and Jimmy's colleagues. At the end of the party each child received a keychain with a miniature toy attached. Several children got keychains with toy cars; others, fire engines or various other small toys. Only Courtney received a keychain bearing a tiny pair of Rollerblades. When Regina saw the little skates, she knew Jimmy had sent them a sign.

Jimmy has left signs for other friends and family members, but his most consistent contact has been with his widow, Regina. "I feel Jimmy's presence; I talk to him every day," she says matter-of-factly. "Not a day goes by that I do not have a conversation with Jimmy or tell him something about what's happened. If I talk to him, I can sense what he is saying back to me. I can hear Jimmy tell me something and then the same words will come out of my mouth. It is almost like what he would be saying.

"I have heard from Jimmy every day. Often, when I've felt very badly or I've been really upset about something, he seems more likely to come to me. Or it can be a situation in which I can't handle something. For example, when I was doing paperwork for the fire department concerning Jimmy, I *know* he was sitting right there with me. I could see him sitting there and even listening to me. I've gotten a sense of him telling me at certain times, 'No, don't do that,' or 'Yes, put it there.'

"It is a very comforting feeling. It is not scary or anything to be afraid of. Even at Jimmy's wake, I felt that he was crying *with* me. He was there in spirit. I have sensed him at different times, but sometimes it is not for a long period. It seems like he cannot be here for a long time. I feel him and then he's gone; he comes and then he goes. Sometimes I can sense him more one day than another.

"I pray for him, that he can go toward the light. I know other loved ones are praying for him also. Knowing that someday I will be with Jimmy again comforts me. A friend of mine who lost her husband has had experiences like mine. She has told me that if I want to kiss Jimmy, to do it. He is still there."

Regina joined a support group offered through a local hospital and run by a bereavement counselor. During each weekly ninety-minute session, group members were encouraged to talk about their losses. Regina looked forward to the meetings, which she found very helpful. However, she felt that they had overlooked the spiritual aspect of grief, including questions about the afterlife and communications from loved ones.

Regina made up her mind that she'd share some of her experiences and ask if anyone else had ever encountered anything like that. Since it was a nonsectarian group and the spiritual seemed to have been avoided, Regina worried about whether the other members would be open to the subject. Most of the group members were Christian, but she knew of one who was Jewish. Most of them were older than Regina, who was thirty-three, the majority being in their fifties.

It was with some trepidation that Regina raised the question at the next meeting. She told of feeling or sensing Jimmy's presence, talked about Courtney and the Rollerblades and a few other incidents. To her surprise, everyone in the group agreed that she was right to interpret those events as signs from Jimmy. Even the bereavement counselor shocked Regina by saying that she too believed that her experiences were genuine.

Emboldened by the positive response, Regina then asked if anyone else had experienced contact with a loved one. To her surprise again, *every* person acknowledged having had an experience—be it a message, a dream, or a sign—from the other side. Several eagerly told their stories, seemingly relieved to discover they were not alone.

Thinking back over that evening, Regina observes, "Nobody criticized it or put it down. I thought some people would not believe or feel it, the type you hear saying, 'When you're gone, you're gone.' But no one in the group felt that way." In fact, the group spent the rest of the meeting discussing books they found helpful and experiences they had. "No one cared *how* the communications were happening," Regina says. "As long as they were happening."

8

THE HEALING POWER OF AFTER-DEATH COMMUNICATIONS

The main reason for healing is love.

—PARACELSUS (1493–1541)

Direct after-death communications are immensely powerful. They can bring comfort, instill hope, reaffirm faith. They can have a practical purpose, whether sending a lifesaving warning or helping someone find a misplaced wedding band. Even when we believe in life after death, we often assume that whatever emotional business is unfinished at the moment of death must remain so. This is one reason bereavement is a major risk factor for depression in both adults and children. Prolonged mourning and depression can result when we feel that our loved one died before we could resolve an issue or simply say the words we now carry so heavily in our hearts. Death, we fear, has closed the door forever. But has it really?

A GARDEN OF FORGIVENESS

"Sandra's" parents divorced when she was five, and she rarely saw her father. Her mother, who worked out of the home and fought a losing battle with depression, was both physically and emotionally distant. More often than not, Sandra was alone. Her adolescence was consumed by helping her mother, whose mental state was deteriorating.

After years of severe depression, her thirty-eight-year-old mother deliberately, fatally overdosed on prescription drugs and alcohol. For Sandra, then only sixteen, the shock of her mother's death made her increasingly introverted and withdrawn. Living with her maternal grandmother, she felt even more isolated. Adding to her grief were the unanswered questions that tormented her every night. Lying in her room alone, Sandra could not stop wondering, *Did my mother love me? If she did, how could she kill herself? What could I have done to stop her?* No matter how many hours she spent in therapy, no matter how often she replayed her mother's last weeks in her mind, nothing changed. Sandra's grief so affected her that she could not even cry.

Weeks after the suicide, Sandra collapsed into bed one night and cried hysterically until she fell into a deep sleep. Within minutes, she was overwhelmed by what she describes as "a beautiful aroma," the fragrance of "a beautiful garden of all different kinds of flowers." Then she saw her mother surrounded by flowers. Stepping forward, she said to her daughter, "I love you, baby. I'm sorry. Don't blame yourself for anything. Mommy loves you. Forgive me. I'm fine now. Go on and be happy." After repeating the message twice, Sandra's mother walked back into the garden. Sandra continued to smell flowers for several more minutes.

Sandra awoke feeling "very peaceful" for the first time in her life. Fortunately, her therapist was open to her patients' paranormal experiences. They discussed the meaning of the dream, which Sandra was certain was a genuine visitation from her mother. Through this brief contact, Sandra's mother helped her daughter achieve a greater understanding of the complex problems leading to her suicide.

"I realized, for the first time in my life," Sandra told her therapist, "that my mother was a good soul in a sick body. But now my mother is fine. She looked so pretty; not tired anymore. I was worried if she was going to be punished because she killed herself. I know now that's not true, because the garden was so beautiful and it smelled so wonderful. She was in such a lovely place, so I know she's okay. I never had such a realistic dream. I really felt like I was with my mother. I'll never forget that."

Did Sandra's dream visitation magically ease her grief and resolve all of her issues with her mother? No. And no reasonable, responsible person would suggest otherwise. However, the visitation did bring

Sandra a measure of comfort and provide a starting point for meaningful work in a therapeutic setting.

Dr. George Bouklas holds a Ph.D. in clinical psychology and is a therapist in private practice, through which he sees and treats many elderly patients. He is among a growing number of therapists who are open to the direct after-death communications and other paranormal events reported by patients. He recalled for us one experience.

"A woman in her mid-eighties had been referred to me by her physician for psychotherapy because she'd experienced a decline in her functioning following a small stroke. During one session in the fourth month of her therapy, the woman sat silently and then looked up toward the ceiling and appeared to be conversing with someone."

Suddenly, she looked at him, laughed, and said, "Ruth says you don't believe she is here in the room with us." Bouklas knew from previous sessions that Ruth was the woman's daughter, who had died as a baby during childbirth. "The uncanny happens often enough in sessions that it is a force to be reckoned with," Bouklas recalls. "I will never forget what happened next. According to Ruth, I was one of three brothers and raised on a farm. I could not fulfill an early vocational choice because of my need for glasses. In college I studied biology prior to switching to psychology. There was more information related to family. All of it was true. Finally the woman ended with a comment that might seem cryptic to an outsider: 'Don't worry about it,' the woman told me, looking up toward the ceiling to get the words right. She told me H was all right, and I had been too concerned about eyes. Then the woman said, 'Ruth asked me if you believe in her now.'"

Bouklas assured her that he certainly did. Earlier that week, Bouklas had visited his grandmother, whose name begins with H, in the hospital where she lay in a coma. "Doctors told me there was no activity in the higher brain. But she seemed to respond to my voice by moving her eyes horizontally behind closed lids. That did worry me greatly, the idea that my grandmother's fertile and conscious mind might be locked within an unmoving body."

Dr. Bouklas asked his patient if Ruth would allow him to ask some questions. The woman checked with her daughter and then told the doctor that it would be all right. "The woman shared with me what she reported were Ruth's words. Ruth was right here among us, with all souls who have been before, are now, and will be. Ruth said, 'We all occupy the same space.' Her mother's pain at losing a child was so great that it seemed to open a window between our plane and this other one. Ruth had visited before and would visit again, I was told. She would be there when her mother needed her. They expected to be fully reunited upon the mother's death."

Three months later, the woman's treatment ended. In Bouklas's words, the patient "demonstrated a successful adjustment." She never spoke again of Ruth, and Bouklas never again saw any evidence of that phenomenon during their sessions.

What does Dr. Bouklas make of such an experience? He does not believe the woman could have researched his life or that she read his mind. "She spoke matter-of-factly and seemed intent on the ceiling, only turning to talk to me after she ostensibly heard from Ruth," he recalls. "That leaves us with the possibility that this is a real phenomenon. This possibility is utterly irksome to the modern intellectual spirit. Perhaps we have to leave the scientific realm to talk about such incidents. It may be more fruitful to investigate their intellectual, emotional, and spiritual meaning to the players themselves. This patient and I partook of a spiritual experience."

Why is Dr. Bouklas so open to paranormal experiences when many of his colleagues are skeptical? "I think modern American psychology has certain axioms and assumptions about the meaning of reality that need to be redefined if one can have these experiences. We have many things that we assume are automatically true in the field of psychology. For example, it's automatically assumed that if an angel appears in a room that it is a pathology and it was created out of the electricity in your brain. American scientists do not question that the phenomenon *could* exist. It's really obvious that the way we see reality is not the way it really is.

"If I hadn't had an experience as a teenager, maybe I would look askance at a lot of the experiences I've listened to from patients. When I was fifteen years old, I walked into my bedroom and was greeted by an angel. The angel was about a foot tall and was floating right in front of me. I attempted to speak to it, but before I could open my mouth, it spoke to me—mind to mind. So in my mind, I thought to it, *You are not real.* It said to me, 'Of course, I'm real.'"

Over the next half-hour Bouklas conversed telepathically with the angel, whom he remembers as "a blonde figure with a beautiful smile, dressed in a white gown. It was fluttering in space. I did not see wings. I'll never forget the creases in its neck as it turned to watch me going around it. It was androgynous, Caucasian, blue-eyed. A beautiful thing, around my age, a teenager at the time. We had a long conversation. At that age, I needed to know that there was meaning in life, that there was a heaven. And it assured me that, yes, it was all true. I asked, 'Is this what you really look like when you're not around me?' 'This is the form we take. This is the form *I've* taken,' the angel answered telepathically."

Reflecting on the experience years later, Dr. Bouklas observed, "It was quite a moving experience." It forever influenced how he regards his patients' paranormal and spiritual experiences. "They're real! I've probably dealt with a thousand elderly people in therapy within the last ten years. Two hundred of them had such experiences. A handful of them had them right in front of me. I treat it as if it's as real as talking about their children and what they've brought for Thanksgiving dinner to the nursing home, or the love a woman had for her husband who died thirty-five years earlier.

"I don't flinch. I totally go along with it. What that does is take the stigma of pathology out of the experience completely. All schools of therapy are now becoming more aware that you should not insult the patient by not believing. What we do in therapy is to flow with the patient and what the patient has to say in order to create the right kind of bond.

"Many of the problems we have when we do psychological research—to try and explain people's experiences—is that we think of time as past, present, and future. But that's Newtonian thinking.

Einstein didn't even believe in time. Modern physicists talk about time-space. Time is not linear at all. It's just that some humans tend to experience it in that fashion. Past, present, and future are dimensionless and are right now. To all my spiritual friends, everything is so obvious. They don't even raise an eyebrow. To my scientific critics, when I bring this up, they act as if it's to their credit that they can tolerate a guy like me in their ranks."

Bouklas then told me about the time he phoned a widely respected psychotherapist at a major university to discuss with him some patients' spiritual and paranormal experiences. With a chuckle, Dr. Bouklas describes what happened next: "He hung up on me!"

Dr. Bouklas was not surprised, and he views the problem philosophically: "People grind their axes. That therapist is grinding an axe. He got spooked by this material. So his patients would never talk to *him* about spiritual experiences and contacts with the deceased. But it doesn't spook me, and so my patients talk to me about their experiences all the time. If, as a therapist, you listen, people will tell you. It's good listening. It's how people get better: they get better by talking to somebody who is really listening and responding.

"Enough scientists have witnessed phenomena such as Ruth to be able to say that our present 'realities' are only a mask set upon the universe. The truth that lies beyond that mask is going to be ever more compelling, and the hunters for that truth will be as gratified and overwhelmed as the men in Plato's writing who forsook the shadows on the cave wall and stepped outside into the light to see what was really going on."

BEREAVEMENT: THE UNCHARTED PATH TO HEALING

How we view death influences how we approach bereavement—both our own and others'. By so completely denying death, our culture does us a great disservice. Not only do we not understand death, we lack an informed, realistic idea of what it means to grieve. In her excellent book *How to Go On Living When Someone You Love Dies,* Therese A. Rando, Ph.D., dispels some crippling, pervasive myths about grief and explains how to deal with loss in a healthy, productive manner.* As Rando points out, grief is a multifaceted, open-ended, and complex process. There is no "correct" time or way to grieve. No two mourners will have the same reaction to a loved one's death, even if they are both grieving for the same person. In addition, grief can be complicated by such factors as the cause of death, age at the time of death, and our relationship with the deceased.

We naturally associate mourning with sadness, loss, and depression. Most would agree that these responses are "understandable" and "acceptable" if not carried to extremes. What we fail to realize is that death provokes a wider range of emotions, including some we may not be comfortable experiencing or expressing, such as anger at the deceased and guilt over our relationship with them. As Dr. Rando writes, "Sometimes you might be angry at the deceased for her omissions and commissions while alive. Such anger may be quite difficult for you to admit, since in our society it is not socially appropriate to speak ill of the dead. . . ."[1]

Can we ever complete the unfinished business of life after someone dies? Sometimes the answer is yes. Tere Soto and Sally Gaines had been closest friends since they met at secretarial school. Like many people, Sally was drawn to Tere's vibrant personality and generous heart. A loving, religious young woman, Tere was a friend you could count on. The two spent hours together, shopping, chatting over coffee, or just visiting. They shared their dreams of the future; both hoped to marry and have children. In fact, they even planned to live near each other. Sally married first, then Tere. Although Sally and her husband relocated to Alabama and Tere made her home in New York, their friendship continued.

Then, just two years after Tere married, she learned she had ovarian cancer. Though devastated, she chose to keep her condition secret. For reasons of her own, she chose not to confide in Sally. Through a mutual friend named Kris, however, Sally learned the truth and longed to reach out to her friend.

---

*In the course of our research, we have seen hundreds of books on the subject of bereavement. We and many people we have interviewed believe that Dr. Rando's works are among the best available and recommend them highly to anyone who is bereaved.

"I never told Tere that I knew," Sally recalls. "I felt slighted, but I was trying to respect her wishes. I didn't want her to know that I was aware of her illness, because she would have been upset. Tere wanted people to be happy. So I pretended I knew nothing, although she was very ill. She didn't want me to go through pain with her.

"Tere wrote me a note that said, 'I'm fine. Everyone's fine. Thank God.' At the time, however, she was very sick and she still didn't tell me. She'd even asked me for a picture of my newborn son. But because I was so busy at the time, I didn't get it to her."

Three months later, Tere died at the age of thirty-eight. Sally was heartbroken, her pain exacerbated by circumstances that prevented her from attending Tere's wake and funeral and an overwhelming sense of guilt. "I felt like I didn't do anything for Tere," she reflects. "I didn't help or call her. I was trying to keep things the way they were. After she died, I regretted that I never sent her the photo of my baby."

At the same time, Sally could not help but be angry with Tere for keeping her secret and making it impossible for anyone to help her. "I was filled with such rage when she died that I wanted to grab and shake her and say, 'How could you do this to me?' I should have told her that I knew about her illness."

About two weeks after Tere passed, Sally experienced a vivid dream in which she was with her friend once again. Tere looked just as Sally remembered her. "She was wearing blue pants and a blue windbreaker jacket. Her dark brown, wavy hair, cut slightly above her shoulders, was beautiful. So was her face. She looked healthy. She looked wonderful, like she did when we were together and had great times."

In the dream, Sally said to Tere the words she regretted not saying when her friend was on earth: "How could you do this to me? I would have been there for you. You didn't give me a chance to help you."

For an instant, Tere appeared to be taken aback. Then she laughed. "I'm fine. I'm fine. Don't worry about me. I'm okay." Suddenly Tere placed her hands in front of her face. This was a gesture Sally recognized immediately. Tere was one to talk with her hands, and she often covered her face to signify regret or apology.

"I woke up thinking, *Well, I told Tere what I'd wanted to say. Now she knows how I feel.* And I felt better about the situation," Sally says. "I'd always thought I would have to wait until I had died and gone to heaven to settle the score. But I was able to do it immediately. Her visit to me in my dream helped me move beyond her death and over-come my feelings of rage at myself. I was able to grow, knowing that I could talk with her, and that she was still with me. I wasn't angry with her anymore.

"The dream visit from Tere was a surprise. But Tere knew that I'd had dreams and visions of my late father and communications of other kinds from him and other loved ones after they died. She was well aware that I was open to someone coming through from the other side. She knew I was going through trouble dealing with her death, and she helped me. Tere just didn't want me to go through the rest of my life being angry at her."

THE HEALING VISION

Samuel Fuchs was more than forty years old when he escaped the Nazi occupation of his native Romania during World War II. For more than eight months, he hid in a forest, where he shared an under-ground bunker with a cousin and a teenage boy. A Jew, Samuel faced certain death if captured by the Nazis. Despite his pleas, his wife refused to join him; she was later captured and sent to the death camp at Auschwitz, where she was killed. Their only child, a nine-teen-year-old son, was serving in the military when he died of typhus in the Ukraine.

The war ended, and like so many Holocaust survivors, Samuel faced rebuilding his life from nothing. In 1951 he emigrated to Israel, where he remarried and became a businessman and farmer. He and his second wife had two daughters and two sons. One daughter, Lily, moved from Israel to the United States in 1970, when she was nine-teen. She had always been close to her father and missed him deeply. Lily phoned home regularly and visited as often as she could.

For years, Samuel had received a monthly check from the German government, reparations for the loss of his wife and son. "My father never used that money," Lily recalls. "He never wanted to touch it. He said it was blood money." As his four children reached adulthood, Samuel withdrew the money from his savings account and divided the $30,000 among them. Lily used her share to start a business specializing in collectible and imported dolls.

On November 7, 1981, the day Lily opened her doll store, she received a phone call saying that her father had died of stomach cancer. He was seventy-nine years old. Following Orthodox Jewish law, Samuel was buried within twenty-four hours of death, making it impossible for Lily to get back to Israel for the funeral. While she respected the religious traditions, she could not help but feel hurt and angry. A month later, however, she returned home for the unveiling of her father's gravestone.

Though apparently gone from her life, Lily's father was never far away. She was back home in the states when she dreamed of him. "He flew into my bedroom when I was having a hard time. I was thinking about him and crying. I saw him in the white shroud in which he was buried," Lily remembers. "He flew in and sat on the corner of my bed and brought me red Macintosh apples. My father had owned a farm in Europe at one time, and there he grew apples. He always loved those red apples.

"I was crying in the dream. I said to him, 'Dad, I need help.' I saw him smile, and then he said, 'Here, my child. Please eat a piece of apple. Don't cry and please don't grieve anymore. It's not good for you. We don't want you to be sick.' Then he flew out, just like an angel.

"I woke up in a sweat and scared because I'd wanted to touch my father, but every time I tried he would move away. I concluded that it was his soul there. I told my husband that I dreamed of my father, that my father was here. My dad came to comfort me. I knew he was not suffering and that he was okay, wherever he was. He looked like he did before he became ill, with his dark complexion, hazel-green eyes, beautiful cherry-red lips, and pepper-gray hair."

Within a year of her father's death, Lily experienced the same lifelike dream visit from him on three different occasions. Each time Samuel said, "Don't cry, my daughter. Don't grieve."

"I have a good friend who is Catholic," Lily told me. "She went to Medjugorje and said that when she was there, something touched her. We all thought she'd lost it. Nobody wanted to talk to her. I always thought she was crazy. But you know what? After it happened to me, no, she's not crazy. Now I believe her when she said that happened."

In 1986, five years after Samuel's death, his youngest son, Hezi, died of bone cancer at the age of thirty-one. "I felt very guilty that he died first," Lily says. "I had a very hard time with that. When we were children, we played a game in which we'd say I was the oldest, so I'd be the one to die first. Hezi was the youngest, so he would die last. But it didn't happen that way. I carried so much grief and guilt for my brother. But I fought and survived it. Hezi was in Israel when he died. I missed him. He was a part of me that was no longer there with me."

In June 1994, Lily returned to Israel for her niece's wedding. The Orthodox Jewish faith requires that the women in the bride's and the groom's families participate in a ritual known as *mikvah*. Housed in a special building, the *mikvah* is a pool of water in which each woman immerses herself while praying. In doing so, she is purified, leaving her sins in the water.

The first to enter the *mikvah* was the bride-to-be, Lily's niece. As Lily waited with the other women for her turn, a strange sensation overtook her. "It was as if something was pulling me, 'Go into the water, Lil. Go in there.' I said, 'No, I'm afraid,'" she recalls. When Lily's turn came, she reluctantly entered the special room. She undressed, showered, and had her nails trimmed, in accordance with tradition. The only other person in the room was the woman who attended to those who entered the water. But "I felt somebody else there besides the woman," Lily says.

The *mikvah* attendant instructed Lily to immerse herself in the

---

*Medjugorje, located in the former Yugoslavia, is a town where apparitions of the Blessed Mother are said to have occurred. For the faithful, the site has become a place of prayer and miraculous healings, not unlike Lourdes, in France.

water three times and told her which prayers to recite. Lily did so once. Then as she readied herself to immerse a second time, she began to cry. "I couldn't stop. I cried like a baby," Lily remembers. She briefly regained her composure, but again found herself feeling a mixture of apprehension and fear, sensing that something mysterious was about to occur. She tried reasoning with herself: "I have to see what was waiting for me down there. Why am I so afraid? What can happen to me?" Once again, she started sobbing uncontrollably, but she went under the water again.

Lily immersed herself for a third and final time. When she emerged, she saw her late father and brother near a wall. "They were walking around and watching me. My father had the same smile he had in the lifelike dreams I experienced. However, this time it was *not* a dream. I felt their warmth; I felt their presence. I felt everything I ever wanted to feel in my entire life. I was healed. I felt that I was cured that day of all my guilt. That's what really happened. You don't know what a relief it was to me. I never thought I'd see my father or brother again.

"The woman attending the *mikvah* knew what was happening. She said something was going on that she had never felt before in more than thirty years in the *mikvah*. She said she never felt such a strong spiritual presence. She advised me not to tell everyone about my experience. I've told only people who believe and understand.

"When I went into the *mikvah*, I was tense, scared, and confused. I didn't know what was going to happen there. I just knew something would. A Christian friend of mine who was there said when I returned from immersing, I looked like I was born again. I was a different person. I felt like I was somewhere else—on a different planet—I can't explain it. My friend knew what grief I carried and how much I suffered through the years because of the loss of my brother and father. But she knew that definitely God had done something. She believed me, that I saw my brother and father."

About two weeks after her niece's wedding, Lily was driving alone in Tel Aviv. Suddenly she had what she describes as "a weird feeling." Then an instant later, she saw shadows on the dashboard and felt both her father's and her brother's spirits near. She clearly heard her father's voice warning her to be careful. She immediately slowed the car, and just in time. Seconds later, a truck pulled in front of her, cutting her off. She slammed on the brakes and skidded, causing another car to hit hers. A second car swerved, missed her, and struck a tree. Remarkably, Lily was uninjured despite the extensive damage to her car.

There is no doubt in Lily's mind that her father and her brother saved her life. "This was the only time in my life that I saw death in front of my eyes," she says. "My father showed me that in a minute, I could be gone. But he warned me, and I was saved."

THE ROSE

"My maternal grandfather, Joseph Tostado, was the closest person I had to a father because I never knew my father," Margaret Wendt explains. "We were very close. I loved my grandfather more than life. Not only did I not have a father, I didn't know my mother until I was older. As a young child, I lived with an aunt. Grandpa was the only one who really loved me, and he told me I was special. He was interested in metaphysics, though he never read books about it. What he knew, he knew from his personal experience, and he taught me about the other side."

Margaret was in her early twenties when Joseph, then past seventy, fell seriously ill with cardiac and pulmonary problems. Joseph, who made his home in San Bernardino, California, was very disappointed that his favorite granddaughter could not be at his side then. When she first learned he was ill, Margaret was abroad. Once home, between caring for her husband and an infant daughter in Chicago, she simply could not go to him. She knew her grandfather's medical problems were serious but did not think they posed an imminent threat. Later, she learned that her grandfather's condition had been graver than she was originally led to believe.

At the first opportunity, Margaret flew west to be at her grandfather's side. By then, he was home recuperating, and while he was happy to see her, he felt he had to tell her how much he missed her. "You didn't come to see me when I was very sick," he said gently. "Everyone else came to see me but you."

"I'm sorry, Grandfather," Margaret replied. "If I'd known how serious your illness was, I would have been here."

"Promise me you'll be here when I die," the old man said, stroking her hair and gazing into her eyes. This warm, loving look was one Margaret knew well, and as she nodded her promise, she thought of how much she loved him. This was one of the few times she ever visited Joseph and did not leave with a rose. He would always give her a rose and say, "You're my rose." She returned home to Chicago three days later, praying her grandfather would recover.

Unfortunately, Joseph soon suffered a relapse and died suddenly. This was the first time Margaret had experienced the death of someone close. "I knew people died," she recalls. "But I didn't think it was going to happen to my family or to me." Overwhelmed by shock and grief, Margaret could not get a handle on the intense guilt she felt over breaking her last promise to her grandfather. She had not been at his bedside, and now he was gone.

"I really think that some part of me died the day he died. I was mortified. I couldn't move or eat, or even wash my hair," Margaret said. "I couldn't believe, as strong as I was, that something affected me that much. I was paralyzed with grief. I really felt I let him down by breaking my promise. I blamed myself."

She returned immediately to California, arriving in time for the wake. "I nearly passed out. I could not look at my grandfather in the coffin. It was so awful that I had to be taken out of there." Loved ones helped Margaret to her mother's house, where she immediately took to bed, sobbing hysterically.

For the next several hours, she lay in a darkened bedroom, her grief and anguish holding sleep at bay. At about three o'clock in the morning, a bright white light washed over the room. "It was like time stood still. The room had become very bright. It was the kind of light that people who report near-death experiences describe. It's the kind of light you only see when the so-called dead come back. You'll never see that kind of light on this side of the veil. There's no such light on this side."

In the light Margaret clearly saw Joseph standing near. "I remember my grandfather's face was white and lighted, yet I saw the pinkish flesh color. But he was not translucent. He looked angelic. His mouth never moved, yet he was talking to me telepathically. I only realized later that his mouth never moved. While I talked to him, it was as if a conversation was all around me. It wasn't that he was just speaking *to* me. I was *in* the conversation. Whatever he said to me, it was as if I was part of the light, part of him."

"Guilt doesn't help anyone," Joseph said to Margaret then. "What he came to tell me was that he'd done a horrible thing by making me feel guilty, and that he loved me and he was at peace. He said he loved me very much and he could see I was dying from grief. That was not good, he said. It was his time to die, he said, not mine. He said he'd come to remove my guilt. He explained he'd always be there for me, but that he'd appear only when I really needed him. He said I could call him when I needed to and he would appear.

"I remember I looked at him, and all of a sudden I went from feeling so ill to feeling so great. One second, I was just so sick and depressed, then quickly I felt so much better. I went from dark to light. He told me he loved me more than anything in the world, and he told me he would always love me. He said I was a very good girl and I never disappointed him. I thought I had disappointed him."

When the vision withdrew fifteen or twenty minutes later, Margaret went into her mother's room. "What happened?" her mother asked, surprised to see her daughter up so late and looking so calm and happy. "You look great. You're okay?" She told her mother she had seen her grandfather. Her mother believed her because she looked and seemed so much better.

Over the coming months, Margaret continued to call on her grandfather's spirit for help. "I would call him when I needed him. I was in art school in the Chicago area, and having a really difficult time traveling and trying to get through school. A few months after he died, I walked into art class and there on my easel was this beautiful drawing of a rose. It was on white paper, a fine pencil drawing colored in with white chalk. I asked everyone around me, Who drew this? No one claimed to have done it and no one knew who did."

That night Joseph returned to her in a vision. "He said that he had left me that rose to let me know that he'd heard me. He didn't remain as long in that vision as he had in the first one. I still have that drawing."

At the time, Margaret was married to a successful, and skeptical, scientist. "I told him I'd seen my grandfather and that I was going to prove that my grandfather comes to me." On a snowy January day about two months later, Margaret and her husband were driving to visit his parents and sister in a Chicago suburb. Margaret predicted that sometime that day, her grandfather would send her a sign: "On the way from here to your sister, I'll see a rose."

"It's snowing outside. You'll never see a rose," her husband answered before pointedly asking, "What's wrong with you?"

As they drove the icy roads, she prayed to Joseph for a sign. A few miles down the road, she suddenly screamed, "Stop the car!" There on a lawn, a large white rose was standing up in the snow, as if someone had just stuck it there. When she returned to the car with the blossom in hand, her husband exclaimed, "This is impossible!"

Obviously not. Joseph had given Margaret her sign.

The following spring Margaret visited a psychic medium in Chicago. This was her first experience with a genuine trance medium, one through whom spirits speak. As Margaret peered into the medium's face, she had the impression that he was taking on her grandfather's countenance. Then the medium began speaking in a voice that Margaret knew was her grandfather's.

"Margaret, you have to stop chasing me when you don't need me and calling me for every little thing. I told you I'll be there when you really need me. I love you, but you have to call me only when you need me, because I've got to go on. I've got to move forward. I have to go to school. I have to do things. I have to learn. But I'll always be there when you *really* need me."

Joseph's message was loving but firm, and Margaret wasn't surprised by his words. "I was calling him for everything," she admits.

Joel Martin and Patricia Romanowski

"Now I only talk to him when I'm really in trouble, and then he'll answer. When he does, it's always about roses. So, for example, when I hear the song 'The Rose,' I know he hears me."

Over the first dozen years after Joseph's death, Margaret experienced four separate visions of him, and he communicated to her through sending signs of a rose several times. Since then, the visions seemed to have ceased. Why?

Margaret thinks she knows. "Because I stopped calling him. Remember, my grandfather said he didn't mind if I summoned him if it was for something important. I grew up. The more I read about the subject, the more I began to understand. All I knew was that I'd seen spirits when I was a child in Catholic school. But then I was told it was evil. Seeing my grandfather kept me alive. I think I would have died if he hadn't come back. I think that's the reason he came to me. It was as if my grandfather gave me a breath of life. He made me feel that I wasn't alone. When you feel you're not alone, you can make it. I think the dead only come back to keep us alive. I know we don't die. I saw my grandfather."

Do people such as Margaret, who claim to have some psychic ability, see or sense the spirit world more clearly than others whose abilities are less developed?

"Yes," Margaret replies. "But I did not see him the first time because I had psychic ability; I saw him because I needed to. But my psychic ability allowed me to see him longer than I might have without it.

"My former husband is a scientist and a 'left brain' person who does not believe in anything unless he can see, taste, feel, and examine it. At the time his mother died, they had many conflicts that went back years. He needed healing. Three days after his mother died of cancer, she just appeared in the middle of the night. She woke him and said she was sorry, and that she'd been very unfair to him. He saw her standing there. She has since come back to ask me for forgiveness. What that's taught me is that they obviously need our forgiveness. So the spirits of our deceased loved ones don't all return for the same reason.

"My grandfather also came to my mother in a vision. But he came to her for a different reason. He came to her because there was an unresolved personal conflict between them. The spirits come to each person for different reasons. The only similarity is that they come to help us. My mother-in-law came to help herself, but I also think she gave her son a sense of spirituality. And it gave me credibility. I think deceased loved ones always come for good. I don't know any who have come for a bad purpose.

"These are important experiences. I've seen spirits and I've talked to them. So why do I still fear death? Because it's still an unknown. You can't explain the experience to me. And yet I've died on the operating table. Years ago I had a near-death experience, and I saw the same light during the near-death experience that my grandfather was surrounded by in the vision. It was a wonderful feeling."

"IT'S TWICE AS HARD OVER THERE"

For the overwhelming majority of people we've talked with, hearing from a deceased loved one is a comforting, joyful experience. Issues may be resolved, questions answered. For a brief, fleeting moment, we know we can believe that love eludes death's grip. Reassuring as that is, however, it would be a mistake to conclude that every direct-communications experience is entirely pleasant. Not every loved one accepts his or her passing or finds immediate contentment and purpose on the other side. In years of talking to people about mourning and bereavement, we have also heard from a substantial minority who feel that other books deliberately ignore stories like their own. For these people, the endless stories of the eternally forgiving and gracious dead—inspiring as they might be—suggest that something is wrong when loved ones return to express dissatisfaction or regret.

Life on the other side seems every bit as complex and challenging as the existence that precedes it, although in different ways. For people whose loved ones come through expressing doubt or unhappiness, this Smiley Face version of life after death is an affront, an insult, a rejection of their reality. For people seeking some validation of their experience, this seems especially cruel. That is why we believe it is very important to include stories, such as Patricia's dream of her father (see chapter 3), that challenge the prevailing and, we believe, inaccurate view of the afterlife.

It is also important to remember that, as a group, those who write and speak about life after death do not make up a representative sampling of contemporary American—much less world—culture or experience. In our years of writing about mediumship, we have often lamented that the overwhelming preponderance of psychics and subjects represented only a fraction of American social and ethnic groups. In addition, most of the subjects and the spirits led typical lives. Whatever other tragedies crossed these spirits' lives on earth, someone cared enough about them to reach out after they had passed.

The survivors of people who mistreated, abused, or abandoned them rarely seek out after-death contact. As a result, we have disproportionately less information about what awaits those who committed heinous crimes or were immoral. Is their experience different from that of someone who lived a so-called average life?

What, we have often wondered, is the after-death experience of someone who lived with degrading poverty, violence, or abuse? Someone who committed murder? Someone who abused a child? Someone who was just plain bad? Who on the other side helps the street gangster, the pimp, or the murderer cross over? Who helps the drug addict or the homeless child who freezes on the street? Is it possible that our current notions about the afterlife reflect only a small band on a much wider spectrum of after-death experience? Is everybody always happy there? Always progressing? Always growing? Can crossing over really solve all the problems we neglected to work on here? Some after-death communications suggest that it may not.

Linda Ackerly's father, Ken, had been battling lung cancer for nearly a decade. A heavy smoker all his adult life, Ken was diagnosed with lung cancer at age forty-eight. After two years of chemotherapy and radiation treatment, Ken's cancer was in remission. For the next six years, he lived an active, normal life. When he was fifty-seven, the cancer recurred and treatment resumed, though doctors were less positive in their outlook.

Ken was hospitalized and feeling as well as could be expected. Although his condition was considered terminal, doctors had no reason to believe death was imminent. In fact, his family had visited him the evening before and assumed he would live several more months. But at around 5 A.M. one morning, his wife suddenly awoke screaming, "He's dead! He's dead!"

Linda, who had been staying with her mother, rushed into her room. "Mom, what's wrong?"

"He's dead! Your father's dead!" she repeated through wracking sobs.

"No, Dad's okay," Linda said, gently holding her mother. "We just saw him last night. You'll go see him today. He's okay." But her mother was inconsolable. Moments later, the phone rang. It was Ken's doctor calling to tell his family that he had passed away within the hour.

The day after Ken's funeral, Linda, her mother, her brother, and his wife returned to their home. The four of them were talking about the funeral and Ken's death, and someone casually asked whether they believed in life after death. They all agreed that they did. "Well, if we all believe in life after death, shouldn't Dad be sending us some kind of sign?" Linda asked. A spirited young woman, she could not resist wondering aloud, "What's the matter with him? Doesn't he love us? How come he's not sending us a sign?"

At exactly that moment, the house filled with the strains of Dean Martin's 1953 hit—and Ken's favorite song—"That's Amore." "That was the song we used to listen to when we were going out to dinner or just having a good time," Linda recalls. "Dad would blast 'That's Amore' on his car tape deck." Linda rushed downstairs where she found her seven-year-old son, George, standing by the tape machine.

"Why did you play that tape?" she asked him. He replied that he did not know. Linda does not think he even knew which tape he had picked, and she is certain he could not have rewound it exactly to begin playing as it did. All he could say was, "I just wanted to hear that song." To Linda, this was more than mere coincidence. The timing was, as she says, "just unbelievable. Here we were upstairs asking for a sign from my father and suddenly, we hear his favorite song. It was pretty amazing. I couldn't imagine it was anything *but* a sign from him. It was too coincidental to be coincidence. I mean, it happened exactly two seconds after we said we wanted a sign. I could see someone being doubtful, if, for example, a day or two passed and maybe you heard the song on the radio. Then you could say, well, maybe so, maybe not. But this? I got my sign."

And it would not be the last. In early spring, about a year after her father's death, Linda drove alone to the cemetery to pay her respects. On the front seat beside her lay a book she had been reading about life after death. As she approached the cemetery gates, she saw a rainbow. It seemed to begin under and arch through and above a cloud. It looked oddly familiar, she thought. Then she looked down at the book. There on the cover was a picture of a rainbow so close it could have been a photograph of the one shining before her.

"I thought it was unusual," Linda says. "The weather that day was mostly cloudy, but it was not raining. I've never seen a rainbow in that way before. It wasn't as if there had been a storm and then it suddenly became sunny. That's when you expect to see a rainbow. I took it as a sign from my father because at that time I was reading that book, and it had comforted me because it helped explain life after death to me. I think it was his sign to tell me that the book was right, that my father did live on, and that maybe he's in a better place."

Nearly two years after Ken's death, he appeared to Linda in a very intense dream. "My father came to my kitchen door," she recalls. "I was standing there with my mother-in-law. I turned to her and said, 'That's my father. But my father's dead. Well, I guess I shouldn't be afraid. It's my father.' It seemed as if he were right there with me. It was like real life. Everything was very vivid, very sharp, and very clear.

"He was dressed casually in slacks and a dress shirt. He looked well, like he did before he got sick. He didn't look unhealthy. But he looked distressed. So I opened the door and my father walked in. He was carrying some papers under his arm. He began to discuss with me some problems I was then having with my business. I said to him, 'Well, since you're dead, I guess I can ask you this. What is it like over there?' My father's answer surprised me. 'Well, if you think that it's hard over here on earth, it's *twice* as hard over there.' He seemed very angry and upset as he spoke to me.

"It seemed that he could not get past whatever problems he'd left on earth, as though he was very angry about what happened to him on earth and perhaps could not resolve it over there. It's been very, very hard for him, I felt. It seemed like he was blaming everyone but himself for his problems. He seemed angry at me, in a way. But maybe that's just how I was perceiving it.

"I think that whatever personal and family problems my father did not resolve in life, he's working through now in the afterlife. My father was always the type of person who would never blame himself. Things were always somebody else's fault. I suppose that now he has to face that, and it hasn't been easy. I've never told anyone else about this. I didn't think anyone would understand."

We tend to view after-death communications as a way for our loved ones on the other side to help us. Yet as we have seen in Linda's case and many others, they also need us to help them, with our acceptance, love, and forgiveness. Just as their lives go on, so does their work and, though in a form we cannot comprehend, the human struggle to be happy and whole. Margaret's grandfather, for example, gently let her know that he was not "on call" all the time, that he has commitments to meet and work to accomplish there. Clearly death does not turn us into "cloud potatoes" dreamily plucking at golden harps and obsessing over every detail in the lives of those left behind. The true healing of grief permits us to accept and move on, both here and beyond.

9

JOURNEYS THROUGH TIME

And in today already walks tomorrow.

—SAMUEL TAYLOR COLERIDGE

Through dream visitations and other forms of direct after-death communication, we can sometimes glimpse the future through precognition. Although it happens much more rarely, deceased loved ones may also help us to see, even to feel, as if we are living in the past. Retrocognition occurs when we experience past events that have not occurred to us, that are not in our personal memories, of which we have no personal knowledge.

Parapsychologists theorize that what we commonly call hauntings may in fact be recurring retrocognitive incidents. Another possibility addresses that old bugaboo time. If our conceptions of past, present, and future are artificial, why couldn't the past occur now or even in the future? The third argument—the choice of skeptics—is that somehow, perhaps subconsciously, we already do know the information and events that we believe are first revealed to us through retrocognitive experiences. Although it is reasonable to assume that this could be the case sometimes, we have found people whose stories prove that retrocognition is real. Further, if retrocognition really were based solely on hidden, unknown memories, nearly all of us would experience it at least once and probably often. That, however, is not so. Except for our momentary experiences of déjà vu, most of us are firmly entrenched in the present.

People often obtain a piece of information through direct after-death communication that they later learn is true. Usually this information was not the whole gist of the communication but a detail one would view as unimportant but for its corroborative value. The next two cases present something entirely different. In both, a spirit—coincidentally a grandfather—took a grandchild on a journey through his past. Why? The most obvious answer would be that in giving their grandchildren information they could not otherwise have known, these spirits made their presence verifiable.

Neither subject was occupied with problems beyond the routine; neither spirit came through to save someone's life or prepare them for future tragedy. On the whole, the content and purpose of these contacts were reassuringly mundane. We noticed that both grandfathers behaved very much as they would have had they continued in this life. Their messages were comforting, and in providing their loved ones here with such rich retrocognitive experiences, they seem to have accomplished what grandparents almost universally do—pass on to their grandchildren a sense of their own pasts and who they are.

"... IN TIME, DOLLY"

Barbara Califano never met her grandfather, who died of a heart attack in 1967, shortly before her parents were wed. However, her father, who loved and missed his father very much, kept his presence alive. "My father used to tell me funny stories about him," Barbara says. "My grandfather was a shoemaker in New York City. He didn't have much money. He and my grandmother raised four children. He was a nice, simple man who cared about everybody else. My father always said my grandfather was watching over us, and that he was with us. As the years went by, I talked to my grandfather like he was there, even though I never knew him."

When Barbara was twenty-one, she went through a rough but typical phase. She was not sure what career plans to make or whether to finish college. And her love life was, in her words, "a mess." Not knowing where else to turn, she asked her father, "Can you talk to Grandpa for me?"

"You can talk to your grandfather," her father replied.

"But he doesn't *know* me."

"No, you talk to your grandfather. He'll answer you," he insisted.

"Yeah, right."

Several weeks after this conversation, Barbara found herself having an incredibly lifelike dream: "It was nighttime and I was on a beach. People were walking toward me. There was a man standing there. I recognized him as my grandfather. Although I couldn't see his face, I knew it was my grandfather. I said, 'Grandpa, Grandpa.' I felt loved, comforted, and protected. I had no fear.

"He greeted me, 'Dolly, Dolly! How are you?' He hugged me. With that, all the people started walking away from us. Then he said, 'Let's get some ice cream. I *love* ice cream.'

"I answered, 'No, thanks. I'm not in the mood for ice cream, Grandpa.'

"'No, come on. Come on,' he insisted. So we went over to an ice cream truck, where someone gave him a little sample of ice cream in a cup. 'Go ahead, you have some,' he said. I answered, 'I don't want it, Grandpa.' So he tasted the ice cream. Then he said, 'I loved ice cream, but it always burned my teeth.' Then he put the paper cup down and said, 'Come on, Dolly, walk with me.'

"He put his arms around me and asked, 'Why are you so sad? Every time I look at you, you're so sad. Why do you cry?'

"'Grandpa, I don't know what's going on in my life. I don't have any money. I don't have any direction. I don't understand why I can't find a decent boyfriend. I don't understand why this is going on.'

"'Dolly, you'll see. You're going to do a lot of good things. You just need some time, and you need patience. There are a lot of good things in store for you, and you'll help a lot of people.'

"'But Grandpa, I don't see it happening. I don't understand. When is it going to change?'

"'You'll see in time, Dolly. In time.' With that, all of the people were coming back toward us, and Grandpa said, 'I have to go, Dolly.' I said, 'No, Grandpa! Don't leave me. *Please* don't leave me.' I was crying. 'Please don't leave me. I'm so lonely,' I begged him.

"'I love you, Dolly. I'm always with you,' he said. With that, the other people took him away."

When Barbara awoke the next morning, her eyes were wet with tears; she had actually cried in her dream. She wiped her eyes, thinking, *What kind of dream was that?*

Barbara told her mother about the dream. Until that moment, she had thought the man she met in the dream was her maternal grandfather, Louis. Remember, she had felt a grandfatherly presence but never saw a face. She naturally assumed that she was with the grandfather she knew; Louis was still alive. But Barbara's mother knew better. "It wasn't your Grandfather Louis. It was your father's father, Antonio, you saw in your dream."

How did Barbara's mother know? "She told me that my grandfather Antonio loved ice cream, but he could never eat it because it used to burn his teeth; in other words, he had sensitive teeth and the cold hurt him. She also told me that he called all his little grandchildren Dolly. Of course, I never knew any of that, because I never knew him. When your parents tell you about a deceased relative, they tend to concentrate on the bigger issues, not details, like the fact that he couldn't eat ice cream."

When Barbara shared her dream with her father, she was surprised to hear him ask, "What did your grandfather look like in the dream?" "I don't know, Dad. I couldn't see the man's face. I just remember that he had big hands."

Her father then told her that her grandfather had large hands. This was another fact that Barbara did not know. "Both my parents cried when I told them about my dream," Barbara recalls. "They couldn't believe that my grandfather was around. When I told my grandmother, she told me to pray for Grandpa; she's very religious.

"I did have one question about the experience that no one could answer: Out of sixteen grandchildren—and Grandpa Antonio only knew a few of us before he died—why did he come only to me? He was very family oriented and he loved children." Here we have to wonder if perhaps he has not come to all of them without them recognizing the visitation for what it was.

For Barbara, the experience changed her life. "When I woke up that morning, all the loneliness and confusion had disappeared. Since then, every time I start to feel anxious about my life, I think of that dream. I think back to Grandpa telling me that it's all going to be okay." Today, true to her grandfather's words, Barbara is helping people. She does public relations work for a local government agency. Among her duties is raising funds for charity, and she recently produced an exercise video for developmentally disabled adults.

"... THAT YOU WILL BELIEVE IN ME"

Michelle and Keith O'Malley became parents of a baby boy on August 2, 1993. They named him Benjamin, after Michelle's paternal grandfather, who had died of emphysema on Christmas Eve in 1978, when Michelle was ten. Benjamin had lived in Schenectady, New York, while she lived in the Portsmouth, Virginia, area. She saw her grandfather annually at the Christmas holiday and during summer vacation.

"I have a few fond memories of my grandfather. I remember the last time I saw him. I knew it was going to be the last time I'd ever see him," Michelle recalled. "My grandmother found a picture of him saying goodbye to me that day.

"It's sad when you lose a grandparent, but I don't really think it affects you when you're young. As you grow older, you think, *Yes, that was my grandfather. I loved him, but he's gone now.* As an adult, however, I became interested in genealogy and wanted to know more about my family's history.

"One day my father and his brother were reminiscing about the old days and their childhood years. It was not a subject I heard them speak about often. They talked about Grandpa Benjamin and told stories about him. It was a side of my grandfather I'd never known about. It really touched me. The stories they shared made me see Grandpa in a totally different light. He was a very strong, proud, and good man. He was quiet, but he had a sense of humor and he loved his family. He accomplished a lot. He worked hard to provide for his family and be a good husband and father. I guess when you're older, you appreciate more, and then you realize you missed knowing the person because you were too young to understand. I told my husband, 'If we ever have a baby and it's a boy, I'm definitely going to name him Benjamin.'"

In November, three months after her son was born, Michelle's grandfather Benjamin appeared to her in a vivid dream. She recognized him immediately. He looked exactly as Michelle remembered. "Grandpa was of Italian ancestry. He was about five-seven or five-eight with classic Italian features: dark brown eyes and black hair that turned gray toward the end of his life. He wasn't breathing with difficulty from emphysema anymore, as he had when I was a child. He asked only, 'Did you make that French toast?' He repeated that question several times."

That was the entire dream. When Michelle awoke early the next morning, she could not shake the dream out of her mind. Why would her grandfather appear so clearly only to ask her if she had made French toast? It seemed preposterous, yet Michelle felt compelled to comply with her grandfather's curious request.

As she walked into her darkened kitchen to prepare French toast for her husband, Keith, she noticed that an oven light that had not been working was now aglow. Michelle was certain that neither she nor Keith had used the oven last night. In fact, Michelle rarely cooked at all, since she and Keith had agreed he would handle kitchen duties while she cared for the baby and tended to the rest of the house. She had no explanation. *How strange*, she thought. After she finished cooking breakfast, she said aloud, "Okay, Grandpa. Here's your French toast."

Keith was surprised to find breakfast made and good-naturedly teased his wife, "My God, what did you do that you needed to make breakfast for me? Wreck the car?"

Michelle assured him that she was not making amends for anything. She did, however, mention to Keith why she decided to cook that morning. Certain Michelle was joking, he replied, "Ask your grandfather what the lottery numbers are the next time you see him."

"Stop. I'm being serious," Michelle insisted. Keith just shrugged, then continued eating, all the while marveling at the delicious French toast, a dish she had never prepared before. Finally Michelle could not stand it anymore; she called her grandmother.

"Did Grandpa like French toast?" she asked.

"Oh, he loved French toast, and he was always asking me to make some," her grandmother said. Michelle hung up feeling that she had her answer. Or did she? It was one unusual dream and one interesting coincidence perhaps. When she shared the experience with her father, Greg, he did not have much to say. Why would her grandfather appear to her after so many years? she wondered. *If* that was Grandpa.

The next day Michelle was napping when she began seeing what she described as fragments of a scene pass before her. She saw "people with a stretcher coming into my grandparents' house and placing Grandpa on it and taking him to a hospital." When Michelle awoke, she was not sure whether the dream was a product of her imagination or a vision of a real past event.

She phoned her mother to ask if anything like that had ever happened. Michelle's mother explained that Grandpa occasionally suffered serious nosebleeds because of his emphysema. From the way Michelle described her dream, her mother confirmed that it was accurate. Yes, Grandpa had been carried out of his house on a stretcher. Michelle hung up with more questions than answers. Why, she wondered, had her grandfather appeared to her twice in two days?

Two days later, Grandpa returned to Michelle in another startlingly realistic dream. Michelle found herself outdoors in the country. Grandpa Benjamin approached her and said, "Tell your father to get a pail of water and meet me at the railroad tracks."

What could Grandpa possibly mean? Upon awakening, Michelle quickly dialed her father. "Dad, I just had another dream about Grandpa. I want to know if this makes any sense to you. Grandpa told me to tell you to get a pail of water and meet him at the railroad tracks." Greg, who hadn't seemed particularly impressed by the French toast incident, fell silent. "Do you know what Grandpa means?" Michelle asked.

After a few seconds, Greg replied, "I know exactly what that means." Michelle's father went on to explain that when he was a young boy, he and his father fished for eels at a place called Frenchie's Hollow, near their Schenectady home. Greg's job was to fill the pail with water and then meet his father, who waited for him near the railroad tracks, with the day's catch.

This was the first time Michelle had ever heard of this; Greg was certain he had never told her about it. After that, Michelle says, "My dad knew I couldn't be making this up. There is no way that I could have known about this."

Around the same time, Michelle recalls, "My son started acting strangely. He was in a crib at the time. He was afraid to stay in his room. Then in the middle of the night, he'd cry out, 'Bird, bird!' We couldn't figure out what was going on. So we moved him into another room and put him in a real bed. But he would sit up at night and carry on conversations, chattering away. He'd stare at the wall and laugh and coo. Again, he was saying, 'Bird, bird.' I told him, 'Benjamin, there's no bird.'"

During a young mother's typically hectic day, Michelle was lifting Benjamin to her hip while trying to open the refrigerator door. Suddenly little Benjamin began excitedly pointing to a small calendar on the refrigerator and crying, "Bird! Bird! Bird!" It took Michelle a few seconds to realize that her son was referring to a picture of an angel flying over houses with a child in its arms. "Bird!" Benjamin squealed in delight, pointing to the image. "Bird!"

"Is that what you're calling a bird?" she asked. Benjamin, still too young to reply, answered his mother nonetheless. Clearly, to Benjamin an angel was a bird, but where had Benjamin seen an angel before? In his room, when he kept repeating the word *bird*, was he seeing an angel? As we now know, it is quite common for children to claim to have seen angels. Researchers who believe angels exist suggest that one reason children seem to see so many of them is that we have not yet trained them to disbelieve their experiences.

Yet Michelle had other reasons to wonder whether little Benjamin was in touch with his namesake. Michelle kept a photograph of her grandfather in the den, and she had shown it to her son and told him who it was. "Sometimes Benjamin would take that picture of my grandfather and sit with it while he watched his favorite video, *Winnie the Pooh*. I think my son saw his great-grandfather both in his dreams and when he was awake. I don't know who the angel is. Perhaps it's my grandfather."

Several times both she and Keith saw their son run through the house saying, "Great Papa! Great Papa!" When Michelle would try to explain, "No Great Papa around. Great Papa in heaven," Benjamin clearly did not understand. Then one day Benjamin suddenly stood up on a chair and, with arms outstretched, pointed at the ceiling and clapped his hands in glee. Michelle turned to Keith. "Does he see something that we don't see?"

Following this intense flurry of visitations, Grandpa Benjamin appeared from time to time to Michelle. But his visits for the next few months were notably brief. In one, "He was smiling, and I'd walk up and hug him, just as I did when he was alive. He asked me, 'How's my granddaughter? How's my girl?'"

On the eve of Michelle and Keith's anniversary, Grandpa Benjamin returned. But this time, he stayed longer and they had a long conversation. "I saw my grandfather in my son's nursery. We were both looking down at my son in his crib. I could *feel* the flannel shirt Grandpa had on. I could smell the Aqua-Velva aftershave he wore and the scent of the wine he drank. I could see myself in the dream. I mean, I saw everything.

"He told me how proud he was of his great-grandson Benjamin and proud of all his children and grandchildren. He said it was a good thing I named *this* child Benjamin because the next one would be a girl. After we looked at the baby, Grandpa sat in my son's rocking chair in the corner of the nursery and started talking to me as I sat at his feet.

"He told me that he can't stay at his old house anymore because new people are there now and the old house isn't the same. 'It's all changed, the attic isn't the attic anymore,' he said. And, you know, I found out that it's true: there are new people in my grandparents' old house, and they *have* changed it all around and turned the attic into a bedroom."

Michelle recalls that her grandfather then said to her, "Remember when I put candy in my pocket for you so you wouldn't be afraid of me? Well, I'm telling you these things because I know you won't be afraid, and I know that you'll believe in me. Ask your dad where his uncle's Purple Heart is. You'll find it wrapped in a flag."

"I don't understand," Michelle replied.

"Just ask your father that," Benjamin insisted gently.

"Okay."

Then Benjamin rose from the rocker and walked out of the baby's room. "Where are you going?" Michelle asked. "Don't worry. I'll return."

"Then I woke up," Michelle says. "It seemed so real that I just had to get up and check my son's room. The baby and his blanket and stuffed animal were in exactly the same positions as they had been in the dream."

"Dad, I had another dream about Grandpa," Michelle told her father the next day. "This is really strange. Did any of your uncles fight in a war? Did anyone earn a Purple Heart? And do you know where a Purple Heart medal is?"

"No, Michelle, I don't know of any of my uncles who fought in a war. So there's no Purple Heart. You're really dreaming this up now, because there is no way."

Disappointed but undeterred, Michelle called her father's brother, but he had no information either. She reluctantly phoned her grandmother. She did not want to bother her with another inexplicable dream or stir up memories of her departed loved ones. But who else might know the meaning of Benjamin's words?

"In a dream, Grandpa told me to ask Dad where his uncle's Purple Heart was. Do you have a Purple Heart?"

"Yes, I do," Michelle's grandmother answered.

"Whose Purple Heart was it?"

"It belonged to my sister Rose's first husband, who was killed many years ago. That would have made him your father's uncle."

Michelle had not known any of this, nor had her father or his brother, who never knew of the uncle who was killed in Europe during World War I, many years before either was born. When Great Aunt Rose passed, Michelle's grandmother inherited her sister's personal possessions, which were now stored away and all but forgotten. Only Grandpa Benjamin and Michelle's grandmother had ever bothered looking through Rose's mementoes. Greg and his brother knew nothing about them—until now. As they soon learned, among them was the Purple Heart. Wrapped in an American flag.

Greg was astonished when he learned about the Purple Heart. "My dad's mouth about hit the floor," Michelle recalls. "He was really skeptical about Grandpa's visits in my dreams until I told him about the Purple Heart."

While Michelle viewed the Purple Heart incident as the irrefutable proof that she was indeed communicating with her grandfather, her grandmother was somewhat alarmed. "At one point, Grandma thought that because these dreams were so right on the money and since I had no way of knowing in advance the things Grandpa was saying, maybe the reason he was appearing to me was that he was coming back for her," Michelle explains. "But Grandpa never said that in any of the dreams. And Grandma, who's eighty-three, is fine. I think she understands better now that was not Grandpa's purpose."

By the summer of 1995, Michelle had written about her dreams of Grandpa Benjamin to the popular network TV program *Unsolved Mysteries*. She had received a positive response, and the show's producers were interested in possibly devoting a future segment to Michelle's experiences.

The next time Grandpa Benjamin came to Michelle in a dream, he told her that he was late for the racetrack. Michelle followed him and another man she did not recognize to a racetrack with very large white bleachers. Then Grandpa turned to Michelle and told her she could not go with them. "But," he added as he quickened his pace, "tell your father I have his lucky pencil. Pack your bags. You're going to the racetrack."

When Michelle told Greg about the lucky pencil, she recalls, "His eyes lit up and he just laughed and laughed." He then explained that when he was a little boy he used to go to the racetrack and try to sell pencils to people making notes in their racing forms. He would tell them that these were special lucky pencils and impudently remind them that if their horse hit, they owed him a tip.

Greg then asked Michelle to describe the man she saw in the dream, which she did, down to a small dark mole near his ear. Greg was stunned: the man Michelle had seen with Grandpa Benjamin was his brother, Dominic, who had shared a concession stand with him years ago. Great Uncle Dominic had died long before Michelle was born, and she had never seen photos of him or heard of his business with Grandpa. As Michelle continued describing the scene of her dream, Greg was convinced she had seen the landmarks, billboards, and buildings around the racetrack at Saratoga, which Grandpa frequented but Michelle herself had never visited. She had also seen them as they had been years, even decades, before her birth.

"I'd never seen or been to any racetrack," Michelle told me. "But I felt like I'd been there. It was strange."

Michelle interpreted the dream to mean that she would be going to Saratoga. In fact, the producers of *Unsolved Mysteries* originally intended to film part of her segment there, but the arrangements proved difficult. When Greg learned they would not be going to Saratoga, he was disappointed, but Michelle was not worried. "Grandpa told me to pack my bags because I was going to the racetrack. And I still believe him. There's some track we're going to." Sure enough, the show's producers arranged to film at a racetrack in Baltimore instead. Again, Grandpa was correct.

In October 1995, Michelle and Keith traveled to Baltimore, where they met the show's producers. As they left their motel for the first day of filming, Michelle noticed rose petals strewn near the front door. Michelle scooped up the petals and put them in her purse. That day's filming involved a re-creation of Michelle's dream visitation in her son's nursery. Even during the reenactment Michelle says she felt her grandfather's presence.

Upon returning home, Michelle decided to do something for her grandfather. She recalled her uncle telling her that Grandpa had a big peach-colored rosebush that he loved. She found a similar bush at a local garden store and planted the bush outside her bedroom window. She also planted some flowers in memory of her cousin Michael, who had died in a car crash at age nineteen, when Michelle was only nine.

Shortly after that, Michelle saw her cousin in a dream. He gave her several personal messages for his family members, which she later passed on. She awoke remembering the ring Michael was wearing: a silver ring with a square turquoise stone. When she mentioned it to her aunt, her aunt began to cry and acknowledged that, yes, Michael had worn such a ring, a gift from his father.

Michelle experienced many other visitations and paranormal, unexplained events. What is remarkable about Michelle's dream visitations is how much detail she could absorb and recall. Clearly, the fact that she could corroborate various aspects of her dreams—the French toast, the pail at the railroad tracks, the racetrack scene, the Purple Heart, Great Uncle Dominic's mole—enhanced her comfort and confidence in the experience. After the first couple of dreams, Michelle did not need to question whether she was really in the presence of her grandfather. She had the luxury of being able to enjoy the visitation, knowing she could probably verify it later. Another result was that Michelle discovered and developed her innate psychic abilities.

"The dream visits come to me when they want to. However, I can meditate, go to sleep, and see Grandpa. People should welcome these contacts with the other side because it's somebody you know. My mother said if these dreams and other experiences would have happened to her, she would have run. I told her, 'Well, if it was your mother and father, would you be scared of them? Don't you know that they love you?' It's not the dead you have to worry about; it's the living.

"They come to us because they love us and because there's unfinished business yet to be done. There's still more that my grandfather has to take care of, and I've got to help him do it. I had one dream in which Grandpa and my cousin Michael walked up together. And Grandpa handed me a beautiful peach rose, and I kissed it. Michael stood there and watched as Grandpa told me, 'You're a good kid, and you've come a long way helping me with my work. But we still have a long way to go.'"

One possible reason Grandpa Benjamin might have come through to Michelle was to reach his son, Greg. "There are a lot of unresolved things he told me in dreams about my father. Things I never knew. For example, Grandpa thinks he should have been more supportive. He asked me to tell my dad that he was sorry. He said that instead of going fishing and doing things with my dad when he was a boy, he should have put his arms around him more, told him he was a good son and that he loved him. He said he was sorry he had been so hard on him. He explained that he never wanted his kids to struggle as hard as he had, and he was so proud of them now."

Grandpa Benjamin also asked Michelle to tell her father that "he doesn't need anything to bring me around. All he has to do is open his heart and mind, and I'll be right there. Tell him to ask his mother for my old radio, and I'll try to let him know I'm around. Tell him that sometimes I like to sit in the chair that used to be next to the bed. And tell your dad that I saw him smile when the baby, Benjamin, walked to him."

It is only logical to wonder why Benjamin chose his granddaughter to communicate through. Why not simply appear to his wife or his son himself? Michelle has pondered that question herself often and thinks she has an idea.

"I think Grandpa probably felt he could use me as a vessel because I'm more open-minded. These messages would probably be more believable coming from me, and people would know it really was from Grandpa, because I hardly knew anything about him."

For Michelle, getting to know her grandfather again has been a positive, loving experience, one that renews her faith continuously. "Sometimes I go to where the rosebush is planted, and I talk to Grandpa. One very cold night in December—there was frost—I found a rose in full bloom. Grandpa had told me in a dream that I'd be rewarded and that my grandmother had something for me. Lo and behold, she did. Grandma gave me a seventy-five-year-old medallion with Saint Theresa on it. The rose is a sign of that saint. Also, my grandmother's sister's name was Rose.

"I don't blame nonbelievers for being skeptical, because I used to be one of those people. But Grandpa is still family. He's still keeping his eye on us. When his work is through, he'll leave. It is out of pure love that he comes back. I want to say that I hope this goes on forever. I would love all my family members to come visit me. But I know it is something that won't last forever, and one day I will have to say good-bye. These dreams and other experiences have changed my attitudes; they have changed me as a person. They have taught me to respect my family and taught me what family is all about."

RORY COMES HOME

Some of our most convincing cases span a time period and involve more than one paranormal event. Here, what later was revealed to be a precognitive dream, several instances of synchronicity, a dream visitation, and the corroboration of a stranger all came together to give a grieving young mother the gift of knowing her son was not dead.

First, it is important to say that Donna Buchanan's dream visitation from her son Rory is highly atypical. For one thing, it was preceded by what now seem to have been precognitive dreams and seemingly coincidental events. What makes Donna's experience so remarkable, however, is that information imparted in the dream led Donna to a stranger who provided corroboration, confirming that the communication from her son was real. The events that preceded and followed formed a cluster of synchronicities that reaffirmed the veracity of the dream. As you read this account, you may be struck, as we were, by how easily Donna might never have found the information she needed. At almost every turn in her journey, Donna witnessed events and happened upon bits of information that in and of themselves meant nothing to her. Yet when taken together and viewed in hindsight, every part of Donna's experience clearly served a purpose and had a meaning.

August 23, 1995, was a beautiful late-summer day, sunny and hot but uncharacteristically dry for New Jersey. Donna Buchanan stood in her driveway, awaiting the return of her fourteen-year-old son, Rory, who had gone with some friends to ride his dirt bike on a nearby road.

Rory was a handsome, loving boy, an excellent student and all-around athlete. With long dark hair, dark eyes, and a winning smile, Rory was a son of whom any mother would be proud. He had always been passionate about physical activity and sports. By the time he was four, he was riding his first pony; at age eight, he got another one. Despite his love of such daredevil sports as dirt-bike racing and in-line (Rollerblade) speed skating, he had never so much as broken a bone. In fact, soon after he took up riding dirt bikes, he took special lessons and a six-month safe-riding course. After that, he rode his bike every day, winter or summer, rain or shine. He seemed to know everything about dirt biking. Donna recalls, "He could take the bike apart and put it back together again."

For the first thirteen years of his life, Rory was Donna's only child. Although he remained close to his father, Wayne, whom Donna had divorced when Rory was just five, mother and son had a special bond. In January 1995, Donna, by then married to Bruce, gave birth to her second son, Rory's half-brother, Randy. Rory loved Randy, who was now seven months old. That August afternoon, as Donna thought about her life, she was more than content. She was, she thought, truly blessed.

She glanced at her watch. It was 3:30. *So maybe Rory is a little late,* Donna thought, *he's a good boy; he'll be home soon.* Suddenly Donna spotted a police car coming up the drive. *What do they want?* Donna wondered. As the two officers approached, she felt a sense of dread. They introduced themselves, then one of them said, "Your son Rory has been in an accident."

"I'm sorry," the other added softly. "He passed away."

Donna screamed so loudly that neighbors came running. All Donna remembers after that is lying on her living room floor, crying and thrashing so violently that it took the two police officers and an emergency medical technician to restrain her. Her legs bruised, her voice so strained she couldn't speak audibly for days, Donna moved through the next few days in a daze. Her doctor thought it best she take a sedative, but her insistence on nursing Randy made that impossible.

Wayne was also contacted, and a few hours later he accompanied Donna to the hospital morgue, where they were permitted to view their son. The police told them that Rory had died instantly when he rode into a steel cable strung across the little-used, densely wooded path he was riding on. Some distance behind Rory, two of his friends caught the glint of sun on the cable ahead and screamed out warnings. Rory, whose vision was obscured in the afternoon glare, tried to stop, but it was too late. The cable caught him by the throat, breaking his neck and killing him instantly. In the few seconds Donna and Wayne were permitted to view their beautiful boy, they saw the ugly, dark bruises that crossed his throat.

Rory's death devastated Donna. Despite the outpouring of support and love from friends, family, and the community—over eight hundred attended Rory's funeral—Donna found it impossible to summon the strength to go on. In the days immediately following Rory's death, she recalled an alarming, bizarre dream she'd had about two weeks before the accident. In it, she saw that someone had killed Rory by choking him. "Then I was strangling that person's mother," Donna recounts. "I never saw who it was who strangled Rory. I said to the woman, 'Your son killed my son. Now I'm going to kill you.' And I was throttling her." Later in the same dream, Donna and Rory had just gotten off one airplane and were waiting together to board another.

It all seemed so real, it took Donna a few minutes to realize that she'd been dreaming. She reasoned that the first part of her dream reflected her concern over a new friend of Rory's that she considered a bad influence. The birth of Randy and again having to worry about every detail of a child's well-being also left her feeling a bit more overprotective toward both her children. As for the business about airplanes, Donna took it as symbolic of the travel Rory had been doing recently, flying to sports competitions around the country.

When she told her son of the dream, Rory shrugged it off. In a strange way, that seemed to give Donna permission to dismiss the dream as well, chalking it up to maternal worry. She never considered that the dream might have been a premonition. That is, until after Rory died.

Now she tormented herself wondering if that dream contained something she had overlooked or ignored, perhaps a sign or message that might have saved Rory if only she had heeded it. Of course, there would be no way to know. However, in light of Rory's passing, other events of that summer took on a new meaning. For example, on an unusually warm day in May 1995, Donna and Rory were driving to a nearby beach. While Rory was absorbed in reading a magazine, a favorite song of his, the Stone Temple Pilots' "Big Empty," came blasting over the car radio. Inexplicably, a feeling of melancholy and foreboding washed over Donna. She later recalled thinking, *You'll always remember Rory when you hear this song.* When she realized what she was thinking, she quickly shook it off.

Three months later, in August 1995, shortly before Rory died, two young brothers drowned as they waded in the shallow, seemingly safe waters off Manasquan Inlet, in New Jersey. The tristate area had just endured a series of violent storms, and authorities had warned that the seas were far more dangerous than they appeared, but some people could not resist. The two brothers drowned when powerful waves pulled them under. The story was widely covered in the area, and Donna and Rory were talking about it when he suddenly said, "When I die, I want to be cremated and have my ashes scattered." Rory then mentioned a specific area that he loved, and after he died, Donna honored his wishes and cast his ashes into the sea there.

In that moment, though, Donna had wondered, *Why is my perfectly healthy fourteen-year-old son talking about this?* Most fourteen-year-olds would not even think of such things. On the contrary, most of them feel absolutely invincible. Again, Donna wondered if Rory could have experienced the same sense of foreboding she had. Did he, somewhere deep inside himself, somewhere beyond the shallow reach of words, know that he was going to die?

Donna would never know. A nurse, she had dealt with death and helped many patients and their loved ones. Yet when it came to her own loss, she was helpless. Despite Bruce's loving support and baby Randy's need for her, she continued to spiral down into a depression that verged on suicidal. Bruce became so concerned that he removed his hunting rifle and ammunition from the house. Donna refused medication and eschewed psychotherapy. As she finished reading a book about a British psychic medium, she began to wonder if indeed Rory was not living on somewhere. That night she prayed to Rory, "Please, you've got to give me a sign to let me know where you are. I need to know."

The next day her parents paid a visit after cashing a large check at a local bank. As her father leafed through the bills, he noticed an unusually ragged, dirty five-dollar bill, which he removed, intending to return it. Suddenly Donna heard her father exclaim, "Oh God, look at this bill!" On the back in green marker someone had written the words: "Read the book." At the bottom, printed in the same hand, was the title of our first book, *We Don't Die*. The writing looked as if it had been there for some time. Donna took this as a sign from Rory, and she smiled for the first time since he died. The circumstances also held further meaning, since every time Donna's father came to visit, he always gave Rory extra spending money—*always* a five-dollar bill.

What first seemed coincidental became a full-blown case of synchronicity when, just five days later, Donna's friend "Carol" phoned. Donna mentioned the five-dollar bill to her, and, without saying anything to Donna, Carol decided she would have her friend "Jane," who knew a lot about this kind of thing, talk to Carol. When Jane called Donna later that day, Donna described the five-dollar-bill incident and the words *we don't die*. Jane was silent for a moment, then said, "You know, there's a book on life after death called *We Don't Die*."

Donna was stunned. She replied that she had never heard of the book but that it could explain the words her father found on the bill. Jane then mentioned that she should also read our second book, and she kindly offered to lend the books to Donna. In them Donna found answers to many of her questions about life after death and the possibility of communication between this dimension and the next. Because these two titles concerned themselves specifically with paranormal, transdimensional communications as facilitated by a psychic medium, not direct after-death communication, Donna found herself hoping that one day through a reputable medium she might hear from Rory, as the subjects of those two books had heard from their loved ones.

About a month after Rory died, Donna was lying in bed late at night, tossing restlessly. She went down and sat in the living room for a while, where Bruce passed her a couple of times but said nothing. Donna secretly hoped he would sit and cry with her, or just give her a hug, but he did neither, feeling that she might need to be alone. Still crying, Donna climbed back into bed and fell immediately into a deep sleep. Suddenly she was dreaming, but it was no ordinary dream. The colors were brighter, the sounds were louder; everything about it seemed more real than real. Donna immediately realized that this was a visitation from Rory.

In her dream, she was very excited. She heard a car in the distance and exclaimed to Bruce, "See? I told you Rory would come back! I told you he was coming back! He's here! He's here now! I told you I heard a car. He's here!" She ran to the front porch and peered out the window into the darkness. There she saw a car she did not recognize. The doors opened, and there stood Rory. Emerging from the driver's side was a boy she had never seen before, small and slender, with a turned-up nose and sandy-colored hair. He looked to be a little older than Rory, perhaps eighteen or nineteen.

As she watched, Rory and the boy walked to the side of the house. Donna cried out, "Where are you going?" to which someone—Donna could not discern who—replied, "They're going to the horses."

"Oh, fine," Donna answered. The next thing she knew, she was opening the front door, and Rory walked in. She thought to herself, *Oh, look at the spotlights hitting him right in the face.* On the side of the house was a light mounted and angled to illuminate the driveway, but there was no way that it could light someone's face where Rory stood.

He looks wonderful, Donna thought, as she studied his face bathed in bright light, a light that seemed to be coming from within him. "He looked at me as if to say, 'I wish you'd cut it out. Here I am now. See me?'"

Then Donna pointed to the boy she did not recognize. "Who's that with you? Who is that?" she asked.

"Oh that? That's Tim Russ," Rory answered without hesitation.

Donna could not place the name. She could not recall Rory having a friend named Tim, and the boy's face was totally unfamiliar to her. Yet he seemed as alive and real as Rory. Then she realized that Rory might not have said Russ. Rush, perhaps? She could not be sure, but she felt the time in the dream precious. She did not ask any more questions.

Suddenly she felt Rory hugging her. "His hug was electric. I could feel him. I could smell him. I could feel his arms around my waist. I was lit up by it. I was thrilled by it," Donna recalls.

The next thing Donna knew, she and Rory were lying on the floor of a darkened room. Bruce was there, too, but also in the dark. Rory's face again seemed brightly illuminated. This time Donna thought it was the moonlight, except that when she looked out the window, there was no moon. Rory placed his head in his mother's lap.

"Rory, do you still have a mark around your neck?" Donna asked.

Rory tilted his head up to show his mother that he did not and then said, "No, no. I don't have to worry about that now."

Donna then turned to Bruce. "See, I told you he was coming back. But the question is, Can we see him during the day?"

In that instant, the dream evaporated. Donna bolted upright in her bed. "I just dreamed—" she gasped.

"Yeah, I know," Bruce said.

"How do you know?" she asked.

"Because you were smiling and kind of whimpering in your sleep. So I didn't want to move a muscle because I was afraid I'd wake you. And I really felt like you were dreaming about Rory."

The couple stayed up for the rest of the night. "I was so elated—excited, frightened, and every emotion you can think of. This was so real. It was so real that I actually jumped up and ran out onto the front porch and looked outside. In other words, I went through the same motions that I'd gone through in the dream. I looked out the window, opened the door, and looked around outside. I even looked at the floor where we were lying and sitting in the dream."

Everything about the dream reaffirmed for her that Rory was not dead but alive, somewhere. While she took some comfort in that revelation, she found her thoughts often returning to the other boy. She knew Rory had no friends named Tim, but she searched through Rory's things, called his friends, scanned the local telephone book, and asked everyone she met if they had ever heard of "this boy Tim," just in case. No one had. Donna kept wondering not only who this Tim was, but why he was with her son. Almost everything else in her dream made sense to her but this.

As before, a series of synchronistic events led Donna to her answer. Four days later, Rory's father phoned to tell Donna about another book she might read: *Our Children Forever*. This, our third book, was written specifically for bereaved parents and presented psychic readings involving children who had died. As Donna read the story of a Long Island boy named Tim Wresch she felt, as she said, "as if someone had hit me in the back of the head."

Tim had been born with two chambers in his heart rather than the normal four. Defying the doctor's gloomy prognosis—that the Wresches should not even consider taking baby Tim home, since he was certain to die soon—Helena and Tim Sr. encouraged their son to make the most of life. Despite his myriad health problems, Tim participated in all but the most strenuous sports, and he excelled in school and several extracurricular activities. He was exuberant and optimistic, even living with the realization that his chances of reaching adulthood were slim. So when doctors from the Mayo Clinic contacted the Wresches about a new procedure that offered Tim's only real hope, they and Tim agreed to take the risk. Sadly, the strain of the surgery proved too much for Tim's already damaged heart, and he died five days later.

As she read, Donna sensed that this was more than simple coincidence. Not only did the boy in the story and the one in her dream share the same first name, but the surnames were remarkably close. In addition, Tim's physical description, even his age—he would have been nineteen at the time of Donna's dream if he had lived—matched. Somehow Donna just knew this was the Tim she had seen in her dream, Rory's new friend on the other side. Yet how could she know for sure?

"I couldn't get this boy's name out of my head. I felt like I had to find his family. It was like I was being pushed to do it," Donna recalls.

The book mentioned that the Wresch family had been active in a local parents' bereavement group, so Donna started there, leaving phone messages for Helena Wresch with several Long Island support group chapters. What Donna could not have known was that on the same evening she was leaving her name and number, praying for an answer, Helena Wresch was feeling particularly depressed: that day would have been Tim's nineteenth birthday.

Luckily, one of Donna's messages found its way to Helena. A week later Helena phoned Donna and introduced herself as Tim's mother. Donna told Helena, who was very open and supportive, of her dream. "It was uncanny," Donna says of their first talk. "Mrs. Wresch said Timmy loved horses. In fact, only three weeks before he died, she had sent him to her sister's home in upstate New York, where they rode horses and dirt bikes." Helena also confirmed that Tim fit the description of the boy in Donna's dream and sent her a photograph of Tim. Donna had no doubt that Rory and Tim were friends on the other side. And Helena Wresch agrees that Rory was just the kind of boy Tim would have sought out for friendship.

Why did Rory appear with Tim? This is one question Donna has considered often. "I believe that as soon as Rory arrived on the other side, he met Timmy Wresch. Rory was concerned about our grief and wanted to let us know that he was all right. He enlisted Timmy's help."

Around Thanksgiving of 1995 Helena dreamed of Tim for the first time in several years. She saw him standing among a group of boys. She noticed he was wearing around his neck a ribbon bearing a large round medal. "Tim, where did you get that medal? Whose is it?" Helena recalled asking.

"You know whose it is," Tim replied.

A few days later Helena received a letter from Donna. In it she found a photograph of Rory wearing the medal he had won weeks before his death for in-line speed skating. Helena recognized it as the medal Tim had worn in her dream. (Donna had no way of knowing about Helena's recent dream visitation from Tim.) As Helena looked at the picture, she knew that Tim's wearing the medal in her dream was a reference to his new friend, Rory. Could there be any further doubt that the two boys, strangers on this side of the veil, were good friends in the afterlife? Could anyone deny that the two were, in some way, still alive?

"When you lose a child, it's a very traumatic experience. You expect to lose your parents, or even a sibling," Donna reflects. "But you don't want to see your child in a casket. That terrible moment when I learned Rory was dead will be with me if I live to be ninety. I'll always remember how that day smelled when the police came to my driveway to tell me.

"It's a shock to your body, mind, and soul. I actually became sick from this. I was always the kind of person who could do three, four, or five things at once—you know, a real juggling act. Now my concentration is shot. I can only do one thing at a time. My body is tired with aches and pains that I never had before. I have no energy. Fortunately, Bruce and I are close. We have the same beliefs, so that really helped.

"I take comfort in the dream visit from Rory. But there is always an element of fear in it. I don't know why. I can't really explain. Maybe it's a residual fear from the shock of what we've been through. I think I'm afraid it could happen again. Rory's death has made me more fearful. I'm afraid to drive, to jump my horse. I'm afraid for Bruce and for my baby, Randy. If I didn't have my baby, Randy, when Rory was killed, I think I would have just blown my brains out that night.

"Sometimes I feel like the souls of Randy and Rory knew each other even before Randy was born. Maybe they had a pact: Rory would stay for fourteen years and then go back. But just before that, Randy would be born, because I couldn't have made it through Rory's death without Randy. I feel that this is true. I don't think there are coincidences. Things happen because they're supposed to, and when they're supposed to.

"I consider my baby, Randy, a gift. Toward the end of my second pregnancy, I was forty-one years old. I hadn't been pregnant in thirteen years. We were amazed. I'd lay in bed at night and ask, 'God, why is this happening now? Why am I getting this baby?' I looked up the meaning of the name Randy. It's Anglo-Saxon for 'a strong shield.' Which Randy is. He's shielding me, and he'll always be my comfort."

Donna recalled a conversation she'd had with Rory before he died. Rory had always called Randy Baby Randy, and on this occasion he told Donna that Randy was going to be Baby Randy for the rest of his life. "You mean when Randy is twenty and you're thirty-three, you're still going to call him Baby Randy?" Donna asked. She was partially kidding and fully expected Rory to say something kidding in return.

Instead, Rory turned suddenly serious and replied, "No, I won't see him then. I'll probably meet him in a war in a desert in Saudi Arabia someplace."

"You're a weirdo!" Donna answered, and they both laughed. After Rory's death, however, the exchange opened new questions for Donna.

"Could Rory have meant that someday Randy will be in a war in a desert? And that Randy will die and meet Rory? I got very upset. I couldn't take that again. Then I heard a voice in my head say, 'Don't worry, Ma. You won't be here.' Does that mean I'll be gone? That I'll have died by then so I won't have to go through that again?"

Hearing from Rory has changed not only Donna's outlook but her whole family's. "We definitely believe it's true," she says. "Both my husband and my ex-husband are receptive and open to psychic experiences. My dad is now a believer; this has changed him. If you had told this story to my mother a year earlier, she would have laughed in your face. I think she's still afraid to embrace it totally, but now she does believe. In retrospect, when she looks back over her life and some of the experiences and dreams she's had, she thinks differently about them. For instance, my mom lost both of her brothers within the past ten years. Then she had a dream about her late brother

Jimmy. In the dream she asked him, 'What are you doing here? You're dead.' 'Oh, no, I'm not dead. I'm fine,' Jimmy answered. At the time, Mom brushed it off as just a dream. But now she's thinking about it.

"Bruce is waiting to see Rory, although he says he's felt him around. On a couple of occasions, when we were watching TV late at night, Bruce looked at me sitting on the couch and said he saw a smoky haze around or near me. I didn't see anything. But both of us have seen pinpricks of light at the same time.

"Meanwhile, I have to live the rest of my life here without him. I find it very difficult. He was our only child for thirteen years. He was the light of all our lives. He was our shining star for so long, and he was turning out to be such a good kid. The high school he would have attended is going to dedicate a tree to him. And there's a memorial fund in his name for in-line skating, as well as a perpetual trophy in his name.

"We had a very close relationship. We were good buddies. We hung out a lot. I miss him as a friend. I mean, not many fourteen-year-old boys kiss their mother goodnight. But he wasn't a momma's boy. He was a wonderful kid.

"We truly believe we will see Rory again and that he is around us. Physically, that doesn't help. However, the dream did help me. Had I never heard anything from him, I know it would have been much worse."

Donna found in her visit from Rory not only comfort in knowing that he still lives, but a new way to view life here on earth. Speaking for her family, Donna says, "I feel that since the dream from Rory, we've reached another level of understanding. Events are happening around us and to us that make me feel that we're going to be blessed by evolving psychically. It's as if something is blooming.

"I believe that there is a continuation of life—that we just go from one plane to the next. Our loved ones who've passed on are still with us. We will see them again. They are closer than we think. We move on and we will see them again. I have to believe that when I pass on and open my eyes on the other side, Rory will be standing there. He'll say to me, 'See, Ma? I told you. It's fine.'"

10

FINDING YOUR PATH TO THE PIERLESS BRIDGE

Faith—is the Pierless Bridge
Supporting what We see
Unto the Scene that We do not—.

—EMILY DICKINSON, POEM NO. 915

For all that it illuminates about the after-death communication experience, Donna Buchanan's incredible dream also leaves us wondering, Why aren't all direct communications experiences like this one? To that, we have no answer. In the last chapter, we warned that Donna's experience was exceptional, as are those of many people whose stories you have read. For every person who has shared an after-death communication, someone has said, "I loved my father so much. Why does he never come to me?" or "My sister had three visitations from our mother, yet I've had none." One of our friends is both amused and confused by a deceased lover who, while neglecting the love of his life, persists in contacting the conservative grandmother who vociferously disapproved of their homosexual relationship. Others have experiences that they find wanting. "My husband came and stood at the foot of my bed," one widow told us. "He said nothing, and then he went away. Will he ever come back?"

People are often frustrated because there are no complete answers to these questions and the entire after-death communication process seems beyond our control. Perhaps because these communications often occur spontaneously, we conclude that we are merely passive receivers in the process, surprise witnesses. If we look at many cases, however, we spot an intriguing trend. For every person whose direct communication appeared "out of the blue," another told of having experienced a crisis, of engaging in prayer or meditation with the deceased in mind, or otherwise appealing for help. Does this indicate that we have the ability to initiate communication from the other side?

We believe the answer is a cautious yes. Before we continue, though, let us look at some other possible means of reaching out to the other side. Humankind's search for evidence of an afterlife and attempts to initiate contact with its inhabitants go back millions of years. History is replete with prophets, oracles, seers, witches, saints, mediums, and others who claimed to have been in touch with the other side. Although not widely recorded, individuals have also explored the possibilities using proven, accepted practices, such as prayer and meditation, and such questionable aids as Ouija boards and techniques like scrying (an ancient form of crystal-, water-, or mirror-gazing) and do-it-yourself séances.

We are not saying that questionable methods don't work. After all, if just one of the millions who have sat around Ouija boards had received a bona fide communication, then we would have to say that it works. However, our focus here is not on the myriad methods, techniques, and practices that may have proved effective sometime, somewhere, under certain circumstances. Books on each of the practices we will be discussing here abound. What we are concerned with here are those practices shown conducive to direct after-death communication experiences, with a special emphasis on those that people we've interviewed mention most. That said, however, it is important to pass on several caveats about any journey into the unknown.

BE PREPARED

Anything is possible. Anything might work. That does not mean, however, that all approaches are equally valid, effective, or safe.

Don't Talk to Strangers

For example, many psychic mediums consider Ouija boards less than accurate and rarely credible. Some even believe that "low spirits" control the Ouija and that they are likely to impart inaccurate information, if any at all. The question of attracting negativity by initiating contact is also a matter of concern. While most New Age books stress the spiritual realm's kindly, loving aspects, it seems that negative, troublesome, even dangerous spirit entities do exist. If people with extensive paranormal experience, such as spiritual teachers and reputable psychics, proceed with caution and respect, so should you.

At the very least a bad psychic experience can be emotionally upsetting and disappointing. Methods such as scrying and using Ouija boards offer many opportunities for projection. For example, one may subconsciously move the planchette to the desired letters on the board. Overall, we feel that the drawbacks and shortcomings of such methods outweigh the possibility that you may receive a true message.

Increase Your Awareness of Received Communications

You may never have experienced an after-death communication, or you may recall an experience that you have always wondered about, or perhaps you have had several. For most people, it is a safe bet that several communications have been received but not processed—not recognized, recognized but not acknowledged, acknowledged but not understood. To analogize for a moment, you can think of after-death messages as valentines. Some will never be opened because their intended recipients never bother looking in the mailbox. No technique or method does more to facilitate direct after-death communications than openness, curiosity, and courage. Direct communications are not monologues, but invitations to conversation. The work of understanding these messages continues long after the phenomenon ceases. As you have read in many of our stories, those who derived the most satisfaction and comfort from their experiences were those who put effort into finding the answers, filling in the picture, and verifying what they did not understand.

For example, we know from our study of psychic readings that mediums and psychics give forth names and information that the subject simply cannot confirm. Sometimes subjects just do not know, but often the name or the connection the psychic sought literally pops into their heads hours, days, or weeks later. If we base an assessment of the reading only on the reading itself and fail to follow up with the subject, we will find many "misses" that were actually "hits."

We might draw the same analogy to dream visitations. Because dreams are the ultimate private, internal experience, and since so many of us are raised to view dreams as the meaningless ramblings of our sleeping inner selves, one cannot even begin to guess how many compelling dream visitations have come and gone. For example, had Donna not read *Our Children Forever*, Tim Wresch would have remained an interesting but minor figure in her dream visitation. Had Donna not had the perseverance to track down Helena Wresch, she would never have received the definitive confirmation of Tim's identity. And had Donna and Helena Wresch not struck up a friendship and exchanged photos, the medal Tim wore in his visitation to Helena would have seemed meaningless.

Rather than follow the lead of skeptics, who would dismiss Donna's entire case as a series of coincidences, we prefer to begin by asking ourselves, What are the odds there could be that many interrelated coincidences? We are not statisticians, but no reasonable person could place the odds in Donna's case at anything better than one in millions, even billions. Indeed, attributing a complex multisubject, multiphenomena experience like Donna's to chance suggests an unscientific, almost superstitious belief that coincidence explains away any other possible source.

It is important to recognize, however, that the pieces of Donna's communication were, for the most part, just that: pieces. Like many loved ones communicating from the other side, Rory delivered messages that were both direct and elusive. Certainly Donna would have been satisfied with a simple "I love you" from her son, yet Rory seemed intent on giving her something far more complex and rich, something she could never question. While Rory made sure his mother got the message, it was Donna's job to discover its every meaning.

We have all had the experience of planning a vacation yet arriving at our destination somewhat disappointed or pleasantly surprised. If the afterlife were exactly as it seems based on substantiated, reliable accounts, everyone who loved or cared about someone they left behind would come back. Yet even if we assume that there are countless visitations and other direct-communication experiences that are never remembered, discussed, or documented, it still leaves countless others whom one might expect to return who yet do not. Do they choose not to return for a specific reason? Do they return and we simply fail to notice them? Or do they return and we rationalize their appearance as the result of some phenomenon we are more comfortable with, like the breeze blowing the curtains (even though the windows are closed)?

Increase Your Level of Sensory Awareness

Once you know what to listen for, what to look for, you may discover that you have had direct after-death communications you did not recognize. When you think about these experiences—whether past or future—try to eliminate words like *impossible, coincidence, chance,* and *doubt* from your mind. When thinking about a possible communication, train yourself to say, for example, "I felt my mother's presence," not "I felt my mother's presence, but . . ." Or "Last night I dreamed that my grandfather handed me a rose," not "You're going to think I'm crazy, but last night I dreamed . . ."

We are all so conditioned to disbelieve that it may take some conscious effort to maintain a positive, open approach. But give it a try. Start with the objective of confirming your experience rather than discrediting it. Seek out the factors that point to its being anything but a coincidence, chance, or your imagination. Consider the date, the day, the time, the circumstances, or anything else that might increase the likelihood that it was a real communication. When something occurs that seems impossible, inexplicable, odd, or strange, look again. Has it happened before? Can you discern a pattern? Does it have any connection to a deceased loved one?

Learning more about all related paranormal phenomena will also help you identify communications from the other side. Think of after-death communications as an opera. People from a wide range of social, economic, and educational backgrounds attend. For some, it is a profound, almost spiritual experience; for others, an expensive, tedious night out. For aficionados, every word, every note, every nuance of the performance is significant. For others, it's just a lot of people singing loudly. Everything about the opera that night is the same for everyone except for how well different audience members are prepared to perceive it.

Learn to be more aware of your environment: the sights, sounds, scents, and textures of your everyday world. Try to slow down and really pay attention to the details of some mundane chore you perform every day, like washing the dishes or turning on your computer or eating a meal. Really think about what you are doing. Try focusing on what you are doing right now: What does this book feel like? How does it smell? How would you describe the typeface? The shade of white these words are printed on? Recall what your spouse or kids had on this morning when they left the house. Try to list the objects on your mantel, the flowers in your garden, or the books on a particular shelf.

Think about your deceased loved ones. In case after case, the key identifying details that cinched a spirit's identity or proved a communication genuine were not great events but everyday details. In her dream, Barbara Califano's grandfather Antonio did not appear hard at work in the shoe repair store she had heard so much about but savoring a treat he could not enjoy before. Remember the days you spent together. What did your loved one enjoy doing? What drove her crazy? What were some of his favorite expressions, places, foods, songs, books, and works of art? Hobbies? Nicknames? Habits? Idiosyncrasies? Favorite colognes? Perhaps visit someplace that was special to you both, or keep around you objects that remind you of them. You may be surprised to discover how many little things you forget. Simply doing this exercise will occasionally bring you closer to those who have crossed over, if only because you are focused on them as living persons.

After just a few of these exercises, you may be surprised at how many bits of information escape our attention every minute. It may seem a time-consuming activity, but in fact, after a little bit of practice, heightened awareness can become as automatic as any other habit.

A woman we interviewed recalled that after her father passed on, she began discovering coins in the most unusual places, at the most unexpected times. She also sensed that her father was close by whenever she saw a coin, and so she made the connection. As a young girl, she would accompany her father on walks. Invariably, they would find dimes, nickels, and quarters, and her father always picked them up and gave them to her. The woman regarded the appearance of the coins as a comforting and reassuring sign of her father's love.

This is a good example of a subtle sign that might have been over-looked or dismissed. For the purposes of this book, we have included many dramatic, exceptional, and verifiable cases. The fact is, most direct communications are subtle, elusive, and brief. That does not mean, however, that they are not important. Recall the story of John Hay, who chose not to ignore what proved to be a life-saving message about his mother. Suppose Rowland Perkins had continued to his Hollywood business meeting instead of listening to the voice urging him to visit his father. These individuals could have dismissed their experiences as imaginary or hallucinatory, but their very real lives would have been poorer for it.

Remember that these people had no other reason to follow their instincts about these communications than what they felt, sensed, or believed. They had no "proof" beyond their feelings, which they wisely followed. Heightening your sensory awareness also helps in distinguishing between true coincidence and genuine meaningful syn-chronicity, the shadow of a moving car on your bedroom wall and an apparition.

PRAYER AND MEDITATION

The most effective way to initiate direct after-death communications is through prayer. The most effective way to prepare to receive after-death communications is through meditation. Through prayer, we send messages of love. We can pray aloud or silently, and we can do it anywhere, anytime. Prayer is simply a thought consciously conveyed with energy and emotion. Psychic readings often mention prayer, and reputable psychics encourage us to pray. Many people report having had direct communications under circumstances that suggested they came in response to prayers or thoughts of their loved one. David Elliot giving his father the Twenty Questions answer (cited in chapter 2) is an example of this phenomenon. And you may have noticed that many dream visitations included here were preceded by pleas, prayers, or highly emotional episodes. Although prayer is usually considered a waking act, we can also pray in our dreams.

We can pray to our loved ones, beseeching their help, sending greetings, or simply talking to them. We can also pray for them. Both are important. When we pray for them, we give them a gift, a surge of love that helps them on the other side. World religions recognize the power of prayer, and all have special prayers for the deceased. Repeated prayers, such as rosaries and mantras, are considered particularly powerful.

It is important to remember that whether you pray formally or informally, every day or simply when you think about it, we need to stay in touch. Most of us would reject the suggestion that we venerate the dead, but in fact we do, in everything from donations made in their memories to the simple prayers we offer. Simply thinking of them fondly, remembering something they did or said or loved, reminds them that they are not forgotten. And neither are we.

It is well known that the late entertainer George Burns regularly visited the mausoleum of his wife, Gracie Allen. He said he did it just to talk to her and keep her up to date on what was happening in his life. No doubt it was cathartic for him. Did Gracie hear him? Burns seemed to think so. He once quipped, "I don't tell her jokes at the cemetery when I visit. She'd heard them all before she died."

Burns understood what we all need to do: pray in positive and loving thoughts, not negative ones. Even in the midst of tragedy, we must not neglect those we have lost. They may need our loving thoughts even more. The father of a sixteen-year-old murder victim told *The New York Post* that he "has daily chats with his slain child at the shrine he erected" near where she was strangled. Some would regard this as morbid, but this father's focus is obviously on the bond between himself and his child, not the how or the why of her death. "I go there every morning," the man told the reporter. "I clean up, I talk to her. It's almost impossible to describe the pain." He tells his daughter, "We all miss you."

The recent interest in the power of prayer is really nothing new. The relationship between prayer and love was expressed beautifully over a hundred years ago by the Reverend Henry Ward Beecher: "I never knew how to worship until I knew how to love." Nineteenth-century parapsychologist F.W.H. Myers once said that "love, empathy and compassion somehow make it possible for the mind to transcend the limitations of the body. We are frequently connected emotionally with one another deeply and lovingly." Compare that to the words of Dr. Larry Dossey, who writes that "empathy, compassion, and love seem to form a literal bond—a resonance—or glue between living things."[1]

If prayer can be described as placing a call, meditation is sitting quietly so that you can hear the phone ring back. Through meditation we free our minds of distractions so that we can devote our full attention to the messages our deceased loved ones may send. We saw the power of meditation in the case of John Hay, whose ability to focus intently at a critical moment saved his mother's life (see chapter 5).

To be most effective, meditation must be studied and practiced. The best-known meditation techniques were developed in Eastern cultures and are practiced in Zen and Tibetan Buddhism, yogic disciplines, and Transcendental Meditation, considered the most easily mastered form. All seek to quiet, block, or silence the busy conscious mind. Anyone can learn to practice meditation, which also has such practical benefits as reducing stress, lowering blood pressure, and encouraging relaxation.

One effect of meditation is an alteration of brain wave patterns to the alpha state, in which we are relaxed but awake. Conscious thought recedes, and the subconscious, nonlogical part of the mind dominates, making it easier for us to recognize paranormal experiences. In meditation, direct after-death communications may occur, as may other paranormal experiences.

The relationship between prayer and meditation is well illustrated in Anne Puryear's poignant account of her fifteen-year-old son Stephen's suicide and their after-death communications. The communications began shortly after Mrs. Puryear prayed to her spirit guides to speak to her late son. Following that, she became "quiet, meditated, and listened." Usually she would feel Stephen's presence in just a few minutes. She and her son began a series of conversations, which others could witness as well. Puryear writes that her communications with her son helped renew her faith. They also enabled him to answer many questions she had about his suicide.

In one conversation, Stephen commented on the problems of direct communication, from his side. As he told his mother: "The souls here try very hard to reach the people they knew. But hundreds of souls simply never get through to anyone because those they are trying to reach don't know that it's really possible to talk to us in this dimension. It can be very frustrating."

VISUALIZATION

Visualization is another enhancement technique that focuses energy on the departed loved one and may draw them closer. When you visualize the loved one, you may want to concentrate on an item that belonged to them or that you associate with them—a piece of jewelry, a photograph, or some other significant object. Although there have been instances where intense visualization seemed to precipitate psychokinetic activity, thoughts of the departed loved one usually prompt subtle signs, such as feeling their presence. We can also combine visualization with prayer, meditation, and dream communication.

ENHANCING DREAM COMMUNICATIONS

Alhough dream visitations occur while we are asleep, we can enhance and enrich them. By doing so, we can become more active in the communications process and actually initiate the visitation. Through a technique called lucid dreaming, dreamers maintain awareness that they are dreaming and can say and do things during the dream that influence how it unfolds. You might wonder how you can exercise conscious will from an unconscious state, and you would not be alone. Some scientists believe that lucid dreaming is not possible, but a growing body of evidence suggests otherwise. Children and some adults apparently have a natural ability to dream lucidly.

There are several current books about lucid dreaming, and we encourage anyone tempted to try it to read up first. While its proponents claim that lucid dreaming can enhance creativity, force psychological change, and improve physical health, they also warn that because it produces dreams that are so real, it can be a disturbing experience for those who are emotionally vulnerable or have psychological problems. A possible spiritual component of lucid dreaming is suggested by the fact that survivors of near-death experiences (NDEs) often show an increased ability to dream lucidly, and some researchers believe that the out-of-body experience occurs in the lucid dreaming state.

Even if you do not have the time, energy, or inclination to pursue lucid dreaming, you can still improve your ability to recognize and remember dream visitations that occur. First, send out the call. Prior to falling asleep, talk to and visualize your departed loved one. Say silently or aloud, "I'm going to contact my departed loved one, and I will then remember my dream when I awake." You may also make your dream wish part of a prayer or meditation that you repeat throughout the day. You are taking the first step toward approaching your dream consciously by simply referring to and thinking about it while in a conscious state. It sounds obvious, but think how little we think of our dreams as something that happens to us.

If you do dream of your loved one, take the time to remember your dream communication: write it down, or record it on tape, preferably before you get out of bed. Remind yourself of the details, even those that seem insignificant. This way you can look back if, for example, a particular image or thought recurs. Just by consciously planning to dream and reminding yourself to remember, you will have greatly increased your ability to recall what you do experience. You may find yourself receiving more dream visitations than you thought possible.

OUT-OF-BODY EXPERIENCES

Can your soul or consciousness travel out of your physical body and return? Yes. During NDEs, some meditative or paranormal states, and physical death, the spiritual self clearly separates from the body. How common are out-of-body experiences (OBEs)? Surprisingly, Dr. Stanley Krippner's late-1970s survey found that three out of ten people believed they had had an OBE. Robert Monroe, who had studied the phenomenon extensively, claimed most of us leave our bodies during sleep.

Out-of-body experiences are the field trips of direct after-death communications. Many people we spoke with described experiences that suggested OBEs, even though they did not use that term and in some cases probably never heard of it. It was not unusual for someone to say that one or several of their dream visitations seemed to have "occurred somewhere else." Several told of awakening with the feeling that they had gone someplace or returned from a journey where they had met their loved one. Experts who believe that OBEs have a role in direct communication suggest that it is easiest to "rendezvous" when the loved one has died recently.

Although OBEs occur during the dream state, they are not dreams (although they may be lucid dreams). OBEs are not that difficult to accomplish. Some believe that the best time to attempt an out-of-body journey is in the hypnagogic state, which occurs shortly before fully awakening, when the mind is awake but the physical body asleep. There is evidence that various other paranormal experiences, such as receiving precognitions, commonly occur in this state.

Tell yourself repeatedly that you are going to have an out-of-body experience and promise your loved one that you will meet him or her. Once you begin to feel that you are dreaming consciously, will yourself to leave your body. Because you are, in a sense, not really dreaming, don't be surprised if your OBE is extremely vivid and realistic. You may need to remind yourself that you are in control of the experience, that you can and will return to your body whenever you wish. That said, it is also important to remember that OBEs can occur when we've done nothing to initiate them. If you find yourself in the middle of a spontaneous OBE, remind yourself that there is nothing wrong and go with it. Obviously, if you find the idea scary, you should not consciously initiate this experience.

ON THE TECHNOLOGICAL FRONTIER
BETWEEN OUR WORLDS

Spirit Photography

One frustrating aspect of direct communications is that they rarely produce photographic, audio, or videotaped evidence. Photographs of spirits are extremely rare; however, some do exist, although, as you will read, most such "recordings" are produced by accident.

In 1993, Tracy Abbott accepted a job in California that would require relocating from New York City. Before moving, she decided to indulge her favorite hobby, visiting homes preserved from the Victorian period. New York has its share of charming, stately old buildings, and Tracy had a favorite: the Old Merchant's House in lower Manhattan, near the Bowery. This gracious three-story house was built by and home to Seabury Tredwell, a wealthy merchant. There he lived with his daughter, Gertrude, who was born in the house and lived there until her death at the age of ninety-three, in 1933. Gertrude was a beautiful young woman doomed to a lonely life of spinsterhood after her father forced her to end her only romance. A virtual recluse, Gertrude rarely left the house.

As Tracy thought of Gertrude's sad life, she could not help but note the dramatic contrast between the beautiful house and its tormented resident. Walking through the rooms, Tracy felt drawn to the third-floor bedroom where Gertrude spent most of her time. As she had throughout the house, Tracy snapped some photographs, using an ordinary 35-millimeter camera with built-in flash. One shot captured a white marble fireplace, upholstered chair, and small wooden table with a Bible.

When the photos were developed several weeks later, Tracy noticed a peculiar image near the fireplace. A white, translucent plume ran the entire length of one photograph. The furnishings behind it were discernible. None of the other photos Tracy took that day showed anything unusual. The image made no sense, and Tracy thought it curious but gave it no more thought than to dub the picture jokingly "Gertrude's ghost."

Tracy forgot the picture until three years later when she was leafing through a guidebook to New York City. The book explained that the Old Merchant's House "was alleged to be haunted by a spirit assumed to be Tredwell's daughter. It was also said that a white aura has been seen above the fireplace." Had Tracy unknowingly captured Gertrude's spirit on film?

From the very first spirit photography in 1861 until the present, controversy has surrounded the field. Spirit photography got its bad reputation during the Age of Spiritualism, when photography was relatively new and the public unsophisticated. In the 1860s and 1870s hucksters passed off double exposures and light-streaked prints as evidence of spirit presences. Looking at some of these alleged spirit photographs today it is impossible to imagine how anyone fell for them, but then if we consider how easily we fall for special effects in movies today, it is not surprising at all. Ironically, the more advanced the technology, the more easily we are fooled.

This is not to say, however, that all purported spirit photographs are fakes. There are a few that have been determined to be genuine, but these are so rare and so often taken by accident that the odds of capturing such an image are close to nil. Professional paranormal researchers have recorded unexplainable forms of light and other unseen shapes at the sites of hauntings, but even then it takes much research and expertise to eliminate conclusively other causes, like technical problems with equipment and film.

I have seen a handful of photographs that are very likely true spirit photographs. In each case, the photographer was not looking for anything unusual, and the images turned up unexpectedly. In every instance, what may be a visual manifestation of a spirit occurs in only one of several photographs taken at the same time with the same equipment. What can we make of these few seemingly random events?

Given the millions of photographs we take every day and the minuscule number of even possible spirit images, we do not recommend loading up on film and spending days shooting in hopes of catching a glimpse of Aunt Minnie. If spirit images were easily captured and appeared on only one-millionth of all the photographs taken in a single year, we would have thousands of possible examples. That just does not happen, which leads us to conclude that there are many other cheaper, more productive, more spiritually evolved methods of making contact.

If you do chance across a photograph that contains an unexplained image, consider the possibilities. If you feel strongly that you may have a true spirit photograph, seek the advice of someone knowledgeable in basic photographic technique and try to rule out other possible causes. You will probably find, to your disappointment perhaps, that photos never lie.

Electronic Voice Phenomena

Electronic voice phenomena (EVP) refers to the electronic recording of spirit voices. The term is also used to refer to the capture of spirit voices and images on computers, televisions, and videotape. The premise behind EVP is simple: voices and images of the deceased that are undetectable to human sense may be picked up and recorded electronically in a form that we can see and hear only when they are played back. This may not be as far-fetched as it sounds, when we think that what we consider possible is determined by what we understand as the limitations of current technology. For example, back in the early days of X ray, the very idea that we could image the human body to detect variations in temperature or show it in three dimensions seemed impossible. Yet today we have thermographic imaging and magnetic resonance imaging (MRI). Anyone with a dog knows that there is a wide band of auditory and visual phenomena beyond normal human perception. Who is to say that spirits are not present in a form we cannot normally perceive but can record?

Many of those involved in exploring EVP are electronics experts, engineers, physicists, physicians, and psychologists. Friedrich Jergenson is generally credited with discovering EVP. He was tape-recording birds near his home, and when he played back the tape, he heard a voice speaking in Norwegian about "nocturnal bird songs." He continued to make other recordings to see if they picked up other voices he did not hear. He claimed to have recorded voices that gave him personal information about himself and provided instructions on how he could better record more such communications. In 1964 he published his experiences in *Voices from the Universe*, which was accompanied with a recording of EVP sounds. Later Konstantin Raudive, a philosopher and psychologist, made more than 100,000 recordings. His research, published in English in 1971, became so widely studied that EVP voices are also known today as "Raudive voices."

EVP communications are often faint and difficult to decipher, though some are clear enough to be heard without headphones. There is no particular pattern to EVPs, although "brief, sometimes cryptic and ungrammatical phrases" can be heard.[2]

Some communications are in foreign languages, others feature voices singing, animal sounds, or what sounds like more than one entity speaking.

EVP researcher Sarah Wilson Estep, who has written extensively about her EVP research, reports that she has received such communications on tape. From some, she claims, she's learned what the other side is like; one voice told her, "It's so pretty." She also tells of a direct after-death communication cluster that began when a woman had a vivid dream in which her late mother told her, "I'm happy. I'm busy."[3]

This dream visitation occurred three times before the woman left a tape recorder on. When the tape was played back, the woman heard what she is convinced was her mother saying "I'm busy." She took this as a confirmation of her dreams.

My own experiments with EVP have been promising but inconclusive. During one of our radio shows, we tried an EVP experiment using highly sensitive, professional-quality equipment. We set up one set of microphones and a recorder in the studio, where a medium gave an incredible psychic reading. We also set up a recorder in the control room, which is soundproof, with microphones in the studio. On playback, we were amazed to hear short bursts of static or electrical noise whenever the medium or a subject asked a question. None of us heard this unusual noise during taping. It occurred only on the tape made in the studio. Although the tape recorder in the control room was being fed by microphones in the studio, none of the sounds turned up on that tape.

This raises the intriguing question of whether spirits make their presence known on tape but not through the usual recording channels. It seems from this experiment that if we did indeed capture EVP, the spirit was recording straight to tape—in other words, not creating any sound that the microphone would detect but instead imprinting an electrical or magnetic pattern directly on the tape itself.

There have also been reports of images or sounds manifesting themselves on televisions, radios, videotapes, and computer screens. According to a television news report in 1995, a team of EVP researchers in Luxembourg unexpectedly saw images on home computers that were later clarified and explained by a series of words that appeared on the same computers. The message said that the other side is similar to life on earth except that "nothing is matter as we know it."

Skeptics argue that spirit voices may be explained by interference from radio and television broadcasts, CB radio, cellular phones, even home intercoms and nursery monitors. They believe that EVPs are just random noises. One cannot dismiss the human propensity to find sense where none exists. (Think back to how many of us were sure we heard "Paul is dead" at the end of the Beatles' "I'm So Tired.")

A paranormal theory suggests that the recordings are not of spirit voices or images but result from our psychokinetic projections. There is some evidence that people with psychokinetic ability can influence previously recorded sounds on audiotape, so this is not as far-fetched as it may sound. Even the otherwise convincing case of the woman hearing her mother say "I'm busy" may possibly be a case of psychokinetic projection.

If you have the equipment and lots of patience, you may wish to experiment with EVP. While serious EVP researchers employ professional-quality highly sensitive microphones, tape, amplifiers, speakers, and other equipment, most experts claim that you can get acceptable results with the equipment you may have in your house. Again, however, we believe it is an uncertain, unpredictable means of direct communication fraught with possibilities for projection. EVP often captures voices and images the researchers do not recognize. We reiterate our reservations about opening the door to spirits unknown. While EVP shows some promise, used improperly it can easily become an electronic Ouija board.

APPENDIX I

"A MASK UPON THE UNIVERSE"

Our Misguided Legacy of Disbelief

Traditional scientific method has always been, at the very best, 20-20 hind-sight. It's good for seeing where you've been. It's good for testing the truth of what you think you know, but it can't tell you where you ought to go.

—ROBERT M. PIRSIG, *ZEN AND THE ART OF MOTORCYCLE MAINTENANCE*

THE HISTORY OF MYSTERY

We can trace evidence suggesting widespread belief in the afterlife back through prehistory. Neanderthal graves more than 100,000 years old contain not only human remains but items such as flowers and food, perhaps intended for use in a subsequent life. As recently as 20,000 years ago, early Homo sapiens interred their dead with cloth-ing, trinkets, tools, pottery, and other items.

Colleen McDannell and Bernhard Lang write in their illuminating *Heaven: A History*, "In the ancient world, belief in life after death was widespread, considered normal, and not generally weakened by skep-ticism. Death ended the visible form of our life on earth, but did not extinguish existence altogether. . . . [T]he complete denial of an after-life remained the exception rather than the rule. The majority of ancient authors, in spite of periods of doubt, assumed that some form of life existed after death."[1]

Humankind has attempted to maintain some form of contact with the dead, most often through ritual and prayer. Among the earliest written records of attempts to contact the deceased is *The Egyptian Book of the Dead*. It predates the birth of Christ by more than a thousand years and was probably passed down orally through generations before that. Consider in *The Egyptian Book of the Dead* a description of the classic near-death experience and the English translation of the book's title: *Pert Em Hru*, "coming forth by day" or "manifested in the light."

Like the later Christians, whom they so profoundly influenced, ancient Greeks believed in an immortal soul that goes to heaven or to hell after death. In the sixth century B.C. the Greek philosopher king Pythagoras was using a kind of early version of a Ouija board to communicate with the spirit world. From approximately the fourth century B.C., manuals, allegedly written by gods, suggesting ways to contact the dead, were popular in Greece.

Roots of the Judeo-Christian Tradition

The promise of eternal life is the cornerstone of Christianity and an important tenet of Judaism, although Jewish belief emphasizes a focus on this life rather than the hereafter. The ancient Hebrews believed in life after death and communed with their dead forebears through private ritual and prayer. Prayers offered by the living empowered the dead, and survivors avoided angering them at all costs, for the living depended on the dead for advice and guidance, often gained through mediums.

According to the Old Testament, King Saul consulted one type of medium, a necromancer identified as the witch of Endor, when a powerful enemy army confronted him. Although Saul had banished mediums and fortune-tellers from Israel and instituted death as the penalty for those practicing such arts, he himself traveled in disguise to consult with a medium (called "a woman that hath a familiar spirit" in the King James version of the Bible). Saul asked the medium to summon the spirit of the prophet Samuel, who asked the king, "Why have you disturbed me? Why do you make me come back?" (I Samuel 28:15). The spirit of the prophet then correctly predicted that King Saul would be defeated and killed in battle.

By the seventh century B.C., attitudes toward the dead had changed. No longer were they viewed as potentially powerful presences but as powerless and unclean, to be avoided whenever possible. Within a few centuries, it came to be believed that the dead and the living inhabited completely separate spheres between which communication and intervention were not only undesirable but impossible. Even with its promise of resurrection and the victory of eternal life over mortal death, Christianity, like most other major religions, has maintained an interesting ambivalence regarding communications with the spirit world. Such communications are not necessarily condemned when they occur spontaneously or seem to be initiated by the other side, as in dream visitations or visions, but the prohibition against voluntarily, consciously, or deliberately summoning spirits is quite strong and widespread. As religious leaders presented it to their flocks, the word from the spirit world to the pious was, Don't call us, we'll call you.

An Eastern View

Before picking up the thread of our Western spiritual beliefs, let's turn eastward for a moment. As we in the West integrate aspects of Eastern religion, philosophy, and healing into our lives, the contrasts between these two world views illuminate the limitations of our long-held assumptions. According to certain Eastern religions, especially Hinduism, Jainism, and Buddhism, the soul not only survives physical death, it does so eternally. The indestructible, eternal soul exists in an endless cycle of death and rebirth known as transmigration or reincarnation. Islam, whose followers make up more than 20 percent of the world population, also teaches that the soul survives physical death and goes on to dwell eternally in either heaven or hell. At roughly the same time that Pythagoras was working with his proto-Ouija board, on the Indian subcontinent Gautama Buddha was founding an offshoot of Hinduism, Buddhism.

Dr. Jong Ree is an Oriental Medicine Doctor who came to the

United States from his native Korea in 1973. That year he was among the first acupuncturists to be licensed by New York State. He spoke to us about after-death communications from a Buddhist viewpoint, shedding some light on the power of love to bridge realms.

"Even now I see my grandmother in my mind," he says. "In other words, I visualize her. And she returns messages to me about whatever personal problems or questions I have. She and I were very close on earth; the love between us bonded us tightly together.

"In Buddhism, there is the belief that everything that exists in the universe is alive—both visible and invisible. There is no beginning and no ending. When man dies, he does not die completely. The soul continues. Unlike Christian belief, Buddhists believe that the soul can only reside when there is a body. Buddhists say that once the soul leaves the dying body, the soul looks for another body to inhabit. Yet I believe the souls of the deceased communicate back to the living on earth through dreams, visions, and other signs."

Jong Ree's explanation of the Buddhist conception of life after death may seem paradoxical to those raised in the Western Judeo-Christian tradition. If the deceased loved one soon reincarnates back to earth, what remains of the spirit to communicate with the living? Buddhists believe that for a short time after physical death—less than fifty days—the spirit resides in the next world before entering a new body to be reborn on this plane. (Highly evolved spiritual individuals, however, may choose not to reincarnate.)

Does the return to earth sever our spiritual bond? No. As Jong Ree explains, "You may think that once the spirit reincarnates into another life, it is no longer 'there,' no longer reachable, but that is not true. You see, it's like a tape recorder or a computer. I believe that when the soul leaves the body, the body's message is recorded onto the soul. Like a permanent tape or a computer memory, it is always there. So though my grandmother has found a new physical body, her spirit is registered in the next world. The spirit is always able to communicate because once you've bonded together when both of you were on earth, that bond endures. It cannot be erased.

"For example, my father died as a young man. For my grandmother, his mother, losing a child was very painful. She always spoke to him after he passed. But she knew that even though his spirit would be reincarnated into another body by the time she died, he would still be there to meet her when she passed. Part of your spirit always remains in the next world."

THE EVOLUTION OF CHRISTIAN ATTITUDES

Despite long opposition by the Christian churches, mediumistic and other psychic and occult practices have survived for centuries. Many consider the New Testament to contain many metaphysical or psychic references. A literal reading of the New Testament suggests that Jesus Christ was psychically gifted, performing a range of miracles that included raising people from the dead (necromancy), discerning spirits (mediumship), his own resurrection after physical death, and levitation. Although attributed to Christ, these powers are more often viewed as emanating from God or as evidence of Christ's superhuman qualities.

Throughout history, such feats, whether performed by gods, messiahs, saints, or religious leaders, have been regarded as anything but the result of purely human capabilities. They are usually attributed to a separate entity, usually God—in which case, it is a gift—or a force of evil, like the devil. To suggest otherwise surely would have spelled the end of religious and political authority over people's lives.*

Through the Middle Ages, what we term psychic phenomena were widely accepted. This included discerning spirits and precognitive dreams and visions. In fact, until the ninth century A.D., belief in the existence of witches was considered in opposition to the Church, which deemed witches nonexistent. Not until Pope John XXII pronounced sorcery a crime in 1326 were those exhibiting psychic abili-

---

*It is not far-fetched to suggest that widespread acceptance of the paranormal would virtually revolutionize society. For a thought-provoking examination of the possible paradigm shift, see Willis W. Harman, "The Social Implications of Psychic Research," in Edgar D. Mitchell, ed., *Psychic Exploration: A Challenge for Science* (New York: Perigee, 1974), 640–669.

ties viewed as in league with the devil or in a conspiracy against Christianity and deserving of persecution. So began the infamous Inquisition. By the end of the fifteenth century, the prosecution of those believed to be witches was in high gear. Authorities estimate that over the next four centuries as many as 200,000 people were tortured and executed. Anyone who spoke of having had precognitive dreams or revealed any contact with spirits was vulnerable to persecution, despite age, sex, or social position. One result is that whatever they knew or recorded of psychic phenomena then went underground.

The First New Age

For the most part, consideration of the spiritual was the province of religion and philosophy. What we might term its secularization began with Emanuel Swedenborg (1688–1772), a Swedish scientist and son of a Lutheran bishop who, among many other things, was a scholar, inventor, and author. He was not deeply religious, though he believed in the soul, and he seemed to have no interest in things mystical. Then suddenly in 1744, the fifty-six-year-old bachelor began having a series of dreams and visions in which he visited spiritual realms, met many religious and historical figures, including Jesus, and spoke with spirits, which he termed *angels*. As a result of these spiritual excursions, Swedenborg claimed to have been "instructed in the true nature of the universe." Two years later, he retired and began publishing accounts of his otherworldly travels. Friends and colleagues thought him mad, an impression supported by his claim of having encountered a race of Martians who dressed in tree bark.

Despite his apparent eccentricities, Swedenborg revolutionized Western thinking on life after death. Why? Before Swedenborg's ideas spread though such works as *Heaven and Hell* (1758), the prevailing Christian view of life after death was one of suffocating stasis. Because God and heaven were considered perfect, they never changed. The good souls who ascended to the higher realms passed eternity among saints and angels, in endless meditation, praise, and prayer. What earlier theologians considered perfection stood in stark contrast to earthly life. Freed of trouble, pain, toil, and fear, spirits in the afterlife were also bereft of loved ones, personality, and change. Not only would we cease living in our physical form, we would also cease to be who we were here on earth.

Swedenborg challenged the existence of this heaven. In the heaven that he visited in his many journeys, the citizens were happy, productive, feeling, sentient beings. Social relationships, work, learning, and the ability of the soul to progress distinguished his modern heaven from its predecessors. "Man after death is as much a man as he was before, so much to be unaware that he is not still in the former world. . . . So the one life continues into the other, and death is only a crossing."[2] Equally significant, Swedenborg believed that we could exist in both this realm and the next simultaneously, that those in the spiritual realm could interact with those still in earthly life. That this revolutionary view of life after death sounds so familiar is a profound testament to Swedenborg's incalculable influence; he also coined the term *the other side.*

Swedenborg's heaven sounds wonderful, but how do we know his visions were not just hallucinations? For one thing, Swedenborg also had a history of remarkable substantiated clairvoyant experiences. In 1759 he was in the town of Göteborg when he perceived a building burning in Stockholm, approximately three hundred miles away. He displayed other psychic abilities, including mediumship, several times. Quite possibly, through lengthy self-induced trances he did indeed travel to the other side. The fact that most mediumistic and psychic descriptions of the realm beyond death closely parallel Swedenborg's is not the result of his vast influence or simple coincidence. If many psychics, survivors of near-death experiences, mystics, or communicating spirits had described a different sort of postmortem existence, we would know it. In fact, accounts of the other side closely follow what Swedenborg claimed to have witnessed.

Among Swedenborg's millions of followers was an American shoemaker named Andrew Jackson Davis. In the mid- to late 1840s he was lecturing throughout the United States on spiritual existence and life after death. He delivered these lectures while in a trance (during one he claimed to have met the late Swedenborg), and in his book *The Principles of Nature* (1847), Davis wrote, "the truth about spirits will 'ere long present itself in the form of a living demonstration, and the world will hail with delight the ushering in of that era when the interiors of men will be opened."[3]

Some interpreted this as a prophetic description of mediumship and the Spiritualist movement* that would soon follow, and no wonder. Davis wrote, "I heard a voice . . . saying: 'Brother, the good work has begun—behold a living demonstration is born.'" The note is dated March 31, 1848. Later in the evening of that same day, in a Hydesville, New York, farmhouse, eleven-year-old Katherine Fox found herself "conversing" with what she believed was a spirit entity. When it answered her questions about the ages of the other children with the correct number of raps, the family was convinced they were in the presence of a spirit.

Shortly after that, Katherine's older sisters, Margaret and Leah, also became adept at communicating with the spirit through a code that used numbers of raps to designate letters of the alphabet. As a result of their spectacular demonstrations, the Fox sisters became national celebrities, and within five years the United States was home to more than 30,000 professional mediums. The so-called Age of Spiritualism had begun.

From there, mediumship's colorful history chronicles the genuinely gifted and the unscrupulous on both sides of the séance table. Just as there were fake mediums, so too there were fake self-appointed debunkers (and not a few dishonest ones, including magician Harry Houdini).[†] Still, the power of spiritualism's message—that some part of us survives physical death and can communicate with us here on earth—was irresistible. Public interest in discarnate communications was so great that in 1854 Illinois Senator James Shields presented the

---

*When we refer to the organized religious movement that flourished between the mid-1850s and the 1920s, we will capitalize Spiritualism; lower-cased, it refers to the general belief in the survival of the spirit after physical death.

†See Appendix II, "A Selective History of Mediumship," in Joel Martin and Patricia Romanowski, *We Don't Die: George Anderson's Conversations with the Other Side* (New York: G. P. Putnam's Sons, 1988).

U.S. Congress with a petition signed by 15,000 constituents demanding that the federal government begin investigating the phenomenon.

Séances were held in the White House during both the Franklin Pierce and Abraham Lincoln administrations, but Lincoln's spiritualist legacy is perhaps the best known (see chapter 2). The Civil War, which claimed over 600,000 lives and left an entire nation in mourning, proved a powerful spur for spiritualism, as would World War I fifty years later.

SCIENCE AND PARAPSYCHOLOGY: MOONWATCHING

In 1882 a group of prominent British intellectuals founded the Society for Psychical Research. Its goal was to scientifically investigate a range of unexplained phenomena, including discarnate communications, deathbed visions, and near-death experiences. In a field of psychical researchers who were often cleanly divided between gullible believers and perpetually skeptical debunkers, the SPR founders were unique. Their stated goal was "to examine without prejudice or prepossession and in a scientific spirit those faculties of man, real or supposed, which appear to be inexplicable on any generally recognized hypothesis."

The SPR produced many important works, including such pioneering studies as *Phantasms of the Living* (1886) by SPR cofounders Edmund Gurney and F.W. H. Myers, with Frank Podmore, an examination of apparitions, telepathy, and deathbed visions, and Myers's *Human Personality and the Survival of Bodily Death* (1903).

From the late nineteenth century through World War I, the subject of discarnate communications and related paranormal experience, such as precognition through dreams, was addressed by many prominent public figures, including authors Mark Twain and Sir Arthur Conan Doyle, the magician Houdini, physicist Sir Oliver Lodge, philosopher William James, and publisher Horace Greeley, to name a few.

Among those who believed the question of communication between the living and the dead deserved greater study was Thomas Edison. In 1920 he told *Scientific American*, "if personality exists after what we call death, it's reasonable to conclude that those who leave this earth would like to communicate with those they have left here." He also believed that life, like energy, could be transformed but never totally destroyed. "I do claim that it is possible to construct an apparatus which will be so delicate that if there are personalities in another existence or sphere who wish to get in touch with us . . . this apparatus will at least give them a better opportunity." Edison was working on such a machine at the time of his death in 1931.*

JUNG AND FREUD: SEEKING THE PSYCHOLOGY IN PARAPSYCHOLOGY

Many unexplained human experiences and abilities have been grouped under the blanket term *parapsychology* (*para* means "beside"). The term was first used in Germany in the late 1800s. The father of modern parapsychology, Dr. J. B. Rhine, adopted it as the official name for his area of scientific inquiry in the 1930s.[†]

At the turn of the century, modern psychology and parapsychology were two relatively new disciplines, both striving for acceptance by the scientific establishment. Sigmund Freud (1856–1939), the father of psychoanalysis, was a member of the SPR. Though he wrote on premonitions, telepathy, and the occult, he categorically dismissed the possibility of life after death. He believed that unexplained phenomena were products of psychological or physiological forces. Although in his later years Freud admitted that he might have pursued parapsychological studies if given the chance, he also feared that psychology's legitimacy as a science would be compromised if it

---

*This may ring a bell with Woody Allen fans, since Edison's gizmo played a role in the plot of his 1982 film *A Midsummer Night's Sex Comedy*.

[†]Recent breakthroughs in medicine, psychology, and physics suggest that phenomena considered "beside psychology" may one day be explained. Breakthroughs in quantum physics, for example, are providing possible theoretical explanations for phenomena that were earlier deemed impossible in light of Newtonian physics. The day science can say what makes the paranormal possible, the field may well be renamed *paraphysics* or *paraneurobiology*.

became too closely associated with what he described in a 1921 letter as the "as yet unexplained sphere of knowledge."

In direct opposition to Freud stands his onetime disciple Carl Gustav Jung (1875–1961). Jung grew up in a family that accepted the paranormal; both his mother and his maternal grandmother were psychic, one cousin was a medium, and he himself had many psychic experiences. The paranormal intrigued some prominent early psychologists and psychiatrists, but none was as comfortable or as certain of its value as Jung.

Freud and Jung differed in their attitudes toward spirituality. Essentially, Jung respected and embraced it, while Freud viewed it as another form of repressed sexuality. In his long career, Jung explored mythology, mediumship, dreams, alchemy, the *I Ching*, and many philosophies and religions. He believed in reincarnation and acknowledged the importance of a belief in life after death. In 1944 he had a near-death experience in which he received what soon proved an accurate premonition of his doctor's death. However, Jung is best known to the general public for developing theories about the collective unconscious and the archetypal, or universal, symbols we encounter in both dreams and our waking life. His theories on the phenomenon of synchronicity are particularly relevant to after-death communications (see chapter 5).

MODERN PARAPSYCHOLOGICAL RESEARCH

Here in the United States, the best-known parapsychology laboratory is the Institute of Parapsychology at Duke University, founded in 1930 by Dr. J. B. Rhine. For the next thirty-five years, Rhine and his colleagues defined parapsychology as a modern science. It was in Rhine's lab that the famous Zener cards (the wave, star, cross, circle, and square) were first used to test the phenomenon he termed *extrasensory perception*, or ESP. Rhine and his wife, Dr. Louisa E. Rhine, researched and wrote about many different psychic areas, which we discuss in the relevant chapters. Rhine began to study mediums in earnest but decided to "back away from the problem of postmortem survival and turn to things we could do experimentally with living people."[4] Shortly before his death in 1980, he encouraged his colleagues to pursue questions about death and postmortem survival.

Besides the practical problems of psychic investigation, there is the matter of scientific discrimination and prejudice. Serious scientific study of the related psychic phenomena has continued, but only on a small scale, and it is interesting to speculate about why that is. Of all paranormal or psychic phenomena, after-death communications are among the least studied, for several reasons. First, unlike telepathy or distant viewing, which may be of some practical value for espionage, proving such communications serves no practical purpose for society. Second, unlike card tests or second-sight experiments, communication with the dead is not easily produced, quantified, or reproduced. Even pro-psi researchers wonder if so-called survival research may have reached a dead end.

Just as we cannot grow moonbeams in petri dishes, we cannot force after-death communications. For now, all we have to study are people's personal experiences, anecdotes, and memories. In the realm of science the term *anecdotal* often commands the same respect as *useless* or *questionable*. After all, an anecdote, or report by an individual, is not like a test conducted in a controlled laboratory or a study with carefully chosen protocols, controls, and statistics. In his brilliant *Parapsychology: The Controversial Science*, Richard S. Broughton, director of research at the Institute for Parapsychology, writes:

> Occasionally you will hear some scientific pundit proclaim there is no evidence for parapsychological phenomena, therefore parapsychology is a pseudoscience with no subject matter to study. That is patent nonsense. For over two thousand years people have been reporting a class of human experiences—the kind commonly called psychic—and for almost as long, scholars and scientists have been trying to understand them. Two millennia of human experiences *is* subject matter.[5]

In his invaluable study of psychic phenomena, religion, and psychology *The Medium, the Mystic, and the Physicist*, Lawrence LeShan puts it succinctly: "The general refusal to deal scientifically with the material gathered in this field seems to be a phenomena *in itself demanding explanation*" [italics in original].[6] In the absence of massive scientific study, we are left with personal anecdotal accounts. Perhaps one day we will be able to look back and regard these early forays into the world beyond as we regard early attempts at flight in relationship to the first moonwalk—only the first steps, just the beginning.

||||||||||||||||||||||||||||||||||||||||||||||||||||||||

APPENDIX II

THE LOVE BEYOND LIFE SURVEY

In my many years of hosting broadcasts on various topics related to the paranormal, I have heard listeners and viewers volunteer thousands of psychic experiences, and I have regularly surveyed them. Following is the latest version of a questionnaire first distributed in the early 1970s, when I began my research into after-death communications.

We invite you to take this survey and return it to us. If you are willing to talk to us about your experiences for a future project, please let us know. We can be reached at the following addresses:

Joel Martin
P.O. Box 5442
Babylon, NY 11707

Patricia Romanowski
bookwrks@village.ios.com

Thank you for your support and interest.

—JOEL MARTIN

DIRECT AFTER-DEATH COMMUNICATION
QUESTIONNAIRE

		Yes	No
1	Do you believe in life after death?		
2	Do you believe communication with the deceased is possible?		
3	Has anyone who has passed on ever contacted or communicated with you *after* their death?		
4	If you answered yes to question 3, what form did this communication/contact take? Check all applicable categories. If more than one, indicate by number in right-hand column how many.		

Check yes/#

- Deceased came in a dream.

- Deceased came in a vision or apparition while you were awake, so that you saw the deceased person appear to you.

- You heard the deceased speaking to you.

- You detected a favorite scent of the deceased.

- You heard a favorite song of the deceased.

- You perceived some other relevant sign
related to the deceased.   _____ _____

  Please explain:

- You had the feeling or sense that the
deceased was present.   _____ _____

- You witnessed an episode of
synchronicity, or meaningful
coincidence.   _____ _____

  Please explain:

- You witnessed the psychokinetic
movement of objects, which you believe
can be attributed to the deceased.   _____ _____

  Please explain:

- You witnessed a thermodynamic effect
("psychic wind" or breeze associated
with the deceased).   _____ _____

- You perceived a visual or audio image on an electronic device (television, computer screen) or medium (videotape, audiotape).
  _____ _____

- You perceived an image of the deceased in a photograph.
  _____ _____

- You survived a near-death experience.
  _____ _____

- You experienced a premonition.
  _____ _____

- You witnessed another person having a deathbed vision.
  _____ _____

- You received a telepathic message from the deceased.
  _____ _____

- You had another experience you believe was prompted by or related to the deceased.
  _____ _____

  Please explain:

5 If you answered yes to question 3, what was the relationship between you and the deceased? The deceased was—

- a stranger
  _____ _____

- a celebrity
  _____ _____

- your mother
  _____ _____

- your father
  _____ _____

- • your step-parent   _____ _____
- • your grandfather   _____ _____
- • your grandmother   _____ _____
- • your great-grandparent   _____ _____
- • some other relative   _____ _____

  Please explain:

- • a friend or neighbor   _____ _____
- • a colleague or coworker   _____ _____
- • your pet   _____ _____
- • other   _____ _____

  Please explain:

	Yes	No
6 Have you had communication/contact more than once with the same deceased person?	_____	_____

If yes, how many times?

	Yes	No

7 Have you ever had a communication/
contact with a deceased person near or at
the moment you were thinking of them?   _____ _____

8 Do you believe that the deceased contacted
you for a particular reason?   _____ _____

Please explain:

What exactly was the message you
received?

	Check yes/#

9 Did the experience leave you feeling—

* frightened?   _____ _____

* comforted?   _____ _____

* reassured?   _____ _____

* dubious about its genuineness? _____ _____

* other?   _____ _____

    Please explain:

Check yes/#

10 Where were you when the
communication/contact occurred? If it
occurred more than once, note number in
right-hand column, for each location.

- At home

- In someone else's home

  Whose?

- At your place of business

- On vacation

- In a store

- At a church, synagogue, or other place
  of worship

- At a cemetery or mausoleum

- At a museum or historical location

- At a theater or other entertainment
  venue (concert, club, movie)

- In a car, bus, airplane, or boat

- In a hospital, hospice, or doctor's office

- At a morgue or funeral home

- Outdoors (at the beach, in the
  mountains, in the desert, in the water)

- At a school, college, or university

- In a professional's office (lawyer, accountant) _____ _____

- In a psychotherapist's office _____ _____

- In a restaurant _____ _____

- At a library _____ _____

11 When did the communication/contact take place? If more than once, indicate number of times in right-hand column.

- Birthday _____ _____

   Whose?

- Anniversary of death _____ _____

   Whose?

- Wedding anniversary _____ _____

   Whose?

Check yes/#

- Birth
  Whose?

- Death
  Whose?

- Funeral or memorial service
  Whose?

- Unveiling or scattering of ashes
  Whose?

- Other death-related ceremony or event
  Please explain:

	Check yes/#

- Graduation

  Whose?

- Other important anniversary
  (e.g., of meeting, dating)

  Please explain:

- Religious holiday

  Please explain:

- Special season

  Please explain:

- Special day

  Please explain:

- Other special event:

  Please explain:

12 When did the communication or contact occur?

- Day

  When?

- Night

  When?

	Yes	No

13 Were you alone when the communication with the deceased occurred?

14 If you answered no to question 13, who was with you when the communication or contact occurred?

- Did that person also experience the communication/contact with the deceased?

15 How did the deceased person who
contacted you die?

- Natural causes (old age, disease)   _____ _____

- Accident   _____ _____

- Suicide   _____ _____

- Murder   _____ _____

- Other   _____ _____

Please explain:

- Don't know or cause unknown   _____ _____

16 When did the communication/contact
occur in relation to the death of the
deceased?

- Immediately after the death, within the
first hours   _____ _____

- Shortly after the death, within the first
month   _____ _____

- Within a year of the death   _____ _____

- More than a year but less than five years
after the death   _____ _____

- More than five years after the death   _____ _____

	Yes	No

17 Did you ever pray for the deceased person who contacted you? _____ _____

18 Do you believe that your prayers or thoughts are received by the deceased? _____ _____

19 Did your after-death communication experience change your attitude toward death? _____ _____

If yes, please explain how:

Check yes/#

20 If you answered yes to question 19, would you say your experience has left you—

• more fearful of death? _____ _____

• less fearful of death? _____ _____

• unchanged in attitude? _____ _____

Please explain your attitude:

Check yes/#

21 In religious/spiritual terms, would you describe yourself as—

- very religious in a traditional sense _____ _____

- somewhat religious _____ _____

- not religious at all _____ _____

- extremely spiritual _____ _____

- somewhat spiritual _____ _____

- not spiritual at all _____ _____

- very New Age–oriented _____ _____

- somewhat New Age–oriented _____ _____

- not interested in New Age beliefs _____ _____

- attuned to Western, Judeo-Christian beliefs _____ _____

- attuned to Eastern religions and philosophies _____ _____

Please explain any or all responses here, if you'd like:

	Yes	No
22 Have you ever had a premonition or precognition of someone dying?	___	___
23 Have you ever consulted a psychic, medium, or channeler in an attempt to receive communications or make contact with the deceased?	___	___
24 If you answered yes to question 23, how would you compare that experience to your direct after-death communication experience?	___	___
25 Would you like to receive future communications/contacts from the deceased?	___	___
26 Do you feel comfortable talking about this subject to others?	___	___
27 Have you ever told anyone about your direct-communication/contact experiences?	___	___

If so, what was their response?

	Yes	No
28 Has anyone else close to you experienced direct after-death communications or other psychic events?	___	___

Please explain:

29 Do you know of anyone close to you or
the deceased who has received a commu-
nication from them?   _____   _____

Please explain:

30 Would you describe anyone else in your
family as psychic?   _____   _____

31 If you have had direct after-death communication experiences, please describe
them:

Please answer the following questions about yourself. All answers will be kept confidential.

Sex:

☐ F ☐ M

Marital Status:

☐ Single ☐ Married ☐ Divorced ☐ Widowed

Age:

☐ Under 21 ☐ 36 to 55 ☐ over 75
☐ 21 to 35 ☐ 56 to 75

Religious affiliation or denomination, if applicable:

☐ Catholic ☐ Protestant ☐ Jewish
☐ Hindu ☐ Moslem ☐ Buddhist
☐ Other (please explain) _____

☐ Agnostic ☐ Atheist

Do you feel that you have psychic ability? _____

Education:

☐ High school graduate ☐ College graduate
☐ Postgraduate study
☐ Other (please explain) _____

You need not identify yourself, but if you choose not to, we would still appreciate your indicating where you live, so we can determine the geographical mix of our responses.

May we contact you for further research?　　　☐ Yes　☐ No

If you answered yes, please understand that your response in no way obligates you to speak with us. In the event that you do, you may request that your particular story not be included in a future book except pseudonymously. Again, all of this information will be kept confidential.

Name _____

Address _____

City _____ State _____ Zip _____

Telephone with area code: _____ ext. _____

When are the best hours to call? _____

Would you prefer we contact you first by mail?　☐ Yes　☐ No

Do you have an e-mail address that you prefer
we use?　　　　　　　　　　　　　　　☐ Yes　☐ No

E-mail address_____
Is this　☐ home?　☐ business?

Please return completed forms and/or any correspondence to:

Joel Martin
P.O. Box 5442
Babylon, NY 11707

or

Patricia Romanowski
bookwrks@village.ios.com

Notes

CHAPTER 1

1. Andrew Greeley, *Death and Beyond* (Chicago: Thomas More Association, 1976), pp. 61–71.

CHAPTER 2

1. James A. Pike with Diane Kennedy, *The Other Side: An Account of My Experiences with Psychic Phenomena* (Garden City, NY: Doubleday & Co., Inc., 1968), pp. 348–349.
2. Jonathan Rosen, "Rewriting the End: Elisabeth Kübler-Ross," *The New York Times Magazine*, January 22, 1995, 22–25.
3. Pike with Kennedy, *The Other Side*, p. 379.

CHAPTER 3

1. Robert L. Van de Castle, *Our Dreaming Mind* (New York: Ballantine, 1994), p. 139.

CHAPTER 4

1. Otis Williams with Patricia Romanowski, *Temptations* (New York: G. P. Putnam's Sons, 1988), p. 163.
2. Louisa May Alcott, *Life, Letters, and Journals of Louisa May Alcott* as excerpted in *Journal of the American Society for Psychical Research* 7, number 7 (July 1913).
3. Karlis Osis and Erlendur Haraldsson, *At the Hour of Death* (New York: Avon, 1977), p. 3.
4. Elisabeth Kübler-Ross, ed. *Death: The Final Stage of Growth* (New York: Touchstone, 1986), p. 5.

CHAPTER 5

1. Andy Warhol, *The Philosophy of Andy Warhol (From A to B & Back Again)* (New York: Harcourt, Brace, Jovanovich, 1975), p. 151.

CHAPTER 7

1. Laura Joplin, *Love, Janis* (New York: Villard, 1992), p. 312.

CHAPTER 8

1. Therese A. Rando, *How to Go On Living When Someone You Love Dies* (New York: Bantam Books, 1991), p. 30.

CHAPTER 10

1. Larry Dossey, *Healing Words: The Power of Prayer and the Practice of Medicine* (San Francisco: HarperCollins, 1993), p. 111.
2. James R. Lewis, "Electronic Voice Phenomena," in *The Encyclopedia of Afterlife Beliefs and Phenomena* (Detroit: Gale Research, 1994), p. 130.
3. Sarah Wilson Estep, *Voices of Eternity* (New York: Fawcett, 1988), pp. 28, 63.

APPENDIX I

1. Colleen McDannell and Bernhard Lang, *Heaven: A History* (New Haven and London: Yale University Press, 1988), p. 1.
2. Quoted in Colleen McDannell and Bernhard Lang, *Heaven: A History* (New Haven and London: Yale University Press, 1988), p. 186.
3. Quoted in Editors of Time-Life Books, *Spirit Summonings* (Alexandria, VA: Time-Life Books, 1989), p. 28.
4. Will Bradbury, ed., *Into the Unknown* (Pleasantville, NY: Reader's Digest Association, 1981), p. 199.
5. Richard S. Broughton, *Parapsychology: The Controversial Science* (New York: Ballantine, 1991), pp. 4–5.
6. Lawrence LeShan, *The Medium, the Mystic, and the Physicist: Toward a General Theory of the Paranormal* (New York: Arkana, 1995; originally published by Viking, 1966), p. 197.

Bibliography

BOOKS

Allen, T. G. *The Egyptian Book of the Dead.* Chicago: University of Chicago Press, 1960.

Atwater, P. M. H. *Beyond the Light.* New York: Birch Lane Press, 1994.

Bradbury, Will, ed. *Into the Unknown.* Pleasantville, NY: Reader's Digest, 1981.

Brandon, Ruth. *The Spiritualists: The Passion for the Occult in the Nineteenth and Twentieth Centuries.* New York: Knopf, 1983.

Broughton, Richard S. *Parapsychology: The Controversial Science.* New York: Ballantine Books, 1991.

Brown, Slater. *The Heyday of Spiritualism.* New York: Hawthorn Books, 1970.

Burns, Litany. *Develop Your Child's Psychic Abilities.* New York: Pocket Books, 1988.

Burns, Stanley B., M.D. *Sleeping Beauty: Memorial Photography in America.* Altadeena, CA: Twelve Trees Press, 1990.

Cayce, Hugh Lynn, and Edgar Cayce. *God's Other Door and the Continuity of Life.* Virginia Beach, VA: A.R.E. Press, 1958.

Chinmoy, Sri. *Death and Reincarnation.* Jamaica, NY: AGNI Press, 1974.

Currie, Ian. *You Cannot Die.* Rockport, MA: Element Books, 1995.

Daniel, Alma, Timothy Wyllie, and Andrew Ramer. *Ask Your Angels.* New York: Ballantine Books, 1992.

Dossey, Larry. *Healing Words: The Power of Prayer and the Practice of Medicine.* San Francisco: HarperCollins, 1993.

Doyle, Arthur Conan. *The History of Spiritualism.* New York: George H. Doran, 1926.

Ebon, Martin. *Communicating with the Dead.* New York: New American Library, 1968.

———, ed. *The Signet Handbook of Parapsychology.* New York: New American Library, 1978.

Editors of Time-Life Books. *Spirit Summonings.* Alexandria, VA: Time-Life Books, 1989.

Epstein, Gerald, M.D. *Healing Visualizations.* New York: Bantam Books, 1989.

Estep, Sarah Wilson. *Voices of Eternity.* New York: Ballantine Books, 1988.

Evans-Wentz, W. Y., ed. *The Tibetan Book of the Dead.* New York: Oxford University Press, 1957.

Fodor, Nandor. *Between Two Worlds.* West Nyack, NY: Parker Publishing, 1964.

———. *Freud, Jung and Occultism.* New Hyde Park, NY: University Books, 1971.

Ford, Arthur. *Unknown But Known.* New York: Harper & Row, 1968.

Fuller, John G. *The Ghost of Flight 401*. New York: G. P. Putnam's Sons, 1968.

——. *The Ghost of 29 Megacycles*. New York: Signet/New American Library, 1981.

Gallup, George, Jr., with William Proctor. *Adventures in Immortality*. New York: McGraw-Hill, 1982.

Garrett, E. J. *Many Voices*. New York: G. P. Putnam's Sons, 1968.

Gettings, Fred. *Ghosts in Photographs*. New York: Harmony Books, 1978.

Greeley, Andrew. *Death and Beyond*. Chicago: Thomas More Association, 1976.

Grof, Stanislav, M.D., and Joan Halifax. *The Human Encounter with Death*. New York: E. P. Dutton, 1978.

Guiley, Rosemary Ellen. *The Encyclopedia of Ghosts and Spirits*. New York: Facts on File, 1992.

——. *Harper's Encyclopedia of Mystical and Paranormal Experience*. San Francisco: HarperCollins, 1991.

Hauck, Dennis William. *Haunted Places: The National Directory*. New York: Penguin, 1996.

Hick, John H. *Death and Eternal Life*. Louisville, KY: Westminster John Knox Press, 1994.

Hooper, Judith, and Dick Teresi. *The Three-Pound Universe*. New York: Dell, 1986.

Houdini, Harry. *A Magician Among the Spirits*. New York: Arno Press, 1972.

Hunter, Stoker. *Ouija: The Most Dangerous Game*. New York: Barnes and Noble Books, 1985.

Jackson, Charles O., ed. *Passing: The Vision of Death in America*. New York: Dell, 1973.

Jacobson, Nils O., M.D. *Life Without Death?* New York: Dell, 1973.

Joplin, Laura. *Love, Janis*. New York: Villard, 1992.

Jung, Carl. *Man and His Symbols*. New York: Doubleday, 1964.

——. *Memories, Dreams, Reflections*. New York: Random House, 1961.

Kübler-Ross, Elisabeth. *Living with Death and Dying*. New York: Macmillan, 1981.

——. *On Children and Death*. New York: Macmillan, 1983.

——. *On Death and Dying*. New York: Macmillan, 1969.

——. *Questions and Answers on Death and Dying*. New York: Macmillan, 1974.

——. *Working It Through*. New York: Macmillan, 1987.

——, ed. *Death: The Final Stage of Growth*. New York: Touchstone, 1986.

Kübler-Ross, Elisabeth, and Mal Warshaw. *To Live Until We Say Goodbye*. Englewood Cliffs, NJ: Prentice-Hall, 1978.

Lande, Nathaniel. *Mindstyles/Lifestyles*. Los Angeles: Price/Stern/Sloan, 1976.

LeShan, Eda. *Learning to Say Goodbye: When a Parent Dies*. New York: Avon Books, 1976.

LeShan, Lawrence. *How to Meditate: A Guide to Self-Discovery*. New York: Bantam Books, 1974.

——. *The Medium, the Mystic, and the Physicist: Toward a General Theory of the Paranormal*. New York: Viking, 1966.

Lewis, James R. *Encyclopedia of Afterlife Beliefs and Phenomena*. Detroit: Gale Research, 1994.

Lukeman, Brenda. *Embarkations: A Guide to Dealing with Death and Parting*. Englewood Cliffs, NJ: Prentice-Hall, 1982.

Lund, David H. *Death and Consciousness: The Case for Life after Death*. New York: Ballantine Books, 1985.

MacGregor, Geddes. *Images of Afterlife: Beliefs from Antiquity to Modern Times*. New York: Paragon House, 1992.

Martin, Joel, and Patricia Romanowski. *Our Children Forever: Messages from Children on the Other Side*. New York: Berkley Books, 1994.

———. *We Are Not Forgotten: George Anderson's Messages of Hope from the Other Side*. New York: G. P. Putnam's Sons, 1991; Berkley Books, 1992.

———. *We Don't Die: George Anderson's Conversations with the Other Side*. New York: G. P. Putnam's Sons, 1988; Berkley Books, 1989.

McDannell, Colleen, and Bernhard Lang. *Heaven: A History*. New Haven: Yale University Press, 1988.

McHargue, Georgess. *Facts, Frauds, and Phantasms*. Garden City, NY: Doubleday, 1972.

Meek, George W. *After We Die What Then?* Columbus, OH: Ariel Press, 1987.

Michaels, Stase. *The Bedside Guide to Dreams*. New York: Fawcett Crest/Ballantine Books, 1995.

Mitchell, Edgar D., ed. *Psychic Exploration: A Challenge for Science*. New York: Perigee, 1974.

Monroe, Robert A. *Journeys Out of the Body*. New York: Anchor Books, 1977.

Montgomery, Ruth. *Here and Hereafter*. New York: Coward-McCann, 1968.

———. *A Search for Truth*. New York: William Morrow, 1966.

———. *The World Before*. New York: Coward, McCann, & Geoghegan, 1976.

———. *A World Beyond*. New York: Ballantine Books, 1972.

Moody, Raymond A., Jr., M.D. *Coming Back*. New York: Bantam Books, 1990.

———. *Life After Life*. Atlanta: Mockingbird Books, 1975.

———. *The Light Beyond*. New York: Bantam Books, 1988.

———. *Reflections on Life After Life*. Atlanta: Mockingbird Books, 1977.

Moody, Raymond A., Jr., M.D., with Paul Perry. *Reunions: Visionary Encounters with Departed Loved Ones*. New York: Villard Books, 1993.

Morse, Melvin, M.D. *Closer to the Light*. New York: Villard Books, 1990.

———. *Transformed by the Light*. New York: Villard Books, 1992.

Morse, Melvin, M.D., with Paul Perry. *Parting Visions*. New York: Villard Books, 1994.

O'Neill, Kim. *How to Talk with Your Angels*. New York: Avon Books, 1995.

Osis, Karlis, and Erlendur Haraldsson. *At the Hour of Death*, rev. ed. New York: Hastings House, 1986.

Parrish-Harra, Carol. *The New Age Handbook on Death and Dying*. Santa Monica, CA: IBS Press, 1989.

Perry, Michael. *Psychic Studies: A Christian's View*. Wellingborough, Great Britain: The Aquarian Press, 1984.

Pike, James A., with Diane Kennedy. *The Other Side: An Account of My Experiences with Psychic Phenomena*. New York: Doubleday, 1968.

Puryear, Anne. *Stephen Lives!* New York: Pocket Books, 1996.

Quackenbush, Jamie, and Denise Graveline. *When Your Pet Dies*. New York: Pocket Books, 1988.

Rando, Therese A. *How to Go On Living When Someone You Love Dies.* New York: Bantam Books, 1991. Originally published as *Grieving* by Lexington Books, 1988.

———. *Parental Loss of a Child.* Champaign, IL: Research Press, 1986.

Ring, Kenneth. *Heading Toward Omega: In Search of the Meaning of the Near-Death Experience.* New York: William Morrow, 1984.

———. *Life after Death: A Scientific Investigation of the Near-Death Experience.* New York: Coward, McCann & Geoghegan, 1980.

Sherman, Harold. *The Dead Are Alive.* New York: Ballantine Books, 1981.

———. *You Live after Death.* Greenwich, CT: Fawcett Gold Medal Books, 1972.

Smith, Huston. *The Illustrated World's Religions.* San Francisco: HarperCollins, 1994.

Spraggett, Allen, with William Rauscher. *Arthur Ford: The Man Who Talked with the Dead.* New York: New American Library, 1973.

Spraggett, Allen. *The Case for Immortality.* New York: New American Library, 1974.

Stack, Rick. *Out of Body Adventures.* Chicago: Contemporary Books, 1988.

Stein, Gordon. *The Sorcerer of Kings: The Case of Daniel Dunglas Home and William Crookes.* Buffalo, NY: Prometheus Books, 1993.

Swann, Ingo. *Natural ESP.* New York: Bantam Books, 1987.

Swedenborg, Emanuel. *Compendium of the Theological and Spiritual Writings of Emanuel Swedenborg.* Boston: Crosby and Nichols, 1853.

———. *Heaven and Hell.* New York: Swedenborg Foundation, 1972. Originally published in Latin, London, 1758.

Tanous, Alex, and Katherine Fair Donnelly. *Is Your Child Psychic?* New York: Macmillan, 1979.

Tanous, Alex, and Timothy Gray. *Dreams, Symbols, and Psychic Powers.* New York: Bantam Books, 1990.

Taylor, Jeremy. *Where People Fly and Water Runs Uphill: Using Dreams to Tap the Wisdom of the Unconscious.* New York: Warner Books, 1992.

Taylor, Ruth Mattson. *Witness from Beyond.* New York: Hawthorn, 1975.

Taylor, Terry Lynn. *Guardians of Hope: The Angels' Guide to Personal Growth.* Tiburon, CA: H. J. Kramer, 1992.

Turner, Justin G., and Linda Levitt Turner. *Mary Todd Lincoln: Her Life and Letters.* New York: Knopf, 1972.

Van de Castle, Robert L. *Our Dreaming Mind.* New York: Ballantine Books, 1994.

Washington, Peter. *Madame Blavatsky's Baboon: A History of the Mystics, Mediums, and Misfits Who Brought Spiritualism to America.* New York: Schocken Books, 1993.

Weenolsen, Patricia. *The Art of Dying: How to Leave This World with Dignity and Grace, at Peace with Yourself and Your Loved Ones.* New York: St. Martin's Press, 1996.

Welch, William Addams. *Talks with the Dead.* New York: Pinnacle Books, 1975.

White, John. *A Practical Guide to Death and Dying.* Wheaton, IL: Quest Books, 1980.

Wilkerson, Ralph. *Beyond and Back: Those Who Died and Lived to Tell It.* Anaheim, CA: Melodyland Productions, 1977.

Williams, Otis, with Patricia Romanowski. *Temptations*. New York: G. P. Putnam's Sons, 1988.

Wilson, Colin. *Afterlife*. Garden City, NY: Doubleday, 1987.

———. *Mysteries*. New York: Perigee Books, 1978.

———. *The Occult*. New York: Vintage, 1973.

Worden, J. William. *Grief Counseling and Grief Therapy*. New York: Springer Publishing Co., 1991.

OTHER SOURCES

Kearl, M. "You Never Have to Die!" Web page about myriad aspects of death, http://WWW.Trinity.Edu/~mkearl/never.html.

Klinkenborn, Verlyn. "At the Edge of Eternity." *Life*, March 1992, 64–72.

Leach, Penelope. "Will I Die?" *Parenting*, April 1993, 105–111.

Menagh, Melanie. "Beyond Death and Dying." *Omni*, Fall 1995, 63–67+.

Morris, Robert L. "Parapsychology at the University of Edinburgh." Web page about the Koestler Chair of Parapsychology, http://moebius.psy.ed.ac.uk/mission.html.

"The Natural Death Handbook," chap. 3. Http://www.newciv.org/GIB/natdeath/ndh3.htm.

Rhine Research Center, Institute of Parapsychology. Web page http://world.std.com/~rhinerc.

Rosen, Jonathan. "Elisabeth Kübler-Ross: Rewriting the End." *New York Times Magazine*, January 22, 1995, 22–25.

Steinfels, Peter. "Psychiatrists' Manual Shifts Stance on Religious and Spiritual Problems." *New York Times*, February 10, 1994, A16.

"Why We Pray." *Life*, March 1994, 54–62.